MOON SHOT

For my Dad, Steve Parry
1943–2008

MOON SHOT

THE INSIDE STORY OF MANKIND'S GREATEST ADVENTURE

DAN PARRY

EBURY PRESS

3 5 7 9 10 8 6 4 2

Published in 2009 by Ebury Press, an imprint of Ebury Publishing

A Random House Group Company

The Random House Group Limited Reg. No. 954009

Addresses for companies within the Random House Group
can be found at www.randomhouse.co.uk

A CIP catalogue record for this book
is available from the British Library

The Random House Group Limited supports The Forest Stewardship Council (FSC), the leading international forest certification organisation. All our titles that are printed on Greenpeace approved FSC certified paper carry the FSC logo. Our paper procurement policy can be found at www.rbooks.co.uk/environment

Printed in the UK by CPI Mackays, Chatham, ME5 8TD

ISBN 9780091928377

To buy books by your favourite authors and register for offers visit
www.rbooks.co.uk

All photographs featured in this book are courtesy of NASA

CONTENTS

Acknowledgements ....(vii)

Prologue 1
1 The Bright Stuff 6
2 Carrying the Fire 22
3 Moving Targets 37
4 Finding a Way Home 53
5 Nowhere to Hide 70
6 Grounded in Safety 86
7 Risks and Risky Remedies 104
8 A Tissue-paper Spacecraft 120
9 Into the Darkness 139
10 Pushed to the Limit 157
11 A Place in History 177
12 'The *Eagle* Has Wings' 193
13 Sneaking Up on the Past 217
14 A Walk on the Moon 230
15 Mission Accomplished 248
Epilogue 266

Notes 275
Glossary 299
Bibliography 301
Index 304

Acknowledgements

Many people kindly gave this book and the TV show it accompanies much generous support and assistance. The factual drama *Moonshot* is one of a number of TV shows produced by Dangerous Films focusing on the history of NASA generally and Apollo 11 particularly. Some were completed before the *Moonshot* project was conceived, but during their production I was enormously privileged to discuss NASA's work with Buzz Aldrin, Neil Armstrong, Gene Cernan, Charlie Duke, Chris Kraft, Gene Kranz, Glynn Lunney, George Mueller and others. Humanity possesses the knowledge and experience to leave our planet at will thanks to the pioneering actions of men such as these, and I remain in awe of their achievements. To those who so patiently helped me with some of the more technical aspects of these achievements, I am grateful. I am particularly indebted to the team behind the exemplary website the Lunar Surface Journal, among them David Harland, Frank O'Brien, David Woods and especially Ken MacTaggart.

Staff at the Johnson Space Center, the Marshall Space Flight Center and other NASA sites have been enormously generous in their assistance to all of us at Dangerous, as have experts at the Smithsonian Institution, particularly Dr Roger Launius. Chris Riley's illuminating suggestions were as entertaining as they were valuable, and I am also grateful to the enthusiastic assistance of Doug Millard at the Science Museum. Thanks too to Ken Barlow and Jake Lingwood at Ebury, and especially to Richard Dale and Mike Kemp at Dangerous, whose kind support is greatly appreciated.

Above all, I'd like to give heartfelt thanks to my gracious and loving wife Saira, who I'm sure on occasion felt she'd been whisked off to the Moon and stranded in lunar orbit. And to Yasmin, I'd like to say that 'Ubba's boop' is finally finished.

PROLOGUE

What would the Moon be like?

While this question fascinated those back on Earth, for Neil Armstrong the Moon was playing no more than a supporting role. Here was a chance for man to achieve something beyond comparison. If it were successful, the Apollo 11 mission would demonstrate that humans, as a species, were capable of escaping from their planet and visiting somewhere a world away from home. It didn't matter much whether the Moon was made of brown rocks, grey dust or even green cheese. To Armstrong, all that really counted was landing safely and then coming home again, without letting anyone down in the attempt to do either.

Standing in the lunar module, the most fragile manned spacecraft ever built, Armstrong was flying at more than 3,000mph, five times faster than a passenger jet. There were no landing pads on the Moon, no ground crew to guide him down; 50,000 feet below him lay nothing more than an uncharted area that was pockmarked by rocks and craters and which was believed to be a little less dangerous than other uncharted areas. If he were to reach his designated target site, Neil would have to gradually reduce his speed to walking pace and then find a relatively benign area to touch down before his fuel ran out. There was little margin for error. Landing too fast on a landscape strewn with boulders could damage the spacecraft and potentially end any hope of returning home.

One way or the other, in the next 12 minutes it would be over and all the hand-wringing, the months of agonising expectation and the endless press questions could finally be laid to rest. The newspapers were fascinated by lunar landscapes. But while rocks and craters captured the media's attention, for a pilot they were to be avoided. As far as Neil was concerned, Apollo 11 wasn't about boxes of stones. Exploring the surface was secondary to the mission's prime objective. None of the early aviation pioneers, who had so inspired Neil as a boy, had regarded their greatest triumph to be a stroll beside their aircraft. Armstrong, like the Wrights, Earhart and Lindbergh before him, knew that nothing was more significant about a test-flight than safely completing it.

Standing beside Neil was Buzz Aldrin, and together the two men would have considered themselves to be flying horizontally face down had they not been in weightlessness. They were also travelling backwards, feet first, using the engine as a brake to reduce their speed. The gleaming white surfaces of their cramped cabin were bathed in sunlight, yet somehow the aura of a brand-new spaceship was personalised by the grubby ways of people. Handwritten notes were stuck on the dull grey instrument panels and here and there other personal items were secured by Velcro or held down by netting. Having taught himself to go to the Moon, man was bringing with him urine bags, food trays and doodles in margins.

While Buzz monitored the instruments, Neil looked through the triangular window in front of him. In timing their journey over the alien terrain below, he discovered with dismay that the crater known as Maskelyne-W had arrived early. They were three seconds ahead of themselves, and three seconds equated to three miles, which would take them beyond the edge of the landing zone. They would be coming down in an area Neil knew to be strewn with boulders, and in a spacecraft with walls so thin you could poke a pencil through them. He knew they would be lucky to avoid any damage. Luck wasn't enough. He had the facility to override the computer and fly the spacecraft manually but this could only be done in the closing stages of the descent. For the moment he must follow the flight-plan.

At 40,000 feet, Armstrong rotated the lunar module by 180 degrees so that he was no longer looking down at the Moon but staring up into space. By repositioning the spacecraft, which was operating under the call-sign *Eagle*, Neil enabled the landing radar to get a clearer view of the surface. Now that they were due to land long he needed as much reliable information as he could get.

Then the yellow master alarm started to flash, a tone sounded in Neil's headset and the computer's yellow PROG light lit up. The computer would help diagnose the problem, allowing Armstrong and Aldrin to decide what action to take based on lessons learned during training. 'It's a 1202,' Neil told Houston after glancing at the computer display. It was a code neither he nor Buzz had ever seen during training, so now they had two problems. The computer could be signalling an immediate need for action, yet incapacitated by uncertainty they could do nothing but wait for advice from home.

The seconds slowly ticked by. Neil was prepared to abort at any moment should it suddenly become obvious that they were in serious trouble. As commander of the mission his decision was final, and if the situation demanded it he would take action, whether Houston had replied in time or not. Conscious that the situation could rapidly deteriorate, Armstrong quickly assessed the performance of the spacecraft's systems. He urgently needed to know whether the alarm required them to immediately abort the flight. In the absence of information, 18 seconds after calling for assistance he was forced to repeat his request, and for the first time anxiety could be heard in his voice.

'Give us a reading on the 1202 program alarm.'

A further five seconds later, Houston finally replied: 'Roger. We're go on that alarm.' Using the jargon of Mission Control, the ground assured Neil that the alarm could be switched off and that it was safe to continue the flight.

Mission Control tried to pass on additional information but the haunting sound of static interrupted the transmission, and for a while communication was intermittent. There were many moments when Neil and Buzz simply didn't know how closely the flight controllers were able to follow the data that was automatically sent back from the spacecraft. This was something they had never practised for. Training simulations had either gone well or something had gone wrong; the question of things-kind-of-being-OK-but-it's-hard-to-be-sure had never arisen, and the astronauts found it distracting. The computer alarm was even worse. It continued to signal a warning, and for Neil and Buzz it seemed that they had a genuine problem. Houston was three days away, and confronted by an error in their timing, broken communications and recurring alarms, Armstrong and Aldrin were relying on pure piloting skills. It was hard to be sure about where they were going to come down, but then it didn't really matter as long as they came down safely. Apollo 11 was no longer confined to the science of computers and trajectories, it was about the art of flying.

Lying on its back, *Eagle* gradually pitched upright towards a vertical position, giving Neil a clear view of the ground ahead. The computer was guiding the spacecraft directly towards a huge crater beside a field of boulders, any one of which could smash the lunar module's landing gear or the engine bell. At less than 1,000 feet Neil took partial control of the spacecraft. Using a hand controller, he cut the descent rate and focused on flying forward, skimming over the dangers below without a word to Mission Control. In Houston the flight controllers were all but paralysed by the tension as it became clear that Neil was delaying the landing. Each man knew that the spacecraft was approaching an altitude just a few hundred feet above the surface that was known to be a point of no return, a part of the flight-path referred to as the dead-man's box. Attempting an abort at this point was fraught with danger. Neil now had to land, safely and quickly, before his fuel ran out.

No TV pictures were being transmitted from the spacecraft so all the flight controllers had to go on was their telemetry. But this didn't explain why Armstrong was taking so long to come down, nor did Buzz's emotionless reading of the instruments.

'3½ down, 220 feet, 13 forward,' said Buzz, reporting on the lunar module's rate of descent, altitude and velocity.

There was no response from Houston.

'11 forward. Coming down nicely.

'200, 4½ down.

'5½ down.

'160, 6 to 6½ down.

'5½ down, 9 forward. That's good.

'120 feet.

'100 feet, 3½ down, 9 forward. Five per cent.

'OK. 75 feet. And it's looking good. Down a half, 6 forward.'

A curt announcement of '60 seconds' from the ground reminded the crew that soon they must land or attempt to abort. To Armstrong, fuel getting low and time running out were mere parts of an equation. There was no need nor time to discuss them with Buzz. Nor did he say much to Houston, only occasionally pressing the switch that would transmit his words. A man with a cool yet agile mind, Neil's ability to conceal much of it from the world was something the world occasionally found frustrating. It barely mattered to Neil that they were now three miles beyond the ideal landing zone, that communications were patchy and that the fuel was low; what mattered as he searched for a safe spot to land was that there were rocks below. The fuel was a concern, but he believed he had enough to do the job.

Supporting Neil with a constant account of their position, Buzz continued to read aloud from the instruments: '4 forward. 4 forward. Drifting to the right a little. OK. Down a half.'

'30 seconds,' called Mission Control.

With their role on this phase of the mission coming to a close, the flight controllers were now no more than spectators, like everybody else. In truth, nothing needed to be said. It was down to Armstrong.

Chapter 1
THE BRIGHT STUFF

Grasping a grey pistol-grip controller with his right hand, Armstrong guided the lunar module down towards his chosen landing point. By manoeuvring the joystick he was able to fire thrusters mounted on the sides of the spacecraft, allowing him to fly in any given direction. But once moving, the lunar module would keep going until the opposite thruster was fired, which meant that maintaining course was a tricky process involving a careful balancing act. After satisfactorily landing the spacecraft, a shirt-sleeved Armstrong casually took off his headset and hopped out of the hatch.

It was Tuesday 15 July 1969, the day before Apollo 11 was due to launch, and Armstrong and Aldrin were taking part in final simulations using a mock-up of the lunar module in the Flight Crew Training Building at the Kennedy Space Center. Equipped with displays showing images of the landing zone, and driven by a battery of computers capable of replicating some of the challenges of space-flight, the simulator at Cape Kennedy[1] was the best available. Here, and in other training facilities, Armstrong familiarised himself with the spacecraft's systems including the joystick with which he would fly the lunar module during the final stages of the landing. For a pilot, the hand controller was an unfamiliar device. In an aircraft, a control stick adjusts the angle of the ailerons on the trailing edges of the wings which roll the aeroplane left or right. The stick also raises or lowers the two horizontal elevators on either side of the vertical tail, pitching the aircraft up or down. By pushing against the air, these adjustable surfaces allow an aeroplane to change direction. In space there is nothing to push against, so these surfaces were replaced with small rocket thrusters that were controlled by the sensitive joystick, based on principles developed in NASA's experimental rocket plane, the X-15.

Straight out of a 1950s sci-fi comic, the X-15 was the stuff of legend. Everything about it was extreme. Slung beneath the wing of an adapted B-52 bomber, the aircraft was carried to altitude before the pilot ignited the rocket engine. Reaching record-breaking speeds in excess of 4,000mph, fast enough to strip paint off its airframe, the X-15 would zoom out of the atmosphere towards the edge of space, where the pilot would briefly experience weightlessness. It would then slice its way back into the thinnest layers of air for the flight down to the ground. In climbing to 50 miles and above, the X-15 was in effect the first manned sub-orbital spacecraft; three of its pilots reached altitudes that entitled them to receive NASA astronaut wings. At such heights the atmosphere was too thin to have any impact on conventional control surfaces, forcing the pilot to rely on the small rocket boosters and the prototype hand controller that were tested by, among others, Neil Armstrong, one of only 12 men ever to fly the X-15.[2]

For Neil, it was not so much a love of flying that took hold of him at an early age, more a fascination with the design and construction of aircraft. Armstrong rarely discusses his personal life, but he revealed in his authorised biography[3] private details about his childhood, describing how he came to build model aircraft out of straw, paper and wood. He still possessed many of the models even after becoming an astronaut. Born on 5 August 1930 in Wapakoneta, Ohio, as a child Neil frequently moved from town to town due to the nature of his father's work in the state auditor's office. Stephen Armstrong had a remote though cordial relationship with his elder child; it was Neil's mother Viola who was to have the greater influence on their son.[4] Like many of NASA's pioneering astronauts, Neil grew up in small country towns many of which were slow to recover from the Depression. 'We were not deprived,' he remembered, 'but there was never a great deal of money around.' All 12 men who walked on the Moon were either the first son or an only child. In Neil's case, a sister, June, arrived when he was nearly three, and a younger brother, Dean, joined them a year and a half later. The three children played happily together, but one abiding memory of Neil's places him quietly indulging in his love of books.

When Neil was 14, the family moved back to Wapakoneta where friends remembered him as being confident and capable but also as a boy with little to say. Those who knew him didn't regard him as shy – he played the baritone horn in the school orchestra and took part in plays – but he was seen as someone who didn't feel the need to say much. Neil was 'a person of very few words' who 'thought before he spoke', class-mates said. His tendency to engage with the world somewhat privately found expression in the construction of those model aircraft. 'My focus was more on the building than the flying,' he told his biographer, Dr James Hansen. 'While I was still in elementary school my intention was to be – or hope was to be – an aircraft designer.'[5]

Unhurried in design projects both at home and at school, Neil came to be known for doing things in his own way without being in any particular rush to set the world alight. He never displayed any 'outer fire', as his brother put it.[6] NASA flight director Gene Kranz said he never saw Armstrong argue; nevertheless he 'had the commander mentality … and didn't have to get angry'. Neil was cool in the old-fashioned sense, in that he tended to keep his distance. His interests weren't confined to model aeroplanes – he once crashed his father's car after the school prom while driving his date back from an all-night diner – but at first glance he was not the kind of person who might expect to find himself in an aircraft flying at five times the speed of sound. Nevertheless, applying his careful (some were to describe it as slow) analytical style of thought to the pursuit of his interest in aircraft design, Neil came to a logical conclusion: 'I went into piloting because I thought a good designer ought to know the operational aspects of an airplane.'[7]

From the age of 15, Neil joined other local kids hanging around Port Koneta, the town's small airfield. He saved his earnings and managed to pay for flying lessons, which he took to so readily he qualified by the time he was 16, before he'd got his driving licence. Hooked on aircraft, Neil opted to study aeronautical engineering at college, notwithstanding that college was expensive and his family couldn't afford it. A solution was possible through the navy, which was offering four-year scholarships in return for a period of service. Armstrong wasn't particularly interested in a military career but he saw it as a means to an end. In 1947, after receiving a 'wonderful deal' from the navy, he began to attend Purdue University in Indiana. Just a year later, confronted with the prospect of war in Korea, the navy began to recruit extra personnel and Neil, aged 18, was ordered to interrupt his studies and report for duty at Pensacola, Florida. While the air force turned out pilots, the navy produced airmen capable of landing on the deck of a pitching carrier, whom they branded aviators. In August 1950, after 18 months' training, Armstrong joined their ranks.[8]

On 3 September 1951, Ensign Armstrong was preparing for his twenty-eighth assisted take-off in three months. After lining up his F9F-2 Panther fighter jet aboard the USS *Essex*, a hydraulic catapult hauled his aircraft from a standing start down the length of the short flight-deck and into the air above the freezing waters of the Sea of Japan. Flying with VF-51, the first all-jet squadron in the navy, Armstrong was just beginning this armed reconnaissance mission over North Korea when his unit ran into anti-aircraft defences. Streaking in at 350mph he prepared for a low-level attack when at 500 feet his Panther, loaded with bombs, struck an air-defence cable that ripped six feet off his starboard wing. Ejecting would have given him only the slimmest hope of reaching safety as few American pilots had returned after parachuting over enemy territory. After reclaiming limited control of the stricken jet Armstrong nursed it back to South Korea where he could safely eject, coming down virtually unhurt in a rice paddy. At a time when ejection seats were still in their infancy, Armstrong's cool handling of the incident won him much 'favourable notice', as a fellow pilot put it.[9]

During five tours of combat and 78 missions over enemy territory, Armstrong lost close friends and experienced freezing Korean winters amid a growing realisation that few people in the States knew what the military were doing in Asia. He fired thousands of rounds, suffered engine failure, survived forays into 'MiG Alley' and many times after landing he discovered bullet holes in his aircraft. Compared to civilian flying, combat – as Armstrong put it – ran the risk of 'more consequence to making a bad move'. He also enjoyed periods of leave in Japan, discovering aesthetic influences that were to stay with him for the rest of his life.

In September 1952, Armstrong returned from the war to finish his degree at Purdue, and there he met 18-year-old Janet Shearon, a home economics student. Attractive and vivacious, Janet was the girl he would some day marry, Neil told his roommate after first meeting her, although it would be three years before he got round to asking her out on a date. 'Neil isn't one to rush into anything,' Janet later said. Outgoing and talkative, she regarded him as good-looking and fun to be with.[10]

When Neil graduated in January 1955, with good though not outstanding grades, he looked for a job as a test pilot. While in Korea his term of service with the navy had officially ended and he had been transferred into the naval reserve, a halfway position between civilian life and the military. For civilians, the most exciting test-flight opportunities were to be found at Edwards Air Force Base, home to a small team from the National Advisory Committee for Aeronautics (NACA). Initially, Armstrong's application to Edwards was unsuccessful, and although the NACA took him on, he was sent not west but east to Cleveland where he was involved in research into anti-icing systems. Then, just five months later, he was invited to swap the grey clouds of Ohio for the Californian sunshine after the NACA found an opening and sent him to Edwards at last.[11]

Neil had once believed that nothing could replicate the great days of aviation, when fighter aces raced about the sky in scarlet triplanes, and heroes and heroines set records in epic flights to distant corners of the Earth. 'I had missed all the great times and adventures in flight,' he felt.[12] But for an ambitious test pilot, Edwards was the place to be. Here, in 1947, Chuck Yeager first flew faster than the speed of sound, taking the rocket-powered Bell X-1 into a new era of high-speed flights that heralded the dawn of the space age. Edwards was where the first US jet had been tested, as well as many of the experimental X-planes, including the X-3 Stiletto and the X-5 variable geometry 'swing-wing' jet. But it was Yeager's achievement that first put Edwards on the map, prompting scores of young pilots to head west in search of golden opportunities.

After marrying Janet, Neil bought a property 5,000 feet up in the remote Juniper Hills region of the Antelope Valley, not far from the air base. It was a rural cabin with basic plumbing, bare wood floors and no electricity, but Neil slowly set about transforming the place into a home fit for a family. In June 1957 Janet gave birth to Eric, whom they came to call Ricky; two years later he was joined by a baby girl, Karen, and then in 1963 by another boy, Mark. Together the Armstrongs lived in the high desert of California, an untamed corner of America lost under endless blue skies.[13]

Edwards was situated next to the dusty salt-pan bed of Rogers Dry Lake. An enormous runway two and a half miles long extended into the lake itself which for most of the year was swept dry by the heat of howling desert winds. Stretching for 25 miles towards desolate mountain ranges, in an emergency the flat lakebed was as useful to dare-devil pilots as it was unforgiving. With its fearsome death toll and harsh climate, its rattlesnakes and sandstorms, Edwards was only marginally less desperate than the kind of air force pilots attracted there by the range of exotic aircraft. What mattered to many was the opportunity to clamber aboard something with an X in its name and push it as hard as possible in a wham-bam moment of ecstasy. However, the small number of engineer pilots, including Armstrong, who were attached not to the air force but to the NACA's High Speed Flight Station sought time to get intimately acquainted with the aircraft in the interests of aeronautical research.

Edwards for Armstrong proved to be a shining highlight of his career. His work was as varied as the aeroplanes he flew: he carried out more than 900 flights in a range of famous aircraft, from the F-104 Starfighter to the KC-135 Stratotanker. While he occasionally evaluated a new aircraft, noting its characteristics and recommending changes, he also flew older types that were fitted with experimental components designed to enhance the performance of the instruments, engines or airframe. A couple of his contemporaries considered other pilots to be better 'stick-and-rudder' men than Armstrong, but he acquired a reputation for a detailed understanding of technical issues and could be consistently relied upon to monitor a test accurately while rocketing through the sky faster than the speed of sound. His unflappable command of the aircraft bought him the time he needed to complete the task in hand.[14]

Sometimes the pressures were enormous. During the early 1950s, an average of one test pilot a week was killed in an air accident; in 1952 alone 62 pilots died at Edwards during a nine-month period.[15] Neil had been introduced to the ugly side of flying while still in Wapakoneta where he witnessed a fatal crash, but it was in Korea that he was first personally touched by loss. On the day he returned to his ship after bailing out, two squadron friends had been killed. Less than two weeks later a Banshee jet, attempting to land on the *Essex*, smashed into a row of aircraft lined up on the deck, burning four men to death. Later, the loss of Armstrong's cabin-mate Leonard 'Chet' Cheshire hit him particularly hard.[16] At Edwards the risks could be more easily calculated, but much of the flying was still inherently dangerous, particularly Neil's work with the X-15, an aircraft he was to fly seven times.

Designed to reach hypersonic speeds above Mach 5, three

X-15s were built by North American Aviation, each so dangerously close to the limits of aircraft performance that they set speed records which still stand today. Managed by a flight control centre equipped with tracking facilities, each flight to the edge of space was first rehearsed in a simulator. Once in the air, the aircraft was accompanied by four chase planes, while on the ground a fleet of vehicles was ready to deal with all eventualities. The pilot, wearing a pressure-suit and squashed into a tiny cockpit, could see little of his sleek black aircraft through the reinforced windows. At the end of his ten-minute test, he would have to lose speed and altitude quickly by flying a specific flight pattern, later adopted by space shuttle pilots. Even then he would be unable to land without first jettisoning the ventral fin slung beneath the fuselage.

On 20 April 1962, as the launch countdown reached zero, Neil prepared to assess a new 'g-force limiter' designed to prevent a pilot from experiencing a force more than five times greater than gravity. Once released, with a sharp lurch, from the B-52 he ignited his rocket engine and zoomed up to 207,500 feet – the highest altitude he would ever reach in an aircraft. At this height he could see the black void of space. He was completely reliant on his rocket thrusters to get back into the atmosphere, but while focusing on a test of the limiter he held the nose of the aircraft up for too long and as he tried to descend the X-15 bounced off the atmosphere back up towards the edge of space. The flight control centre urged him to follow the correct course, but Neil found that by the time he had managed to cut back into the upper reaches of the atmosphere he was screaming past the airfield at a speed of Mach 3. Turning round 45 miles south of Edwards, he was confronted with the uncomfortable thought that he might have to ask for permission to bring his rocket-plane into the traffic pattern of Palmdale municipal airport. When he eventually came within sight of the southern tip of Edwards the chase jets caught up with him and the control centre helped co-ordinate the landing as Armstrong raced in just a few feet above the desert floor.

During the post-flight debriefing a flight manager asked one of the chase pilots how close Neil had been to the trees.

'About 150 feet,' came the reply.

'Were the trees 150 feet to his right or to his left?' asked the smirking manager.[17]

Yet for all the record-breaking altitudes and speeds achieved by Armstrong and the other X-15 pilots, there was a growing sense that America was being left behind in the attempt to send a man into space. In October 1957, the legendary aircraft streaking about the blue skies above Edwards were overshadowed by a football-sized satellite. It did little more than transmit a radio signal back to Earth, but it was unmistakably un-American. Russia's successful development of Sputnik propelled the Cold War into space, prompting a sense of shock that rippled in many high-level directions. There was a widespread belief that if the Russians could send a ball across the United States, they could surely send nuclear warheads. But instead of bombs, a month later Sputnik 2 carried a dog, Laika, into orbit, extending Russia's bid for recognition as the world's leading technical nation. For the first time the NACA realised that Moscow was preparing to send a man into space,[18] something that would deal a major blow to American esteem and put the US on the back foot for years to come. Washington was forced to act.

Less than a year after Sputnik, the NACA was replaced by the National Aeronautics and Space Administration (NASA), and its managers were given a specific brief: put a man in space ahead of the Soviets.[19] But what could a man actually do in space? Would the high g-forces, weightlessness and the undiscovered problems of orbital flight allow him to do anything at all? These questions shaped the search for recruits, and eventually 110 military pilots, each with a college degree and at least 1,500 hours' flying time, were invited to apply.

Armstrong, a civilian, was not asked. In any event, it is unlikely that he would have agreed to swap the successful X-15 programme for an unproven project where a man would be shut up in a capsule and blasted on a short trajectory largely controlled from the ground. 'Spam in a can' Yeager called it, though Armstrong himself was not quite so scornful. He saw that space represented a new challenge. 'I thought the attractions of being an astronaut were actually not so much the Moon, but flying in a completely new medium,' he said later.[20]

In April 1959, seven men were selected to take part in the fledgling manned space programme, named Project Mercury. All were white military men despite the fact that thirteen women later proved they could pass the demanding round of tests, including Jerrie Cobb. Cobb, who had set records for speed, distance and altitude, sought support from Congress, and a memo noting her impressive qualifications was laid before Vice President Lyndon Johnson – who promptly dismissed her cause with the comment 'Let's stop this, now.'[21] NASA argued that one day capsules would support two or more astronauts in a confined space, making it difficult to accept women into the programme. However, as writer Andrew Smith put it, 'anyone capable of contemplating the myriad nasty ends available to an astronaut could probably learn to bare his arse in front of a lady without bursting into tears'.[22]

After being accepted by NASA, the Mercury Seven began preparing for America's first manned missions. The United States expected to become the first nation to send a man on a sub-orbital flight, in a mission that would be a triumphant coup for the West. In the first weeks of 1961, however, doubts remained concerning the safety of the capsule and its rocket, and both had yet to be man-rated in a test-flight. Instead of an astronaut, the capsule would first carry Ham, a four-year-old chimpanzee, and on 31 January Ham was launched on a flight lasting nearly 17 minutes. Then on 12 April the Russians, once again ahead of the Americans, launched Yuri Gagarin not just into space but into a complete orbit of the Earth. The coup had been pulled off, not by NASA but by Moscow. In the States, a contemporary newspaper cartoon by John Fischetti showed one chimpanzee telling another

'We're a little behind the Russians, and a little ahead of the Americans.'

On the day when he first flew faster than sound, Chuck Yeager had been unable to close the aircraft canopy unaided, after breaking a couple of ribs two days earlier while riding a horse. He had told only his wife and a fellow pilot about the accident, asking his buddy to secretly rig up a device that would help him secure the hatch. This anecdote comes from the writer Tom Wolfe, who wrote about the rugged, pioneering ways of pilots like Yeager, and his contemporaries the Mercury Seven. Only men with the 'right stuff', who rode horses through the desert, were able to fly experimental flying machines powered by rockets and testosterone, while ignoring eye-watering pain. Men like Yeager could 'break the sound barrier' (although there was no such thing), and if you asked them nicely they could even possibly squeeze spinach from a tin using just their hands. Wolfe's pilots are lone heroes, 'single-combat warriors' living on the edge, having taken over the mantle of the cowboys who occupied the wild deserts of the West before them. Such bravado was embraced by many of the air force pilots at Edwards. Men like Yeager were dismissive of the more studious type of airmen, some of whom came to be recruited as astronauts.[23] It was said that anyone who would want to sit in a Mercury capsule would have to 'wipe the monkey shit off the seat first'.[24] Some of these air force men were not actually entitled to become astronauts themselves because they did not have a college degree, such as Yeager. Priding himself on his 'balls out' attitude, Yeager regarded NASA's airmen as 'sorry fighter pilots' who rated 'about as high as my shoelaces'.[25] But it was NASA's research pilots who would prove themselves capable in the agency's blossoming space programme.

In May 1961, Alan Shepard became the first American to reach space, his Mercury capsule being carried to an altitude of 116 miles by a Redstone rocket. During this and subsequent Mercury flights, the astronauts' work in weightlessness exceeded all expectations. Encouraged by their early success, NASA began to plan for more complicated missions in preparation for the ultimate ambition, a journey to the Moon. Such a flight would rely on orbital mechanics, lunar trajectories, docking procedures and machinery complex enough to safely carry a crew nearly a quarter of a million miles and back. More technically complicated than anything achieved by man before, such a mission would require years of studious preparation. Notwithstanding Wolfe's adulation of heroics, only those with the bright stuff would be up to completing such an adventure.

In April 1962, NASA asked for applications for a new class of astronauts. Applicants had to be test pilots who were currently flying high-performance aircraft and who had a college degree in engineering or one of the sciences. They could be no taller than six feet and no older than 35. Although it wasn't explicitly mentioned, it was clear that one way or another they would be involved in the preparations for a lunar landing. As well as new personnel, such ambitious plans would require spacecraft and rockets bigger and stronger than anything that was currently available. Two months earlier, Project Mercury had successfully achieved its goal of putting a man in orbit. John Glenn, a former marine, circled the Earth three times, but his hardware fell far short of the capability needed to get to the Moon. The rockets propelling the first two Mercury flights were not much more powerful than the XLR-99 engine installed in the X-15.

In May, NASA's plans for the future were set out at a conference in Seattle, and among those speaking was Armstrong, who delivered a presentation on hypersonic research flights. The conference was held alongside the Seattle World's Fair, whose guests included John Glenn. By proving that NASA was capable of orbital flight, Glenn had demonstrated that proposals for more adventurous missions deserved to be taken seriously. It was clear that the design and engineering challenges posed by flights into space promised to go beyond anything on offer elsewhere. For a pilot captivated by powered flight since childhood the new opportunities were too exciting to resist. Still, never one to rush things, Armstrong waited until he got back from Seattle before submitting his application. It arrived at the Manned Spacecraft Center in Houston in early June, missing the final deadline by a week.[26]

()

At Cape Kennedy on 15 July 1969, after leaving the simulator Armstrong returned to the crew quarters, from where he called his parents in Wapakoneta. Sounding cheerful, he told them that he and the rest of the crew were ready for the launch, scheduled for 9.32am local time the following morning.

'Will you call us again before you leave?' his father asked.

'No, I'm afraid I won't be able to call again,' Neil softly replied.

'We asked God to watch over him, and then we had to say goodbye,' his mother later said.[27]

After lunch (why was it always steak, he had once asked Janet) there was little to do except try to relax and maybe steal a breath of fresh air. The crew were given access to a cottage on the coast where they passed the time swimming and relaxing on the beach. That evening they called their wives and ate an early dinner. Jim Lovell, the commander of the backup crew, told Armstrong, 'This is your last chance to tell me if you feel good. Because if you do I'm going to have myself a party.'

While the astronauts themselves maintained an air of business as usual, around them their support team felt a rising sense of tension. 'We were the ones who were a little uptight,' Dee O'Hara, the crew's nurse, later said. After driving to the space centre from her hotel, Dee told Neil, 'You wouldn't believe the number of people who have come to watch the launch.' Neil gave her a brief smile and said it was inevitable people were going to make 'a big deal out of it'. Dee was surprised by Armstrong's cool assessment of what to the rest of America promised to be the biggest scientific accomplishment in the country's history.[28]

Tight security operated throughout the 88,000 acres of the Kennedy Space Center as a million sightseers from all corners of the country descended on eastern Florida. From Titusville to Melbourne, thousands of cars converged on a huge region stretching as far west as Orlando. With the freeways blocked by the worst jams in Florida's history, some drivers used the wrong side of the road since no-one was heading in the opposite direction. Only the wealthy, or well-connected, managed to avoid the crowds by arriving in private aircraft and then boarding one of the hundreds of boats choking the Banana River. Meanwhile thousands of people, who were already settled among barbecues, beer coolers and bottles of pop, were either lounging around or else trying out their cameras, telescopes and binoculars. Somewhere out there was a rocket and a bunch of guys who were going to fly on it and there were persistent debates about which direction to look in. Hotel rooms had long since sold out but late-comers were allowed to set up camp-beds in lounges and lobbies. By the waterfront, caravans, tents and awnings lay scattered among camper vans and station wagons as revellers prepared for the countdown beach parties that would run through the night. A 'lift-off martini' would set you back $1.25, while for those who really wanted to live it up there was the 'moonlander', consisting of crème de menthe, crème de cacao, vodka, soda and a squeeze of lime, topped with an American flag. Food and drink were still available but local stores had sold out of alarm clocks by lunchtime.

While for some Apollo 11 represented exploration, prestige and glamour, all wrapped up in a neat metal tube, beyond the fanfare on the beaches others believed that America was falling apart at the seams. Many felt the whole event was a costly mistake that ignored the social problems battering the nation. As the parties were getting under way, the Reverend Ralph Abernathy, successor to Martin Luther King as head of the Southern Christian Leadership Conference, led more than a hundred campaigners to the gates of the space centre in protest at 'this foolish waste of money that could be used to feed the poor'. As far as Abernathy and his supporters were concerned, relieving poverty was surely a priority over the search for moon rocks that was costing the nation $24 billion. Abernathy wanted to know whether the largest commitment of resources ever made in peacetime was really worth it. He was met by NASA Administrator Thomas Paine who addressed the protesters' concerns before inviting a delegation to watch the launch from the VIP area.

For the vast majority of America, however, the moral arguments were a distraction from a feat of engineering that represented all that was great about the country. American expertise had built this rocket, heroes would sit in the top of it and there were only a few hours left before everyone could see it for themselves. 'Apollo 11 gave a lot of nice people a chance to get acquainted,' said Texas car dealer Jay Marks. He and a friend had loaded up their sons and driven east to Cocoa Beach, a Florida playground that had been frequented by off-duty astronauts since the days of Mercury, and which was now overflowing with people from out of town. Throughout the day the southern sunshine had given way to heavy clouds, but undaunted by the weather, everywhere everyone shared the feeling that history was about to be made.

Ten miles beyond the most congested areas stood the object at the centre of all the excitement, the anguish and the hope. On launch-pad 39A, the towering Saturn V rocket waited in the one place on the coast that was relatively peaceful. With no-one aboard, and not yet carrying any fuel, the vehicle could be largely left alone until the pre-launch activity began. Yet this rocket, the most powerful machine ever built, was impossible to ignore. As dusk descended, the second tallest structure in Florida (the tallest was the building in which the Saturn V had been assembled) was brilliantly lit up by floodlights, its white panels glowing softly against the forbidding clouds behind. This was the vehicle that was going to achieve something men had dreamt of for millennia. That was the plan at least.

Like all astronauts' wives before a launch, Janet Armstrong had been trying to prepare herself for any eventuality. Having been driven to a spot three miles from the launch-pad, Janet and her children gazed at the monumental sight before them. With clouds obscuring the Moon, she stood lost in her thoughts until forced to retreat to the car when a gentle rain began to fall.[29]

Chapter 2

CARRYING THE FIRE

Standing 363 feet tall, from a distance the Saturn V looked more like a peaceful monument than anything capable of reaching orbit. But as lightning lit up the night sky, technicians began to busily prepare the slumbering rocket for its improbable flight to the Moon. At 11pm the launch-pad team began cooling the booster's empty fuel tanks before filling them with six million pounds of propellants. The RP-1 kerosene was allowed to remain at room temperature but the pale blue liquid oxygen had to be kept extremely cold to prevent it returning to gas. It boiled at a temperature of minus 182.96°C; positively balmy compared to the liquid hydrogen that was held at minus 252.87°C. The propellants were pumped into insulated tanks resembling giant thermos flasks. As the tanks slowly began to fill, glistening chunks of ice formed on the outside of the rocket. Some of the liquid oxygen was allowed to boil off, and as the tank was replenished excess gas was released into the atmosphere to prevent a dangerous build-up of pressure. Streams of vapour rolled down towards the ground, and the rocket looked as if it were exhaling on a cold winter's morning.

The sections of the vehicle that would fly all the way to the Moon weighed more than 103,000lb (51 tons). To get them there meant first raising them off the ground, then pushing them up through the atmosphere so quickly that they reached orbit before they could fall back again. Orbit was just 100 miles from the ground; the Moon, however, was the best part of 239,000 miles away. To complete the journey the rocket would have to break free of Earth's gravity, which meant burning fuel for another five minutes and 53 seconds. All in all, to put the spacecraft on course for the Moon required such a heavy load of fuel that its weight compressed the relatively thin external skin of the booster. When fully laden, the rocket shrank by eight inches.

Once depleted, the Saturn's heavy fuel tanks had to be dropped over the Atlantic to reduce the burden on the engines. This required the rocket to be made of three separate sections. The first stage – fuel tanks, engines and all – would fall away at a height of 36 miles, at which point the second stage would take over, pushing the rocket up to an altitude of 101 miles before it too was dropped. To assist each separation process, small thrusters were placed at strategic points along the Saturn's length so that the entire vehicle carried a total of 41 rocket engines. Between them, the first two stages of the Saturn V produced enough energy to supply the city of New York for an hour and a quarter.[1] After the second stage was jettisoned, the third-stage engine would then ignite, sending the spacecraft into orbit. Built by different contractors in separate locations, the three stages (together referred to as the 'launch vehicle') had been transported to Cape Kennedy and bolted together in the Vehicle Assembly Building (VAB), an enormous hangar with a floor plan covering an area of eight acres.

On top of the third stage sat an instrument unit carrying the rocket's guidance system, and above this came the three modules that would continue all the way to the Moon (together referred to as the 'spacecraft'). The lunar module was sealed inside a conical 'adapter' that rested on the instrument unit, and on this sat the cylindrical service module which carried oxygen, electrical power and other critical supplies for the command module that was attached above it. The conical command module, the principal section that would be occupied by the crew, was just 11 feet five inches high. At the very top of the stack (or 'space vehicle') was an abort rocket which was capable of pulling the command module clear of danger during the launch. The stack, consisting of nearly six million parts – a labyrinth of fuel lines, tanks, pumps, gauges, sensors, circuits and switches – was put together by more than 5,000 technicians using computer-assisted cranes and an assembly tower, which at 398 feet was taller than the Saturn itself. The entire vehicle was completed on 14 April.[2]

Connected by horizontal access arms, and together weighing 12 million pounds (6,000 tons), the vehicle and the tower rested on an enormous steel platform inside the VAB. The tricky thing about the VAB was that it was three and a half miles from the launch-pad. Fortunately the platform was mobile and could be collected by a vehicle and driven to where it was needed. The vehicle capable of collecting a Saturn V rocket and its accompanying tower and driving both to the launch-pad boasted a set of statistics that rivalled the booster itself. The six-million-pound 'crawler transporter' trundled along at 1mph on giant caterpillar tracks; each of its 'shoes' alone weighed a ton. More than 500 gallons of fuel were consumed during its six-hour journey along a road the width of an eight-lane motorway.[3] Once the rocket was in position at Launch Complex 39A, the transporter retreated.

Specifically designed and built to accommodate the Saturn V, the pad was equipped with fuel lines encased in a protective vacuum (small leaks were stopped using tampons soaked in water that quickly froze in place). It also offered a concrete blast-room, designed to protect the crew from an exploding rocket. Built directly under the pad and capable of holding 20 people for up to three days, in an emergency the bunker could be entered via a 40-foot slide that ended in the 'rubber room'. The pad was managed by a team of technicians who reported to the Launch Control Center, an enormous blockhouse built beside the VAB, from where the overnight preparations were directed.[4]

At 4.15am, Neil Armstrong, Michael Collins and Buzz Aldrin were woken by the Director of Flight Crew Operations, Deke Slayton. Deke had originally been selected as one of the Mercury Seven, but after being unceremoniously grounded by a heart condition he had been moved to a management position and had never flown in space. He joined the crew for breakfast (steak), accompanied by Bill Anders from the backup crew and the artist Paul

Calle, who sat sketching in a corner. Half an hour later, the astronauts began the arduous process of putting on their pressure-suits. All being well, the bulky suits could be removed a few hours into the mission, but an emergency during the early stages of the flight might mean they would have to be worn for days. The procedure began with each man rubbing a special salve on his buttocks before strapping on a condom-style device to collect urine, followed by a nappy for anything else. After attaching sensors to their chests, Armstrong, Aldrin and Collins put on 'constant wear' long-johns before being assisted into their airtight suits.

On Earth, when drawing in breath your lungs rely on the fact that their sucking action is readily met by a quantity of air heaped into the body by the weight of the atmosphere pressing down from above. Without external pressure, the lungs would struggle to function. Worse still, the natural forces within your body would no longer be held in check; blood, and other fluids, might try to burst free. Keen to avoid this, the astronauts would artificially maintain pressure within the command module, allowing them to remove their suits. These were only worn to protect the men in the event of a sudden loss of pressure during vulnerable moments, such as the initial journey into space. Each suit consisted of an inflatable bladder that allowed an artificial degree of pressure to be imposed on the body. To stop the bladder ballooning once inflated, its human shape was maintained by a web of stiff fabric, bellows, inflexible tubes and sliding cables, all of which were woven together to produce the familiar spacesuit. Two types were available: Armstrong and Aldrin wore a heavier 55lb variety capable of protecting them on the surface of the Moon, while Collins wore a lighter 35lb suit.

Once they had donned their 'Snoopy hats' (soft caps fitted with earphones and microphones), the astronauts completed the suiting-up process with the addition of a pressure helmet, a clear polycarbonate bubble. The suits were then filled with pure oxygen, which in space would allow them to replicate only a fraction of the pressure of Earth's atmosphere (3.7 psi as opposed to

15 psi). However, pressure as low as this allowed nitrogen within the body to break free of solution and collect in painful bubbles – a condition known to divers as 'the bends'. In its mildest form this effect is familiar to all of us: it's thought that 'cracking knuckles' can be attributed to bursting bubbles of nitrogen. In space, nitrogen collects in joints, particularly elbows and knees, and to prevent this the astronauts purged their body of the gas by breathing pure oxygen for more than three hours before launch. Dependent on portable supplies of pure oxygen, connected to the suit via a tube, the three men were sealed off from any physical contact with friends and colleagues waiting to bid them farewell. 'You peer at the world, but are not part of it,' wrote Michael Collins. He secretly found pressure-suits to be unsettling and even claustrophobic, so much so that he had once considered confessing all and leaving the programme.[5]

In the weeks before the flight, Collins had attracted almost as much press attention as Armstrong, for the fact that he would *not* be walking on the Moon. As the only member of the crew who would remain aboard the command module throughout the mission, he had been repeatedly asked about his fears of isolation. Despite the growing press attention he maintained a sang-froid that later earned him a reputation as Apollo 11's philosopher. Unencumbered by Neil's focus or Buzz's ambition, Michael occasionally managed to indulge a sense of detachment from his role as the command module pilot, not to mention the mission overall, and even NASA itself.

This relaxed attitude to life developed during childhood when he learned to adapt to the succession of new homes and schools that were part and parcel of life in a military family. His distinguished father, Major General James Collins, had served in the Philippines in 1911, where he had flown aboard the wing of a Wright Brothers aircraft. During an appointment to Italy as a military attaché, Michael, his fourth child, was born, in Rome on 31 October 1930. After returning to the States, the family moved to Governor's Island in New York Bay, then to Baltimore, Ohio, and Texas before being sent to Puerto Rico where they lived in a 400-year-old house. To ten-year-old Michael it seemed that no other home could offer such an immense ballroom, gardens teeming with tropical animals, and a brothel at the end of the road. Later he remembered that the girls would 'toss me money if I would talk to them but I never would'. Through his father's connections and varied postings, Michael came to acquire a broader understanding of the world than some of his NASA contemporaries.[6]

At school he was capable and athletic, and while he developed a love of books he also became known as a prankster. 'I was just a normal, active, troublesome kid. I liked airplanes and kites, and climbing trees and falling out of them. I didn't like school much.' He also shared Armstrong's interest in model aircraft, but for Michael it was an occasional hobby that was never as important as football and girls.

Following the family tradition, Collins attended West Point Military Academy, principally for a free education rather than to pursue an interest in the army. He could have made much of the fact that his father was a general and his uncle, a corps commander on D-Day, was now the army's chief of staff. But Michael played down his connections, to the point that after graduating in 1952 he declined to join the army at all, choosing the air force instead. After training at Nellis Air Force Base in Nevada, in 1954 Collins was sent to an F-86 fighter squadron that was soon transferred to Chambley-Bussières, a NATO base in north-eastern France.

At Chambley in early 1956 Michael met 21-year-old Patricia Finnegan. Pretty, with a vivid smile, Pat was a graduate in English who was working for the air force as a civilian. To her, Michael looked 'just as dashing, just as white-scarfy, as the others', but she was impressed by his knowledge of fine wines and French cuisine, along with his love of books and interest in the theatre. She thought he was simply 'lots and lots of fun', and above all she admired his approach to life: 'It was, and is, that everything will be OK; that everything will work out.' They married on 28 April 1957, and returned to the States a few months later.

Initially Michael had intended to complete his required four years in military service before finding something he was more suited to (his mother had suggested the State Department), but in France he found that flying had become a passion. Rather than leaving, he looked at how he might channel a restless desire for fulfilment. Collins felt the best way to get on was to become a test pilot, and he sought to accumulate the hours required by the air force's test pilot school at Edwards. Flying a variety of aircraft, Michael moved from post to post until August 1960, when the school eventually accepted him.[7] As a trainee test pilot, Collins learnt to 'observe, remember, and record every last movement of a bucking, heaving, spinning plane', doing so with such proficiency that on graduation he was the only member of his class assigned to test fighter jets.

During 1961 the number of available test-flights began to dwindle and Collins found himself casting his eye further afield. Rumours that NASA was about to hire a second group of astronauts were confirmed in April 1962, and Collins, in contrast to Armstrong's dawdling, applied 'before the ink was dry on the announcement'.[8] Manned space-flight was still in its infancy, and with scant information on the long-term effects of orbital missions NASA felt obliged to inspect the health of its applicants in great detail. Candidates were strapped to a table and their cardio-vascular response measured after they were jerked upright. In other tests, cold water was poured into one ear, 'eyeball pressure' was assessed, and one foot of bowel was examined using a rectal 'steel eel'. After being poked, prodded and pierced, Collins felt that 'no orifice was inviolate', the medics only giving way in order to allow the psychiatrists to take over. When asked to describe a sheet of white paper, Collins wondered what he should say. 'Perhaps I see a great white moon in it, or a picture of Mother and Dad, with Dad a little larger than Mother. Second-guessing the shrinks is not easy.'[9] He scored highly in the two-month selection process, but his lack of postgraduate study and his limited test-flight experience were deemed insufficient compared to the likes of Armstrong, and ultimately he was rejected.

Just nine men were successful, including Armstrong, despite his late application. This was thanks to the support of Dick Day, a friend who had already made the move from Edwards to Houston. An expert in flight simulators, Day had been appointed as assistant director of the Flight Crew Operations Division and in this capacity he acted as secretary to the selection panel. He admitted that he and a number of others valued Armstrong's experience and wanted him to apply, so when Neil finally got round to it Day quietly slipped the late application into the pile along with the rest.[10]

In October 1962, while the New Nine settled into the space programme, Collins went back to Edwards, where he set about building the experience he needed. Fortunately the air force had begun to teach the science of orbital flight to hand-picked graduates of its test pilot courses, and Michael was able to spend six months acquiring the knowledge he lacked. In June 1963 NASA again asked for astronaut applications, and after another session with the 'steel eel', Collins was successful.[11] Accompanied by Pat and their three children Kate, Ann and Michael junior, in October 1963 Collins headed south to Texas.

By the time the fourteen new recruits arrived in Houston, NASA was preparing to take the next step towards one day reaching the Moon. In the end there had been six Mercury flights, the longest lasting a little over 34 hours. This mission had provided valuable data, but a trip to the Moon might last anything up to two weeks and many questions had yet to be answered. Just how dangerous were the belts of radiation surrounding the Earth, which threatened to harm anyone venturing near them for too long? How long was too long? At least their location could be identified; solar flares, on the other hand, which also posed a radiation risk, were in 1963 largely unpredictable. After arriving on the Moon, would the crew and their 'lunar lander' spacecraft vanish into a thick blanket of dust, as suggested by Professor Thomas Gold of Cornell University? Other eminent scientists feared that if the lander did successfully settle on the surface, a charge of static electricity would attract so much dust that nobody would be able to see out of the windows. No-one was going to fly all the way there and back without actually stepping out of the spacecraft, but how could an astronaut be protected from the vacuum of space or the extreme temperatures of light and shade? The Moon was pockmarked by countless meteoroid craters, but just how often did meteoroids hit the surface? Continuously? Did lunar soil contain pure metallic elements that would spontaneously combust when carried by dirty boots into the pure oxygen that filled the lander's cabin?[12] What should the lander even look like?

The years 1963 and 1964 were dominated by the search for answers to questions such as these, early results being drip-fed into training sessions. Since everything was geared towards a lunar landing, the training included a series of geology lectures. The Mercury veterans grumbled about learning to describe grey, lumpy stones as 'hypidiomorphic granular, porphyritic, with medium-grained grey phenochrists', but to the new recruits the lectures brought the Moon a little closer. Nevertheless, Collins sometimes found the lessons a little dull, particularly when he found himself trudging along on the back of a mule after one of the field trips. 'From supersonic jets at Edwards,' he later wrote, 'I had progressed all the way to kicking a burro up out of the Grand Canyon.'[13] Between lessons, the Mercury Seven, the New Nine and the Fourteen, as the press referred to them, toured launch facilities at the Cape and inspected the new Mission Control Center in Houston. They also underwent survival training, learning to live off the land in deserts and jungles in case they came down somewhere beyond immediate reach of help. During environment training they were exposed to the noise, vibration and weightlessness of space-flight, enduring trips in what was then referred to as the 'zero-g airplane', better known today as the 'vomit comet'. As well as attending the training sessions, each astronaut also had to take on a particular area of research, representing the Astronaut Office in design meetings and test sessions. Armstrong worked on flight simulators;[14] Collins was asked to help develop pressure-suits and other equipment that would be used during space walks (properly referred to as extra-vehicular activity, or EVA).

Many of the difficulties accompanying a flight to the Moon were to be explored during a series of orbital research flights, and accomplishing a successful EVA was close to the top of the list. The Mercury capsule was too small for most of this work (it was said you didn't board it so much as put it on), and by 1965 its replacement was ready to fly. Capable of accommodating two people for days at a time, the bigger Gemini spacecraft replaced Mercury's small hatch with wide hinged doors. It was intended that during the first Gemini EVA an astronaut would open the doors, stand up and simply look around. But, as before, Russian advances forced NASA to quicken its pace. On 18 March 1965, Soviet cosmonaut Alexei Leonov became the first person to leave his spacecraft during a flight. Pictures released to the international press showed him waving to the camera as he floated comfortably above the Earth. But with the Soviet secrecy that was typical of the time, the Russians did not reveal the difficulty Leonov experienced in returning to his spacecraft, Voskhod 2. While floating in space, his pressure-suit ballooned and despite an anxious struggle during which he suffered the first symptoms of heatstroke, he was unable to climb back through the airlock. After losing 12lb in body weight, Leonov was forced to partially deflate his suit – a dangerous move under any conditions. The Russians found through hard experience that returning to a spacecraft after an EVA was far from easy. Collins independently came to the same conclusion while taking part in tests aboard the zero-g aircraft. In a memo, he warned that an 'extravehicular astro requires all his strength and agility to get back inside the spacecraft'.[15] It was a lesson NASA was slow to learn.

Astronaut Ed White, Collins's close friend from West Point, strenuously objected to the warnings, going on to make the whole process look easy while performing America's first EVA three months after Leonov.[16] With nothing to do but enjoy himself, White found he could easily move through space using blasts of oxygen from his 'zip gun'. For more than 20 minutes he freely floated above the Earth until ordered back into his spacecraft by Mission Control. The public fell in love with Ed's boyish enthusiasm, and his triumphant accomplishment encouraged NASA to race ahead with ambitious plans for future EVAs.

Next to leave his spacecraft was Gene Cernan. Secured to the outside of the rear of Cernan's capsule was a backpack equipped with small thrusters, which he was intending to fly as if he himself were a mini spacecraft. On 5 June 1966, Cernan huffed and puffed his way back towards the backpack, known as the 'astronaut manoeuvring unit'. Lacking sufficient handrails and footholds, and breathing heavily, he suffered sunburn on his lower back after tearing the outer layers of his pressure-suit while trying to drag himself along the spacecraft's hull. Once in position, he found it so difficult to complete his task that he was forced to take frequent rests. With his visor fogging and his body beginning to overheat it was clear he was in serious trouble. As his pulse soared to around 195 beats per minute, the flight surgeon in Mission Control feared Cernan would lose consciousness. The experiment was abandoned, and after Cernan returned to the hatch Tom Stafford struggled to pull him back into his seat. Once they had repressurised the capsule Stafford felt compelled to break procedure by firing a jet of water into Cernan's face to help him recover. Had Cernan not made it back aboard the capsule, rather than cut his tether and leave him in orbit it is likely that Stafford would have strapped him to the side of the spacecraft where his body would have been cremated on re-entry.

Despite Ed White's success, NASA knew 'diddly-squat' about EVA, Cernan later wrote. His experience showed that the agency had not yet developed the training, procedures or equipment required to complete a successful EVA. There was much to learn before anyone could contemplate walking on the Moon. At least on the lunar surface it would be easier to move about. But those responsible for the development of the spacesuit, including Collins, would have to come up with a more robust design incorporating an improved cooling system.

In the meantime there were just three Gemini flights left, all would involve EVAs, and next to go was Michael.

( )

With just three hours remaining before the launch of Apollo 11, Collins moved through the corridors of the Manned Spacecraft Operations Building, smiling at old friends and colleagues from inside his pressure helmet. By prior arrangement, one of them handed him a brown paper bag containing a gift for Guenter Wendt, the technician in charge of the launch-pad. Collins and Wendt frequently fished together, and Michael enjoyed poking fun at Guenter's claims to have caught a spectacularly large trout. In celebration of Wendt's stories, Collins decided to present him with a tiny trout that had been frozen and secured to a wooden plaque above the words 'Guenter Wendt Trophy Trout'.

Clutching his bag, Michael stepped out into the early-morning sunlight, and with the press looking on he, Neil and Buzz clambered aboard the van that would take them on the eight-mile journey to the pad. On the way, the crew crossed the Banana River where, five miles downstream, Janet Armstrong was waiting aboard a boat.[17] The only one of the three wives to attend the launch (Pat Collins and Joan Aldrin had chosen to stay at home to avoid the press), along with her children Janet was accompanied by astronaut Dave Scott and *Life* magazine reporter Dora Jane Hamblin. Meanwhile, ashore, more than 5,000 people were taking their places in an enclosure three and a half miles from the launch-pad – deemed to be the closest point where spectators would probably escape serious injury from an exploding Saturn V. The clouds had cleared, and although it was still early the humidity was climbing and the temperature was already in the high eighties.

In the VIP stands, former president Lyndon Johnson was joined by senior NASA managers, led by Tom Paine. Beyond the Cape, millions of Americans were watching the live television coverage, among them President Nixon in Washington and hundreds of soldiers, sailors and airmen in Vietnam. Many astronauts had friends stationed in Asia, where already nearly 34,000 Americans had been killed, and some felt guilty that rather than serving alongside them they were being treated as celebrities. Gene Cernan, along with Tom Stafford, had made headlines just two months earlier following their part in Apollo 10. Cernan felt that Vietnam was his war, yet he was safely in America where he was regarded as a hero. The commander of US troops in Vietnam, General Westmoreland, had however managed to overcome any similar worries about where he ought to be and was also watching the launch from the stands. He was joined by cabinet ministers, foreign dignitaries, businessmen and half the members of Congress, together with a scattering of stars including aviation pioneer Charles Lindbergh, comedian Jack Benny, and Johnny Carson, host of NBC's *Tonight Show*.

Nearby around 3,500 reporters from 55 countries were gathered in the press enclosure, their numbers swollen by the throng that had witnessed the astronauts depart aboard the van. It was a moment some felt to be shaped by the hand of history, and venerable reporters like Eric Sevareid found themselves ascending into lofty rhetoric. 'You get a feeling,' Sevareid told the equally venerable Walter Cronkite, the CBS anchorman, 'that people think of these men as not just superior men but different creatures. They are like people who have gone into the other world and have returned, and you sense they bear secrets that we will never entirely know.'[18]

Wearing nappies and carrying a dead fish, the astronauts meanwhile were lumbering across the deserted launch-pad, still breathing through a tube. Previously they had seen it only as a hive of activity. 'Did everyone know something we didn't know?' Michael Collins later asked in jest. The only thing that exuded life was the rocket itself. Absorbing electrical power, exhaling oxygen and loaded with a million gallons of propellants, the vehicle hissed and groaned as it adjusted to its fully laden weight.

A high-speed wire lift whisked the crew up the tower to the highest swing arm, at the end of which the tiny White Room adjoined the command module. There wasn't room for all three men to board the spacecraft at once, so while Aldrin waited on the tower, Armstrong led Collins across the access arm, accompanied by Guenter Wendt. A technician with thick glasses and a caricature accent, Wendt had served as a flight engineer aboard German night fighters during the war. Nicknamed the Pad Führer by the astronauts, the term was not always used in admiration of his good-humoured though committed style of leadership. In the sterile atmosphere of the White Room, a smiling Guenter gave Neil a farewell gift in the form of a 'key to the Moon', a four-foot-long Styrofoam key wrapped in foil. In return Neil presented him with a card that had been pushed under his watchstrap by suit technician Joe Schmitt. It read: 'Space Taxi. Good Between Any Two Planets'. Clasping a rail inside the spacecraft, Neil swung his legs through the hatch and pulled himself over to the commander's couch on the left-hand side of the cabin. Behind him, Collins presented the trophy trout to Guenter[19] before he too swung himself into the command module, sliding over to the couch on the right with the assistance of Fred Haise, a member of the backup crew who had spent 90 minutes preparing the cabin for launch, working his way down a 417-switch checklist.[20] After Buzz had taken his position in the centre couch, Schmitt connected the astronauts to the spacecraft's oxygen supply and communications system and then climbed out of the hatch, followed by Haise, who shook each man's hand as he bid them farewell.

The suggestion that 'beneath the bravado, astronauts naturally felt fear' is something of a cliché. 'What was there to be afraid of?' Buzz later asked. 'When something goes wrong, that's when you should be afraid.' For the first time man was going to the Moon, where wonderful sights were waiting to be described, but rather than give the job to a coterie of wilting poets NASA had recruited test pilot types for a reason. Through a combination of personality and training, Armstrong, Aldrin and Collins, once strapped into a cockpit, were just not the kind of people predisposed to fear. 'What would be the point?' was the way it seemed to them. Apollo 7 astronaut Walter Cunningham described how he had silently besought those around him to 'please launch and get us away from all that hand-wringing'.[21] Nevertheless, there was no getting away from the fact that here was a machine designed to generate an enormous prolonged explosion. But just how controlled was it exactly? When looking for a title for his 1974 autobiography, Collins was asked to sum up space-flight in a single phrase. For him it was like 'carrying fire to the Moon and back', and in wondering how this might be done his editor received the suggestion 'carefully, that's how, with lots of planning and at considerable risk ... the carrier must constantly be on his toes lest it spill'.[22]

At launch, the point when a 'spill' was most likely to occur, the whole vehicle weighed more than 3,300 tons, 90 per cent of which was fuel; the command module together with the crew took up just 0.2 per cent of the overall weight. The amount of fuel, the size of the engines and the extensive safety precautions left no-one in any doubt that the crew would have to tread a fine line in terms of retaining control of the whole assembly. The prospect of watching the rocket ascending upon a stream of fire while three men sat at the mercy of its explosive force sparked a shared sense of awe among the thousands of spectators. The Saturn V was the only manned machine ever built that was powerful enough to leave not just the ground but the Earth's entire sphere of influence, the edge of which lay 186,437 miles away. As the minutes ticked by, the test of the crew's ability to control such power drew closer.

At 7.52am, technician John Grissinger closed and locked the hatch, then he, Wendt, Haise and the rest of the small 'close-out' team descended the tower, leaving the astronauts alone in the cabin.

Chapter 3
MOVING TARGETS

With three of the command module's five windows covered by a protective shroud, the cabin was illuminated by a scattering of small lights that cast reflections in the men's transparent helmets. Lying on their backs and surrounded by dull grey hardware, Armstrong, Collins and Aldrin were busy making their final checks. An hour and 20 minutes before lift-off, still scheduled for 9.32am, Neil was monitoring the guidance system, his right elbow brushing against Buzz. Above, beneath and around them lay stowage lockers, harness supports, manuals and checklists, batteries, two computer displays, fire protection panels, 12 reaction control engines, pyrotechnic devices, helium tanks, drinking water facilities and 57 instrument panels supporting more than 800 switches and gauges. Tucked away were tapes containing music selected by the crew, and an opal chosen by Guenter Wendt which was to be presented to Mrs Wendt after it had travelled to the Moon and back. As well as items necessary for Holy Communion, among them a small quantity of wine, the men were also taking with them 2.4 ounces of plutonium 238, intended to heat one of the lunar experiments; snacks such as bacon squares, and meals including spaghetti and meat sauce; fragments of *Flyer*, the Wright Brothers' aircraft that was the first to achieve powered flight; two full-size American flags at the request of Congress; and TV broadcasting equipment for the benefit of the rest of the world.

If successful in reaching its destination, Apollo 11 promised to take mankind somewhere new – and it seemed to the crew that virtually all of mankind had given them a trinket to take along for the ride. For Michael there was a sense of tension that came 'mostly from an appreciation of the enormity of our undertaking rather than from the unfamiliarity of the situation. I am far from certain that we will be able to fly the mission as planned. I think we will escape with our skins, or at least I will escape with mine, but I wouldn't give better than even odds on a successful landing and return. There are just too many things that can go wrong'.[1] Squashed in beside Buzz, Michael had minor tasks to complete, 'nickel and dime stuff' as he called it. 'In between switch throws I have plenty of time to think, if not daydream. Here I am, a white male, age thirty-eight, height 5 feet 11 inches, weight 165 pounds, salary $17,000 per annum, resident of a Texas suburb, with black spot on my roses, state of mind unsettled, about to be shot off to the Moon. Yes, to the Moon.'[2]

Beyond the rocket and its pad, 463 people directed the final preparations from consoles in Firing Room 1 of the Launch Control Center. At one point Jim Lovell, Neil's backup, came over the air, asking again whether Armstrong felt OK to fly. 'You missed your chance,' Neil replied.[3] At the 56-minute mark, public affairs officer Jack King announced that parts of the countdown checklist were 15 minutes ahead of schedule. 'That's fine,' Armstrong had said, 'so long as we don't launch 15 minutes early.' With less than 40 minutes to go, launch controllers tested the Saturn's destruct system. Should the rocket tumble out of control near a populated area, the destruct system could be remotely activated. After passing the 15-minute mark, the booster no longer drew on an external electrical supply but began to rely on its own resources. At five minutes and 30 seconds from lift-off, the destruct system was armed,[4] and at three minutes and seven seconds the launch sequence came under the control of a master computer in the firing room. At 17 seconds, the Saturn's highly advanced instrument unit, built by IBM, began independently to monitor the rocket's stability.

'T minus 15 seconds,' announced King, 'guidance is internal ... 12, 11, 10, 9, ignition sequence starts.'

In 1961, Alan Shepard's Redstone rocket had produced 80,000lb of thrust. Less than nine seconds before the launch of

Apollo 11, fuel cascaded into the Saturn's five F-1 engines, the most powerful of their type ever built. After reaching maximum output, together they generated a ground-shaking 7.5 million pounds of thrust.

'6, 5, 4 ...'

Strapped down tightly inside the dull cabin of the command module, the men could see little through the hatch window. The first indication that they were on their way would come when the mission timer on the main instrument panel began to register the seconds, minutes and hours that had elapsed since ignition.

'3, 2, 1, zero. All engines running, lift-off! We have a lift-off, 32 minutes past the hour. Lift-off on Apollo 11.'

The engine-bells ignited in a blinding flash of light, each soon producing more thrust than the three main engines of the space shuttle combined. Now they were lit, they could not be shut down. Come what may, the crew knew they were at least going somewhere. All being well they would be in space in less than 12 minutes.

Boiling plumes of fire plummeted down through the launch platform, then were briefly sucked back towards the engines before rolling down to ground level. As 25,000 gallons of water washed across the face of the platform, huge clouds of flame, reaching temperatures of 1,900°F, were channelled away from the pad via long trenches filled with water. With the engines now burning 15 tons of fuel a second, more than 40 tons of propellant were consumed before the rocket even left the ground. Fountains of flame instantly vaporised the water in the trenches, producing clouds of steam that could be seen for dozens of miles around. Behind a protective sand bunker nearly 3,000 feet away 14 people in flame protection gear were waiting on armoured personnel carriers, ready to help the astronauts in an emergency. Further afield, teams of doctors, safety officials, ordnance experts and recovery specialists were stationed beside roadblocks surrounding the space centre. The five swing arms that were still connecting the vehicle to the tower were rapidly pulled aside, and as the engines' exhaust fumes thrust downward in a relentless force of energy they generated enough pressure to push the 36-storey rocket slowly off the ground. More than 17,000 gallons of water a minute were sprayed over the swing arms to preserve them as flames gushed from the 14-foot-wide engine-bells at a rate four times faster than the speed of sound.

The spectators saw the steam but at first heard nothing. Fifteen seconds later a noise could be sensed rushing at them. When it arrived it overwhelmed them, a resounding deep bass crackling that shook the ground. Australian journalist Derryn Hinch, packed in among the press corps, later found bruises on the tops of his thighs, caused by his shuddering desktop. (In tests carried out during poor weather conditions in Alabama, the sonic energy of five F-1s had reverberated so strongly off the cloud ceiling that minor earthquakes were felt 40 miles away.) Nurse Dee O'Hara cried as she saw the rocket rise into the clear blue sky. Photographers forgot their cameras and just stood and watched along with everyone else. In the VIP stands, the protester Reverend Ralph Abernathy considered himself to be 'one of the proudest Americans as I stood on this soil'. Aboard her boat on the Banana River, Jan Armstrong exclaimed, 'There it is! There it is!'[5]

Inside the command module, the astronauts were shaken so much they found it difficult to see the altimeters to check they were actually moving. The sound of the launch rumbled through the cabin like a distant express train. Buzz felt 'there was a slight increase in the amount of background noise, not at all unlike the sort one notices taking off in a commercial airliner'.[6] Four of the engines could be gimballed, and as the rocket lifted off the ground it threw itself this way and that, struggling to keep away from the tower. To Michael, the first ten seconds felt 'very busy', and he believed the three of them were maintaining only the thinnest veneer of control. He compared the rocket's jittery action to a 'nervous lady driving a wide car down a narrow alley. She can't decide whether she's too far to the left or too far to the right, but she knows she's one or the other. And she keeps jerking the wheel back and forth.'[7]

In an emergency, Armstrong was responsible for swiftly selecting one of a number of abort procedures, as determined by the rocket's velocity and altitude. The booster was the first of its type equipped with a manual override system that allowed the commander to fly it himself should it deviate from its course.[8] If the crew were to lose control altogether, Neil would turn the abort handle beside his left knee, which would instantly ignite the rocket mounted above the command module. This would quickly carry the cabin clear of trouble. Emergencies aside, the Saturn remained free to guide itself, and as its speed rapidly increased, the fast-changing situation required intense concentration. 'You have to do things right away and do them properly,' Neil later said, adding that he 'listened to indications over the radio as to which [abort] phase you were in or about to enter'[9] while simultaneously monitoring the instruments.

After clearing the tower, the rocket maintained course by rolling over to 18 degrees from vertical, while control on the ground transferred from the Cape to Houston. In the Mission Control Center, flight controllers and backroom staff assessed more than 1,300 telemetry measurements that were automatically sent from the rocket. The launch team then gave updates to astronaut Bruce McCandless as he helped Armstrong through the abort options.

McCandless: 'Apollo 11, Houston. You're good at 1 minute.'

Armstrong: 'Roger.'

McCandless: 'Stand by for mode 1 Charlie.'

McCandless: 'Mark.'

McCandless: 'Mode 1 Charlie.'

Armstrong: 'One Charlie.'

Approaching four miles in altitude and climbing at nearly twice the speed of sound, the rocket's rough ride was beginning to quieten down. Thousands of awestruck spectators along the eastern coast of Florida were left stunned by the sight of the tiny white needle balanced on top of a towering column of smoke. Above the exhaust fumes, a plume of fire hundreds of feet long was driving the astronauts forward at 6,000mph, so fast that as they sank back into their couches they felt as if they weighed more than four times as much as normal.

McCandless: 'Apollo 11, this is Houston. You are go for staging.'

After the giant F-1 engines had burned for just two minutes and 42 seconds, the 138-foot first stage fell away from the rest of the vehicle. While soaring up to an altitude of 36 miles, the lowest reaches of space, the rocket had travelled at such a speed that it had been compressed lengthwise. When the first stage was dropped, the rest of the booster snapped back to its true proportions, throwing the astronauts forward against their harnesses.[10] The five J-2 engines of the second stage then ignited, pushing the spacecraft up past the 60-mile mark. At this point the abort tower was jettisoned, carrying with it the command module's protective shroud and thereby allowing sunlight to stream in through the windows. At this height the Saturn was scything through the thinnest regions of the atmosphere.

More than six minutes after ignition, the second stage was depleted and it too was jettisoned, eventually plunging into the Atlantic 2,300 miles from the coast. Apollo 11 was now powered by the single J-2 engine of the third stage (known in NASA's jargon as the S-IVB). Pitching over towards a flatter trajectory, the crew were presented with a spectacular view of the curvature of the Earth as the ocean stretched away before them. Finally, at a point 1,461 miles downrange, the instrument unit stopped the engine. The astronauts were now coasting at more than 17,400mph, on an orbital path 103 miles above the world. Just 11 minutes and 49 seconds after launch – before the spectators had had time to return to their cars – Armstrong, Aldrin and Collins had arrived in space.

Buzz felt that 'The Earth ... has an almost benign quality. Intellectually one could realize there were wars under way, but emotionally it was impossible to understand such things. The thought reoccurred that wars are generally fought for territory or are disputes over borders; from space the arbitrary borders established on Earth cannot be seen.'[11]

On the ground, the cabin had been filled with a mixture of oxygen and nitrogen. During the ascent, the cabin pressure had been allowed to drop from nearly 15 to 5psi, and at the same time the crew's life-support system purged any remaining nitrogen to leave an atmosphere consisting of 100 per cent oxygen. Protected from the threat of nitrogen, the crew were able to remove their helmets. These had to be carefully stowed to stop them floating about the cabin in the liberating conditions of weightlessness. Releasing the straps on his couch, Collins moved forward towards the middle of the display panel. By slipping underneath it, he could pull himself into the lower equipment bay, on the far side of the command module. This was the only place in the spacecraft where an astronaut could stand up, his head rising towards the apex of the cabin. At the top lay a hatch, through which the crew would later be able to enter the lunar module once they had retrieved it from its protective position inside the adapter.

Moving about in the equipment bay, Michael removed a Hasselblad stills camera from a locker, then called over to Buzz: 'How would you like the camera ... I'll just let go of it, Buzz; it will be hanging over here in the air. Coming up – it's occupying my couch.'

The crew had spent a lifetime living with gravity, and now that it was no longer present, their hearts were working overtime. The men experienced a pounding in their ears and throats until their bodies were able to adjust. The first pictures Buzz took show that their faces were puffed up with blood, and though the redness receded the crew continued to look fuller than when on the ground.[12] With gravity no longer pulling down on the fatty tissue beneath their eyes, Michael believed that Neil and Buzz looked 'squinty and decidedly Oriental'.[13]

An hour and 20 minutes into the flight, as the spacecraft

passed from the dark side of the Earth into sunrise, an arc of rich crimson light rolled back the blackness of space with a majesty that took Michael's breath away.

'Jesus Christ, look at that horizon!'

Armstrong: 'Isn't that something?'

Collins: 'God damn, that's pretty; it's unreal.'

Armstrong: 'Get a picture of that.'

Collins: 'Oh, sure, I will. I've lost a Hasselblad ... has anybody seen a Hasselblad floating by? It couldn't have gone very far – big son of a gun like that.'

After a couple of minutes searching, the camera still hadn't appeared.

Aldrin: 'But you want to get it before TLI.'

Collins: 'I know it. That's what I'm worried about.'

After eventually recovering the camera, Collins looked out of the window.

Collins: 'Trees and a forest down there; it looks like trees and a forest or something. Looks like snow and trees. Fantastic. I have no conception of where we're pointed or which way we're going or a crapping thing, but it's a beautiful low pressure cell out here.'

Having entered a 'parking orbit', the spacecraft travelled around the world one and a half times in less than three hours, giving the crew and the ground a chance to make sure everything was working. Once it was established that all was OK, at two hours and 43 minutes into the mission the crew received permission to re-ignite the third-stage engine. By burning the engine a second time, in a manoeuvre known as trans-lunar injection (or TLI), they would escape from orbit and begin their journey towards the Moon.

Mission Control: 'Apollo 11, this is Houston. Slightly less than 1 minute to ignition, and everything is go.'

Collins: 'Roger.'

Collins: 'Ignition.'

Mission Control: 'We confirm ignition, and the thrust is go.'

Mission Control: 'Apollo 11, this is Houston at 1 minute. Trajectory and guidance look good, and the stage is good. Over.'

Armstrong: 'Apollo 11. Roger.'

Mission Control: 'We show cut-off.'

Mission Control: 'Apollo 11, this is Houston. Do you read? Over.'

Aldrin: 'Roger, Houston. Apollo 11. We're reading a VI of 35,579 ... over.'

Armstrong: 'Hey, Houston, Apollo 11. That Saturn gave us a magnificent ride.'

Mission Control: 'Roger, 11. We'll pass that on. And, it certainly looks like you are well on your way now.'

Armstrong: 'We have no complaints with any of the three stages on that ride. It was beautiful.'

In a mission to the Moon, an obvious thing to do would be to point your rocket towards it and fly in that direction. But in attempting to do this, you'd be likely to miss. The Moon is a moving target, travelling at 2,286mph as it orbits the Earth over a 27-day period. When flying towards it, the trick is to aim at a point where you think it will be once you've completed the three-day journey out to its orbital track. It was a while before NASA could demonstrate an ability to do this accurately and reliably. Ranger 3, a probe launched in 1962, was designed to examine the lunar surface but due to an incorrect course change it missed the Moon by 22,000 miles. It remains trapped in lunar orbit to this day. Ranger 5 also failed to reach its target, problems with its power supply causing it to miss by 450 miles. Later, more advanced probes demonstrated that such difficulties had been overcome – so although the TLI burn put them on a course towards an empty point in space, the crew of Apollo 11 confidently expected the Moon would eventually meet them. Indeed Armstrong, Aldrin and Collins intended to arrive with such accuracy they knew that if they never fired their engine again they could expect to be carried round the Moon by lunar gravity and automatically sent back to Earth. Known as a free return trajectory, this technique was adopted as a safety measure since it gave the crew a chance to come home even if they ran into trouble after TLI.

Such intricate manoeuvres had to be carefully worked out by specialists, including astronauts. While Collins assessed EVA equipment and Armstrong worked on simulators, the third member of the crew, Buzz Aldrin, focused on mission planning. Buzz had once been a member of Houston's rendezvous and re-entry panel, but when he found that the panel was not performing the work he expected of it, he drew attention to himself by switching to the trajectories and orbits panel.[14] Within the Astronaut Office such actions occasionally won Aldrin a bad press, his true nature and motivation sometimes being misunderstood. Being misunderstood was something that had haunted Buzz since childhood.

( )

Born in Montclair, New Jersey, on 30 January 1930, Edwin Aldrin Jr was the third child and only son of a distant and demanding father. After studying under Dr Robert Goddard, a leading pioneer in rocket science, Aldrin senior (who used the name Gene) served as a pilot during the First World War and later came to know Orville Wright. Gene Aldrin completed a doctor of science degree in electrical engineering at the Massachusetts Institute of Technology (MIT), then cut a dash as an aide to General Billy Mitchell, who was stationed in the Philippines. In 1928 Gene left the military to become a stockbroker; through luck or judgement, he sold his stock just three months short of the Wall Street crash. Taking a job with Standard Oil, he travelled the world in a style that for an oil executive managed to include a good deal of adventure. He was commended by Mussolini, flew himself over the Alps, and crossed the Atlantic aboard the *Hindenburg* zeppelin. Gene subsequently became an aviation consultant, making use of his connections with Charles Lindbergh, Howard Hughes and Jimmy Doolittle.[15]

When Edwin junior was born, his two older sisters, Madeline and Fay Ann, came to call him 'brother'. Fay Ann, who was just learning to speak, pronounced this as 'buzzer', which was later condensed to Buzz. He saw little of his adventurer father, and was largely brought up by his mother, his sisters, Anna the cook and Alice the housekeeper. There was a sensitive, almost vulnerable side to Buzz, more pronounced than any comparable quality in either Armstrong or Collins. His childhood was marked by a quest for his father's approval, that even in adulthood proved to be somewhat elusive. During the Second World War, Gene Aldrin was away from home even more than he had been in previous years, serving in the South Pacific and in Europe. Buzz later wrote that whenever he came home 'the visits were always short and, it seemed to me, rather remote'. While, as children, Neil and Michael pursued hobbies that fulfilled personal interests, Buzz sometimes took part in things that were likely to win him attention. These included picking fights in pursuit of a 'much-wanted shiner', in order to impress the crowd he wanted to hang around with.

As much a loner as Neil and Michael, Buzz enjoyed solo activities such as pole-vaulting, swimming and cycling, but also played at quarterback for the school football team. His average grades at school brought disapproval at home, and as he grew older he came to realise that a better performance was required. 'My father never gave direct instructions nor stated goals,' Buzz later wrote, 'but what was expected was somehow made clear.' Making a decision to improve his schoolwork he threw himself into this ambition, so much so that by the time he graduated from West Point, in 1951, he came third out of a class of 475. His father wanted to know who came first and second. 'Third place doesn't hold quite the appeal to him that first place does,' Buzz remembered.

In deciding to join the air force, Buzz pursued his own ambitions rather than following his family's wishes. Instead of West Point, his father had wanted him to attend the navy academy at

Annapolis, Maryland. The two had fought over the subject, Aldrin senior eventually giving way. Subsequently Gene wanted his son to fly multi-engine aircraft, while Buzz hankered after fighters. Again Buzz won the day, but at some cost since his successes were tinged with conflict and defiance.

Tenacious, competitive and with a point to prove, Buzz flew 66 combat missions in Korea, shooting down two MiGs. After returning to the States, in 1954 he married Joan Archer, the daughter of family friends. Bright, articulate and with a master's degree from Columbia University, 'she had a way of smiling at me I couldn't figure out', Buzz wrote. 'It either meant, "I've got your number, buster," or "Try and catch me." Both, I think now.'[16] Joan came to think of him as a 'curious mixture of magnificent confidence bordering on conceit and humility'.[17] Indeed a fellow air force officer quietly took Buzz aside after a few beers one night and told him he was too competitive and too insensitive to others, but that he had great potential and he wouldn't want to acquire a reputation as an egotist. 'He must have spoken the truth,' Buzz later recalled, 'because the truth can sometimes hurt and I had tears streaming down my cheeks. I thanked him.'[18]

In 1956, Buzz was transferred to Bitburg, Germany. In Bitburg, Aldrin began to think about his future and considered applying to the air force's experimental test pilot school at Edwards. Instead he decided to earn a postgraduate degree, and he asked the air force to send him to MIT where his father had studied some 40 years earlier. Beginning his studies just a few months after NASA selected the Mercury Seven, Buzz chose for his doctoral thesis the subject of manned orbital rendezvous techniques. Rendezvous, the science of two spacecraft finding and approaching each other, would be an essential component in any mission to the Moon. It was not, however, a traditional subject of study for an air force pilot. It was becoming clear that Aldrin's ambitions lay in other directions.

After starting his doctorate, Buzz wrote to NASA during their search for a second group of astronauts, suggesting they drop the requirement for test-flight experience. NASA declined. In early January 1963, after completing his studies Aldrin was briefly posted to the air force's space systems division in Los Angeles, and from there he was sent to the Manned Spacecraft Center to assist with government experiments that were being prepared for the Gemini flights. He, Joan and their three children, Michael, Jan and Andy, together made the journey to Houston. Then in June, when NASA asked for applications for a third group of astronauts, Aldrin found that the requirement for test pilot experience was no longer mandatory and he quickly applied.

After enduring the series of rigorous selection tests, alongside Collins, Aldrin was in his office one day in September when Deke Slayton called and invited him to become an astronaut. 'Shoot, Deke,' Buzz replied, 'I'd be delighted to accept.' In common with almost everyone who received *the call* from Deke, Buzz accepted in as relaxed a style as he could muster, later saying, 'I was determined to look casual and self-assured and from somewhere deep in my conditioning, that attitude materialised.' In contrast to Armstrong, who genuinely was casual and self-assured, Buzz later described himself as being 'out of my head with excitement'. Whereas Armstrong had been too busy to worry about whether he would be selected,[19] Buzz wrote that he had become 'so oriented to the goal of becoming an astronaut that I felt being refused would bring about destruction, deep disappointment from which I might never recover'. For Aldrin, much was at stake. Many years later he once introduced his father as 'the man who propelled me into the astronaut business', which, said Buzz privately, 'was a bit of an under-statement. An under-statement that paled beside the expectations Edwin Eugene Aldrin had for his lastborn child and only son.'[20] Joining NASA was a moment of triumph Buzz had long been working towards. But in many respects membership of such an elite group of high-achievers meant that life was to become more complicated.

Aldrin's doctoral work – and vocal championing of his own ideas – eventually earned him the nickname Dr Rendezvous.

Armstrong later said it was true that Buzz knew more about rendezvous matters than anybody else in the Astronaut Office, adding that 'he didn't hide that fact but he didn't take advantage of it either'.[21] Another fact Buzz found it hard to hide was his confusion over how crews were selected for flights. Decisions were made behind closed doors, largely though not exclusively by Slayton. Thirty astronauts were available for the ten manned missions of the Gemini programme, and each flight required two crewmen. In theory there were 20 places to fill, but some astronauts were to be selected for a second trip. Deke paired potential candidates according to their skills and compatibility, giving command positions to the Mercury veterans and handing out the remaining seats to the more promising newcomers.

Inevitably some of the 14 recruits were chosen to fly ahead of their envious peers. Buzz was among those who had to wait. For six years he had been studying hard for an opportunity that now lay just outside his reach. As frustrating as it was, he knew he could not adopt the direct approach he had used in confrontations with his schoolmates, or later, when fending off his father. His father, having kept him at arm's length, awakened in Buzz a need to go the extra mile. All along, Buzz had found that determination and achievement could overcome the difficulties in his life. But now things were different and he was unsure how to take the softly, softly approach. When he ran out of patience, Buzz decided to talk to Deke directly. After reminding Slayton just how experienced he was in the field of rendezvous techniques, Buzz went on to say, 'I had no idea at all how the selections were made, but that I felt it was honest to at least state that I had some pretty good qualifications'. The conversation dried up in an awkward silence until eventually Deke said he would take the matter under consideration. Subsequently, Slayton and the NASA hierarchy deemed that Buzz had been brash.[22]

Aldrin decided to share the problem with colleagues. He frequently discussed the 'astronaut business' with his close friend and fellow air force pilot Charlie Bassett, who was due to fly aboard Gemini 9. As crew after crew was announced, it appeared that the only thing that raised a man's chances of being selected was previous experience as the member of a backup crew. Anyone on a backup crew could reasonably expect to fly three flights later. Finally, Buzz was told that he was to be part of the Gemini 10 backup crew, which meant he might fly aboard Gemini 13 – a poor place to be in a programme with 12 flights, two of which were unmanned. Bassett's forthcoming mission was of great interest to Buzz since it was to include a rendezvous, and the two frequently discussed Charlie's preparations.

Early on the morning of 28 February 1966, Charlie and his fellow crewman Elliot See flew from Houston to St Louis to inspect their spacecraft. Amid bad weather, See, who was piloting their two-seat T-38 jet, was struggling to land and after coming in too low he attempted to go round again, but it was too late. The jet tore into the very building where the spacecraft was being prepared and both men were killed. In the aftermath, their backups, Tom Stafford and Gene Cernan, became the prime crew, Cernan subsequently carrying out the dangerous EVA Charlie had been training for. In the weeks after the accident, those preparing for successive missions moved one flight forward. Through the loss of his close friend, Buzz moved from Gemini 10 to backing up Gemini 9, which put him in line to fly on the last flight, Gemini 12 – in theory. When he explained the changes to Charlie Bassett's widow, Jeannie, she told him, 'Charlie felt you should have been in it all along. I know he'd be pleased.'[23] Aldrin later described this as one of the most uncomfortable moments in his life. But the Gemini 12 line-up was not yet confirmed. The final decision on whether Buzz would fly was to be addressed by Slayton and the NASA hierarchy.

()

At her home in Houston, Joan Aldrin and her children Michael, 13, Janice, who was nearly 12, and Andrew, 11, had watched the launch of Apollo 11 on television. Sitting alongside Jeannie

Bassett, Joan had fallen silent during the final seconds of the countdown; while watching the rocket race away from the Earth she didn't say a word for the first seven minutes of the flight.[24] The live TV coverage had struggled to keep up with the booster's furious pace and soon all that could be seen was a billowing column of smoke, as if the rocket had finally been consumed by the fire trailing behind it. The men were not due to return for another eight days.

Chapter 4

FINDING A WAY HOME

During trans-lunar injection the crew fired the third-stage engine for less than six minutes, but it was enough to increase their speed to more than 24,000mph. 'We started the burn at 100 miles altitude,' Collins later wrote, 'and had reached only 180 at cut-off, but we are climbing like a dingbat ... At the instant of shutdown, Buzz recorded our velocity as 35,579 feet per second, more than enough to escape from the Earth's gravitational field.'[1] Following a course that would put them some 40 degrees ahead of the Moon as it travelled on its path around the Earth, Neil, Michael and Buzz were now heading directly towards deep space.[2] A quarter of an hour later, Mission Control lost contact with them. While this was a routine irritation during any space-flight, for the families it was worrying. In Houston, Janet Armstrong, Pat Collins and Joan Aldrin were able to hear everything for themselves. A 'squawk box' loudspeaker, installed in their homes, broadcast the repeated attempts to restore communications.

Mission Control: 'Apollo 11, this is Houston. Our preliminary data indicates a good cut-off on the S-IVB. We'll have some more trajectory data for you in about half an hour. Over.'

Mission Control: 'Apollo 11, Apollo 11, this is Houston. Over.'

Mission Control: 'Apollo 11, Apollo 11, this is Houston. Over.'

Armstrong: 'Hello, Houston. Hello, Houston. This is Apollo 11. I'm reading you loud and clear. Go ahead. Over.'

Mission Control: 'Roger, 11. This is Houston. We had to shift stations. We weren't reading you through Goldstone. We show pyro bus A armed and pyro bus B not armed at the present time. Over.'

Armstrong: 'That's affirmative, Houston. That's affirmative.'

Mission Control: 'Roger.'

Mission Control: 'Apollo 11, this is Houston. You're go for separation.'

Listening to the radio messages, Pat Collins tried to hide the tension behind a calm smile as she prepared to address the press gathered on her front lawn. She and her children – Kate was ten, Ann seven and Michael six – had watched the launch on television, accompanied by friends and relatives. Before stepping outside, Pat had told the children, 'Be polite, say that you thought it was nice or whatever you thought, and don't say too much.' The reporters were gathered around a fallen oak tree that had been brought down overnight by a thunderstorm. It had attracted quite a bit of attention in the Collins household and already somebody had called offering to chop it up. 'But that's my wishing tree,' sobbed Kate.[3]

Meanwhile, more than 3,000 miles above the Earth, Michael Collins was preparing for his first big test of the flight. Three and a quarter hours into the mission, Apollo 11 consisted of the command module, followed by the service module and then the adapter, the long cone-shaped container holding the fragile lunar module (which was normally abbreviated to LM and universally referred to as the 'lem'). Beyond this was the instrument unit and then finally the S-IVB third stage. Having completed the TLI burn, the third stage was no longer needed. Before it could be discarded, however, the lunar module had to be extracted from the adapter. As the command module pilot, for Michael this would be one of the most complicated and delicate manoeuvres of the mission.

Swapping seats with Neil, he climbed into the left-hand couch and for the first time took control of the spacecraft. Pushing a switch to detonate pyrotechnic charges, Michael separated the command and service modules (shortened to CSM) from the rest of the vehicle. Then, by increasing his speed by just half a mile per hour, he was able to edge ahead. After 15 seconds, he pitched the CSM up by 180 degrees so that he was looking directly back towards the adapter, now 100 feet away.[4] Deprived of the CSM, the top of the slender container opened up like the petals of a flower. Four panels splayed open and then broke away entirely, revealing the precious cargo contained inside. Slowing down by the smallest margin, Collins allowed the adapter to approach them. With the Sun shining brightly on his target, he could see the LM crouching snug inside its shell. Meanwhile Buzz, who like Neil was largely a spectator during this part of the journey, was recording Michael's progress using a 16mm camera. Inch by inch, Collins flew the command module towards the LM, gently docking with it. Once he had accurately lined up the two vehicles Michael quickly operated a mechanism which automatically fired 12 spring-loaded latches, securing the connection between the LM and the command module.

Collins was dissatisfied. 'That wasn't the smoothest docking I've ever done.'

'Well, it felt good from here,' Armstrong reassured him.

Ten minutes after separation, Collins had completed the first part of his task. Sliding out of his seat he scrambled under the console in front of him and slipped into the lower equipment bay. Once he'd opened the hatch at the top of the command module Michael would later have to clear the elaborate docking mechanism out of the way. For a bon viveur who had somehow wound up as an astronaut, such fiddly mechanical work had proved difficult in training and he wasn't looking forward to doing it for real.

Armstrong: 'Well, Buzz is getting comm right now.'

Collins: 'Yes, let Buzz do his high-gain thing, and I'll get ready to go dick with the tunnel.'

On opening the hatch, Michael was struck by a smell of burning, resembling 'charred electrical wire insulation'. Later he would say it was 'enough to knock you down ... it was one strong odour'. Other astronauts have since noticed a similar sensation after completing a docking, some describing it as the 'smell of space'. (British scientists researching this phenomenon link it to 'high-energy vibrations' in particles associated with the solar wind.) Fifty minutes later, sitting back in his couch, Collins eased the command module away from the adapter, and like a cork from a bottle the LM came away with it. With its legs still folded, its protective gold foil shining in the sunlight and its two iridescent windows glinting like eyes, the LM resembled a giant insect drawn from its protective chrysalis. Flying through space, 12,600 miles from the Earth, Apollo 11 now consisted of two spacecraft, each capable of supporting a crew. Safely secured together, the two vehicles pulled ahead of the spent third stage as they continued their flight to the Moon.

( )

The decision to bring a second spacecraft along – with all the extra weight this implied – was one of the reasons why the Saturn V had needed to be so big. Controversial though it was, the LM was *the* vital component in the only viable plan to get to the Moon. When first raised, this plan was considered so risky it was barely taken seriously. It originated during the agency's first major discussions on the lunar landing and relied on concepts so ambitious they triggered one of the most emotionally charged rows in the history of NASA.

The debate arose a year before Shepard's Mercury flight, in 1960, when NASA's Space Task Group was looking for projects that could be pursued after the Mercury programme. Responsible for planning and developing manned missions, the group was led by Dr Robert Gilruth. Initially, his task was 'to put man in space and bring him back in good shape – and do it before the Soviets', but his brief later expanded. Based at the Langley Research Center in Virginia, Gilruth was a gifted aeronautical engineer who managed his team with the air of a Victorian gentleman, his reticent manner, old-fashioned values and paternal style of leadership masking his immense political acumen. Although Mercury remained the priority, Gilruth was looking towards the future. One idea involved a flight orbiting the Moon, a proposal which came to be called Apollo, after the Greek god of light. By October, staff at NASA HQ in Washington felt Apollo needed a clear objective and it was suggested the project should involve a series of manned lunar landings.[5] Beginning on 5 January 1961, ideas on how one might land on the Moon were presented to the agency's senior managers, and during two days of briefings it became clear that there were a number of ways this could be done.

A popular plan, known as direct ascent, suggested launching a huge rocket and sending it directly to the Moon where it would fly all the way to the lunar surface. This idea was depicted in films such as *Destination Moon* (1950) and adopted by Tin Tin and other space-travelling heroes. Already NASA was working on designs for a massive booster, named Nova, that would carry enough fuel to support its payload through two launches, the first from Earth, the second from the Moon. But from the start it was clear that landing such a huge rocket tail first on the Moon contained many challenges, not least the notion of an elevator that would carry the crew down to the surface.[6] Many believed it would be easier and safer to land a smaller spacecraft on the Moon, though this too brought problems. How, for example, could a small spacecraft travel all the way from the Earth to the Moon and back? During the January briefing sessions, it was suggested that a small vehicle should be launched into orbit where it should rendezvous with other rockets which would supply it with the fuel for the return trip to the Moon (no existing booster could carry the whole lot into space in one go). This idea, known as earth orbit rendezvous (or EOR), was supported by Dr Wernher von Braun, a rocket engineer from Germany, caricatured by Peter Sellers in the film *Dr Strangelove*.

Von Braun came to be fascinated by the prospect of space travel during his teenage years, and later pursued his interest in rocket engines by designing missiles for the German army during the 1930s. A shrewd political operator, von Braun found it expedient to join first the Nazi party and then the SS, while developing what became the V-2 rocket.[7] He also permitted the use of slave labour. Twenty thousand people died at the Peenemünde and Mittelwerk plants while building the V-2, the world's first ballistic missile.[8] After von Braun and his team surrendered to the American army in 1945, they were sent to the States together with examples of the V-2 and boxes of supporting documents. Continuing their work, they gave the army a leading edge in developing large liquid-fuel rocket engines, supersonic aerodynamics, and guidance and control systems. Their Redstone booster was used in America's first live nuclear missile tests (and later in the initial flights of Project Mercury). In 1958, a modified Redstone, the Jupiter-C, launched the West's first satellite, Explorer 1. Meanwhile von Braun was working on designs for a more powerful booster, named Saturn – 'the one after Jupiter'. This was intended to be able to send large payloads into Earth orbit, or smaller loads into lunar orbit. By 1959, plans for the Saturn rocket had become integral to the army's Project Horizon, a proposal for a military camp on the Moon, which was just as optimistic as the Lunex Project, the air force's dream of a lunar base staffed by airmen. In the spring of 1960, von Braun was told that he and his team were to be transferred from the army to NASA, and in July he became the director of the new Marshall Space Flight Center in Huntsville, Alabama. In this capacity he was invited to attend the landing discussions in January 1961.

The briefings led to the creation of a planning group which was set up in mid-January, more than two months before Gagarin's flight. Based at HQ and chaired by the Assistant Director of Manned Space Flight, George Low, the group looked at the various ways of landing on the Moon, particularly direct ascent and EOR. Direct ascent was favoured by influential members of the team including Max Faget, the designer of the Mercury capsule. Faget was asked to examine a third idea, involving a rendezvous not in Earth orbit but in lunar orbit, but he wholeheartedly dismissed it and the group barely returned to the subject again. Low's preliminary report[9] suggested manned flights to the Moon using EOR could be possible as early as 1968, while direct ascent could become a reality between 1970 and 1971. In addition to their work on a lunar landing, the group also agreed to support a second generation of spacecraft intended to maintain a presence in space after Mercury. This programme, which evolved into Project Gemini, laid the groundwork for future missions to the Moon, as did simultaneous development of the Saturn booster, the F-1 engine and hydrogen technology.[10]

On 22 March 1961, NASA's senior managers discussed some of these plans with John F. Kennedy, the country's dynamic new president. A written summary, sent to the White House the next day, included references to 'manned circumlunar flight in 1967', Saturn rockets, and a landing that could be 'achieved in 1970' using Nova.[11] A month later, on 11 April, George Low briefed a Congress committee on plans for a lunar landing, even though nobody had yet flown in space. To demonstrate that manned missions were possible he intended to a show a film of the successful sub-orbital flight made on 31 January by Ham the chimpanzee, but he ran out of time before the committee adjourned. That night Gagarin orbited the Earth, and by the time Low returned to Congress the country was smarting from Russia's success. Low later admitted that 'we thought it would not be in our best interests to show how we had flown a monkey on a sub-orbital flight when the Soviets had orbited Gagarin'. Under pressure, NASA managers told the Congress committee that Russia might even be aiming to land a man on the Moon in 1967, the fiftieth anniversary of the Bolshevik revolution.[12] Then, just as Gagarin was getting used to his new status as an international hero, American pride was further dented by the Bay of Pigs debacle, which began just days after his triumphant flight.

Kennedy had to quickly find a way of restoring national prestige. Focused on domestic priorities, he was less than dazzled by the idea of orbital flight. But with the Cold War at its chilliest

Kennedy recognised that a public show of affection towards space was necessary to score major political points. With the Russians chasing a claim for technical superiority, Kennedy was advised to beat them to it. 'This is, whether we like it or not, in a sense a race,' he told James Webb, NASA's newly appointed administrator.[13] Even if Mercury succeeded in putting a man into orbit, a race towards something more ambitious in space was only just beginning. The question was, what should the prize be?

On 20 April, Kennedy sent a memo to Vice-President Johnson asking whether 'we have a chance of beating the Soviets by putting a laboratory in space, or by a trip around the moon, or by a rocket to land on the moon ... ?' Johnson replied that a manned Moon landing was far enough in the future to allow the United States the possibility of achieving it first. It was an argument supported by Gilruth, who saw the project as being so technically difficult the US and Russia would each have an equal chance of success regardless of their current position. For the moment, however, Gilruth remained preoccupied with the more modest objectives of the current missions. For him great relief came with the first successful Mercury flight on 5 May. Millions of TV viewers were enthralled by the first US manned rocket launch, but behind the scenes America's ambitions were already being propelled towards bigger ideas.

In deciding to back a manned landing, Kennedy gave NASA the relevant parts of a forthcoming speech proposing a flight to the lunar surface in 1967. Since they still did not know how such a mission could practically be accomplished, NASA's managers urged him to put back the date. On 25 May, Kennedy told a joint session of Congress, 'I believe that this nation should commit itself to achieving the goal, before this decade is out, of landing a man on the Moon and returning him safely to Earth. No single space project ... will be more impressive to mankind or more important ... and none will be so difficult or expensive.' The question of how far Kennedy was prepared to stomach the costs involved remains a subject of debate, but publicly he needed to send the right signal. The president recognised that such an effort in such a short timeframe would require a monumental commitment on a wartime scale. 'It will not be one man going to the Moon,' he added, 'it will be an entire nation. For all of us must work to put him there.'[14] Gilruth doubted it could be done in the time available.

Given a shot in the arm by the commitment from Kennedy, NASA managers commissioned studies on the various landing options. Once it was realised that a huge rocket such as Nova could never be developed within the president's deadline, and the whole idea of direct ascent was left to sink into a fug of equations. With Nova stranded on the drawing board, interest veered towards von Braun's work on EOR. Although his rockets were smaller and more feasible than the Nova, his vision of two spacecraft successfully finding each other for a safe rendezvous in space remained a daunting prospect. At least if the rendezvous failed, the astronauts could be quickly brought home.

This was a comforting thought compared to the nightmare inherent in a proposal put forward by NASA's Langley Research Center. Supported by John Houbolt, a tenacious engineer with a passion for his work, the Langley plan also involved a rendezvous in space but suggested this take place not above the Earth but three days away, above the Moon – an idea that 'horrified' Low.[15] Direct, to the point of being blunt, Houbolt refused to let the idea drop. He suggested that lunar orbit rendezvous (LOR) required only a very small capsule to be sent to the surface of the Moon. Unencumbered by the resources necessary for a six-day round trip to and from Earth, the capsule would only have to fly from lunar orbit down to the surface and back again. It would then rendezvous with a bigger vehicle for the journey home. Small and lightweight, it would be far easier to land than the large spaceship envisaged in EOR, never mind the mammoth Nova. In fact, Houbolt argued, LOR was 50 per cent lighter than direct ascent. Nevertheless, the plan meant that men returning from the lunar surface would have no way of getting home if they failed to find the vehicle waiting for them. The Moon was more than 2,000 miles wide. Yet if it were difficult to find a moving target as big as this, how was anyone going to be expected to find a small orbiting spacecraft? If things went wrong, there would be no hope of rescue. Forced to contemplate the prospect of dead astronauts perpetually trapped in orbit around the Moon, in June staff at headquarters rejected the idea.[16]

Difficult as they were for some to accept, Houbolt's proposals were inspired by a logic that could not be dismissed. Nova was too impractical and EOR raised too many technical questions. Houbolt knew there wasn't time to pursue anything other than LOR, but for months he found there was 'virtually universal opposition – no one would accept it – they would not even study it'.[17] 'The critics in the early debate murdered Houbolt,'[18] von Braun later remembered. Bypassing several layers of management, six days before Kennedy's announcement Houbolt had put his arguments in a letter to the second most powerful man in NASA, Robert Seamans. Kennedy's deadline only served to harden Houbolt's opinions, and in November – still facing opposition to his ideas – he wrote to Seamans again. 'Do we want to go to the moon or not?' he demanded, asking, 'why is a ... scheme involving rendezvous ostracized or put on the defensive?'[19]

Over time, senior figures slowly came round to Houbolt's point of view including, in January 1962, Gilruth. He had been instructed to take his Space Task Group from Virginia down to Houston and there set up a site under the new name of the Manned Spacecraft Center. Once in Houston, Gilruth's group began to look seriously at LOR, while von Braun's team at the Marshall Space Flight Center continued to study EOR. Each side sought the commitment of headquarters, and with tensions running high an argument on the subject broke out within earshot of the press while Kennedy was visiting Marshall.[20] Without a decision, it was impossible to move forward. Aware of the difficulties of EOR – and of the president's deadline – in June von Braun came to accept that the only viable option was lunar rendezvous. It was the final move in the game: on 11 July 1962, NASA decided in favour of LOR. 'It is my opinion to this day,' Low wrote twenty years later, 'that had the Lunar Orbit Rendezvous mode not been chosen, Apollo would not have succeeded.'[21]

With Apollo free to move forward, Gilruth was now able to devote his attention to the fledgling Gemini programme, believing this would provide the experience in space-flight needed to fly to the Moon. Beyond spacesuits and extra-vehicular activities (EVAs), a pressing priority was to begin work on rendezvous techniques. Any lunar landing relying on a rendezvous in space would be impossible if Gemini failed to prove it could be done. On 3 June 1965, shortly before Ed White began the first US space walk, the commander of Gemini 4, Jim McDivitt, tried to fly alongside the abandoned upper section of their two-stage rocket. Although such a manoeuvre had never been performed before, McDivitt assumed it would be relatively straightforward. But each time he attempted to approach the rocket stage he found that it mysteriously moved further away, and amid concerns over using up fuel he was ordered to abandon the experiment. By the time Gemini 5 reached orbit two months later, new training techniques had been developed and the spacecraft was fitted with a radar system. The crew successfully flew from one point in space to another, demonstrating for the first time an ability to reach a pre-determined position in orbit.

Only through practical experience of orbital mechanics was NASA able to get to grips with the difficulties of rendezvous. McDivitt had expected to catch up with his target by firing his engine, with the intention of going faster. Actually the burn simply pushed him into a higher orbit, which left him travelling more slowly relative to anything at a lower altitude – like a spent rocket stage. With the target in sight, McDivitt ought to have slowed down. In doing so he would have become more vulnerable to the pull of the Earth's gravity, which would have taken him down to a lower – and faster – orbit. When he was in the right position he could have fired his thrusters and climbed back up to meet his target. Such logic wasn't for the faint-hearted. Once digested it was supplemented with side orders of apogee adjusts, phase adjusts, plane changes and coelliptic manoeuvres, spiced up by the differences between near-circular and elliptical orbits. In short, a successful rendezvous requires an understanding of the relationship between a spacecraft's speed and its height above the Earth (or the Moon).

While Gemini 5 proved the theory, it did not approach any target but simply completed a rendezvous with an empty point in space, following a plan designed by Buzz Aldrin. It was left to the next two missions to show that NASA could indeed perform a rendezvous as required by LOR. Relying on his basic flying skills and supported by a computer, on 15 December 1965 Mercury veteran Wally Schirra flew Gemini 6 to within one foot of Gemini 7. The two spacecraft orbited the Earth three times while flying in formation, at one point maintaining their positions so accurately that neither crew had to fire their thrusters for 20 minutes. The Russians had not yet managed to do the same thing with a similar degree of accuracy, and for the first time in the space race NASA was edging ahead.

The next stage was docking. Rendezvous involved two spacecraft finding and approaching each other, but only by demonstrating an ability to dock could NASA show that LOR was feasible. The first test was given to Gemini 8, to be commanded by Armstrong. Neil had been part of the backup crew on Gemini 5 before becoming one of the few astronauts to be given a command position on his first flight. Approaching from behind and below, Armstrong rendezvoused with an Agena target vehicle (a converted rocket stage). After gently approaching it at three inches per second, on 16 March 1966 he completed the first successful docking. 'Outside in airless space,' Armstrong later recalled, 'there was only silence, but in the cockpit we heard a slight thud. We relaxed for the first time.'[22] The final moments took place during darkness; Armstrong remembered that 'you saw stars up above, and down below you might see lights from a city or lightning embedded in thunderstorms'.[23]

Neil, and his pilot Dave Scott, had been warned that the Agena may have been experiencing guidance problems, and soon after docking they found they were being rolled over. They stopped the problem by using the Gemini spacecraft's own thrusters, but only when they turned the Agena off did they feel that they had the problem under control. Then it started again. Armstrong noticed that the fuel used by their thrusters had dropped to 30 per cent and it dawned on him and Scott that the problem was not with the Agena but with the Gemini. The roll reached the point where Armstrong felt that the 'stresses might be getting dangerously high', and the two spacecraft might break apart.[24] He wanted to pull away from the Agena, but with dangerous levels of 'rotation in all directions' he knew he risked a collision. Eventually he was able to pull away, but the problem returned, and with the spacecraft now revolving faster than one revolution per second it was quickly becoming one of the most dangerous moments in space-flight history.

'The sun flashed through the window about once a second,' Armstrong noted. Out of radio contact with the ground, the vehicle was spinning round and round so fast that the crew, now suffering from tunnel vision, were close to losing consciousness.[25] 'I could tell,' Armstrong later said, 'when I looked up above me to the controls for the rocket engine that things were getting blurry.'[26] He had no choice but to shut down the thrusters. Investigating the problem in the analytical style he developed as a test pilot, Neil successively fired each of the small boosters and found that one had become stuck in the 'open' position. By activating the re-entry control system he was able to fly the spacecraft safely, but according to the mission rules this action obliged him to return to Earth as soon as possible. Less than eight hours after launch, a decision was made to end the flight early. Armstrong felt frustrated and depressed at being unable to complete the mission, but his cool handling of the emergency won him much praise within NASA's higher echelons.[27]

Next to fly were Tom Stafford and Gene Cernan aboard the

ill-fated Gemini 9 flight. They had hoped to dock with a second Agena, but when it dived into the Atlantic shortly after launch it had to be hurriedly replaced with another target device which itself malfunctioned once in orbit. After its protective shroud failed to detach properly, Robert Gilruth called a meeting in Houston to discuss the problem. Buzz Aldrin, serving as Cernan's backup, suggested that Gene try to remove the shroud during an EVA – an idea that appalled Gilruth. 'What in hell did you say?' Deke asked Buzz a few days later. 'He's all pissed off at you. Said he had had great confidence in you and now he wants you taken off Gemini 12.' After Buzz explained what had happened, Deke ordered him to wait in his office. While Aldrin paced up and down, Slayton chased after Gilruth, returning three hours later. 'Everything's cool, you're on,' grunted Deke, adding, '... but listen Buzz, why don't you use me as your translator from now on?'[28] Although Slayton had rescued his career, Buzz had inadvertently made things more difficult for himself. He now needed his mission to be a success more than ever – and relying on the success of a Gemini mission was a risky strategy.

While the science of rendezvous was now well understood, docking had been achieved only once, and even then it had been aborted early – and never had a range of tasks been successfully completed during an EVA. With just three flights left, NASA was struggling to achieve the objectives necessary to convince Washington and the country that it was able to fly to the Moon. As well as national prestige, billions of taxpayers' dollars were at stake.

Gemini 10 launched on 18 July 1966, and much was expected of its crew, which included Michael Collins. To the joy of those on the ground, Collins and his commander, John Young, successfully docked with an Agena in low orbit. Together the two spacecraft then climbed to a record 475 miles – higher than any previous flight. 'I don't know whether to laugh or to cry,' Collins later wrote, 'when I think of all the pioneer aviators who have aspired to this record and who have put their reputations, money and lives into seeking it, and now John and I are handed it on a platter.'[29]

As Collins prepared for the first of two EVAs, Mission Control urged the astronauts to talk more about what they were doing. In return they were given news of home, including an update on a game between the Houston Astros and the New York Mets. 'Jesus Christ!' an exasperated Collins later said. 'Here I am asshole deep in a 131-step EVA checklist and they want to talk about baseball! One little boo-boo at this stage of the game and all the oxygen will depart my suit and I will die, and they will be talking about the colour of the infield grass.'[30] His first EVA involved taking pictures while standing up in the open hatch, and although the spacecraft was in darkness Collins found that there was 'just enough of an eerie bluish-grey glow to allow my eye to differentiate between clouds and water and land ... We are gliding across the world in total silence, with absolute smoothness.'[31]

Once the EVA was completed, Collins and Young rendezvoused with the Agena previously abandoned by Armstrong. Still tethered to the Gemini, Michael climbed out of the hatch and pushed himself away. 'Flying' through empty space towards the booster, Collins became the first person to meet another vehicle in orbit, and while hanging on to the Agena's docking adapter (last used by Armstrong's spacecraft four months earlier) he controlled his movements with a gas-gun similar to that used by Ed White. Although restricted by a lack of handholds, he retrieved an experimental panel which had been collecting micrometeoroids, thereby accomplishing a primary objective of the mission. Collins encountered occasional difficulties in mobility, and concerns about the spacecraft's limited fuel eventually forced him to cut short his EVA before he could complete a thorough testing of the gas-gun.

By the time Gemini 10 returned to Earth, NASA could show that the difficulties of rendezvous and docking had been mastered, yet still EVA remained a worrying challenge. During the next mission, Dick Gordon's space walk had to be brought to an early halt after he began to grow increasingly tired. This left it to the final flight in the programme to accomplish the last of Gemini's objectives. It would be down to Buzz.

As he and his commander, Jim Lovell, approached Guenter Wendt, moments before boarding their spacecraft in November 1966, a home-made sign on Lovell's back read simply 'The', and another on Aldrin's said 'End'. In the hope of avoiding any further EVA problems, Buzz was required to complete a series of basic mobility tasks which he considered as 'nothing more than the average suburban handyman might perform in his garage on a Saturday afternoon'.[32] A monkey could carry out such tasks, Buzz felt, on one occasion going so far as to ask those around him for a banana. (Later in Houston, Buzz recalled, 'parties unknown to me kept a supply of bananas in my office'.[33]) His principal task was to demonstrate that he could operate easily while weightless. During preparations for Gemini 10, a facility in Baltimore had shown that by training under water an astronaut could replicate some of the conditions of weightlessness. Collins didn't make use of this, being far advanced into his training programme, and Gordon felt the same way. When Aldrin discovered what was possible in the pool he spent much time practising under water, becoming the first astronaut to train substantially for his mission in this way.

Although Buzz was frustrated by the lack of a more challenging objective, he looked forward to the chance to participate personally in a rendezvous. Shortly after arriving in space the vehicle's radar failed, and Aldrin – the master of rendezvous techniques – suddenly found himself blessed with an opportunity to show the world that all his hard work on the subject was not just an obsessive pursuit but was of practical application. Aldrin had brought with him the charts he had spent years working on, both at MIT and later in support of the pioneering rendezvous mission achieved by Geminis 6 and 7. Using these, and a sextant, he was able to guide Lovell towards a manual rendezvous with their Agena target vehicle. Later, during his EVA, Buzz successfully manoeuvred himself over to the Agena, as Collins and Gordon had done before him. But his underwater training paid off, and after comfortably returning to the spacecraft he felt fresh and alert. Later, during his next task, he unpacked equipment stowed at the rear of the vehicle – finding along the way a bright yellow picture of a banana – before methodically tackling the rest of his objectives. Working '160 miles above the surface of the Earth there was no awareness of height at all', Buzz later remembered. 'I was secure and comfortable – though encumbered – in the spacesuit. I felt enclosed and safe.'[34] Aldrin went on to complete a flawless EVA lasting more than two hours. Two further EVAs, performed while standing in the open hatch, were also successful, and by leaning out of the spacecraft Buzz could all but hear the huge sigh of relief on the ground. He spent a total of five hours and 26 minutes exposed to the vacuum of space, all the while calmly controlling his mobility.

Aldrin had flown into space fearful of being doubted by Gilruth and Slayton; he came back a man NASA needed to get the job done. Dr Rendezvous, who on occasion had been a subject of amusement among his colleagues, had demonstrated prowess in space, and in the Astronaut Office nothing counted for more. Gilruth was delighted. At the post-flight party he told Joan how pleased he was, both with the rendezvous charts Buzz had prepared and with the overall success of the EVAs. For Buzz, 'those were the very words I needed to hear'.[35] Project Gemini had ended on the triumphant note all involved had hoped for, not least Aldrin. All the years of hard work, all the misunderstandings, all the frustration and tension had culminated in a clamour of achievement that was a defining moment in his life.

But amid the sense of relief was something else. 'I felt an almost overwhelming sense of fatigue mixed with a vague sadness,' Buzz later said. 'I yearned for sleep so strongly.' He was unable to leave his bed for five days, at the time blaming exhaustion. In truth, he missed the signs of something more sinister that was to haunt him in the years to come.[36]

Chapter 5

NOWHERE TO HIDE

After retrieving the lunar module the crew began a series of housekeeping tasks, starting with a three-second test of the powerful engine attached to the service module. Although the TLI burn had accelerated them to more than 24,000mph, for thousands of miles to come they would be flying against the Earth's gravitational pull which began to slow them down the moment the burn finished. If the Earth had its way, sooner or later they would fall back into the atmosphere. When Collins took control of the spacecraft, 20 minutes after TLI, they were 3,000 miles out and already down to 18,000mph. But although the vehicle was slowing down, the burn had pushed it to such a speed that eventually it would be able to break free of the Earth's hold, allowing the crew to coast towards outer space. They were banking on the Moon intersecting their journey but there was a long way to go before they would know whether the calculations they were relying on were correct.

The empty third stage, still travelling behind them, threatened to follow them all the way. To avoid a risk of collision, at four hours and 41 minutes into the flight signals were transmitted from the ground sending the last remaining section of the Saturn booster towards a path around the Sun.[1] While this was happening, the crew had a chance to update Mission Control on what they could see. In Houston (an hour behind the Cape), it was 1.24pm.

Armstrong: 'Well, we didn't have much time, Houston, to talk to you about our views out the window when we were preparing for LM [lunar module] ejection. But up to that time, we had the entire northern part of the lighted hemisphere visible, including North America, North Atlantic, and Europe and

Northern Africa. We could see that the weather was good all – just about everywhere. There was one cyclonic depression in northern Canada, in the Athabasca – probably east of Athabasca area. Greenland was clear, and it appeared to be we were seeing just the icecap in Greenland. All North Atlantic was pretty good; and Europe and Northern Africa seemed to be clear. Most of the United States was clear. There was a low – looked like a front stretching from the centre of the country up across north of the Great Lakes and into Newfoundland.'

Houston: 'Roger. We copy.'

Collins: 'I didn't know what I was looking at, but I sure did like it.'

Houston: 'OK. I guess the view must be pretty good from up there. We show you roughly somewhere around 19,000 miles out now.'

Bruce McCandless gave the astronauts a list of routine tasks that were necessary to maintain healthy living conditions in the cabin. He also wanted the crew to verify their navigation details, but it was more than nine hours since they had eaten and Michael had other priorities.

Collins: 'If we're late in answering you, it's because we're munching sandwiches.'

Houston: 'Roger. I wish I could do the same here.'

Collins: 'No. Don't leave the console!'

Houston: 'Don't worry. I won't.'

Collins: 'Flight doesn't like it.'

The flight director, or 'Flight', at this point was Cliff Charlesworth for whom Collins had previously worked during a stint in Mission Control. He had served in a position that was originally known as 'capsule communicator' but which was now usually abbreviated to 'CapCom'. Of the hundreds of people working in the Mission Control Center only the CapCom, who was always an astronaut, was cleared to talk to the crew in space. Charlesworth, the lead flight director for the entire mission, was coming to the end of his first shift after watching over the launch and TLI. Cool-headed and relaxed, he was known as the 'Mississippi Gambler'[2] by the flight controllers sitting at the banks of computer consoles in front of him. Working in the windowless Mission Operations Control Room (abbreviated to MOCR and pronounced 'moe-ker'), Charlesworth and his team were bathed in a dull blue-grey light as they studied their monitors and quietly chatted to one another. During a mission the room was operational for 24 hours a day, the 20 or so controllers sitting in a disciplined atmosphere of intense concentration amid a stale odour of cold coffee, sweat, food and cigarette smoke. Between them, the flight control teams played a vital role in monitoring more than 350 telemetry measurements automatically transmitted by the command and service modules. Additional data would later be sent by the LM. To help them manage the vast mass of mathematical equations relating to the changing position of the spacecraft, the controllers were supported by teams of backroom staff, including representatives of the companies that built the hardware. By wearing headsets plugged into their consoles, the controllers could talk to their specialists working elsewhere in the building, and to the flight director sitting behind them.[3]

Facing three ten-foot-high screens set in the wall in front of them, the controllers sat in four rows raking up towards the back of the room. Their job titles, working practices, even the way they talked, were originally shaped by NASA's first flight director, Chris Kraft, a stocky engineer with a stern manner and forthright views on almost everything. Many of the decisions made by Kraft during the Mercury flights remain in practice today, and he has since come to be recognised as the father of Mission Control. The Mercury control room had been based at the Cape, but prior to Gemini 4, and Ed White's headline-grabbing space walk, Kraft and his team moved to Houston where they were given purpose-built facilities equipped with computers and an internal radio network.

Since Kraft had found that the quickest way to swap messages with the spacecraft was through acronyms and jargon, each controller was known by an abbreviated version of his title. In the front row – referred to as 'the trench' – on the left-hand side sat the technician who monitored the rocket stages, operating under the call-sign Booster. Next to him was the retrofire officer (call-sign Retro), who was responsible for abort procedures and the spacecraft's re-entry into the atmosphere. He assisted the flight dynamics officer sitting beside him, call-sign FIDO (pronounced like the dog's name), who studied the spacecraft's flight-path. On his right sat the guidance officer who would monitor the LM's computer and radar during the landing (call-sign GUIDO, to rhyme with FIDO). Behind them, in the second row, the 'systems people' sat on the right, including the electrical, environmental and communications controller (EECOM) and the guidance, navigation and control officer (GNC). Across the aisle on the left sat the CapCom, who was often accompanied by at least one other astronaut, and sitting at the end of the row was the flight surgeon. The flight director sat in the middle of the third row, and during a mission he had absolute authority. 'His decisions during a space flight are the law,' wrote Kraft, adding that managers could only overrule a flight director by firing him. Kraft said that during his Mercury and Gemini missions he had the feeling that 'I'm Flight. And Flight is God.'[4]

By 1969, Kraft had become the director of flight operations and in this capacity he appointed four flight directors to support Apollo 11, each with his own team of controllers. During the critical moments of a mission Bob Gilruth, Kraft and other senior figures sat at the back of the room, in 'management row'. Minutes before the launch of Apollo 11, Kraft had asked so many niggly questions that Charlesworth had been forced to tell his boss, 'Chris, if you don't settle down, I'm going to have to ask you to leave the room. You're making me nervous.'[5] Risking the wrath of God, Kraft gave a thumbs-up and sat back in his chair. Nobody argued with the flight director.

Six hours into the mission, Charlesworth's green team handed over to the white team of Gene Kranz, a former fighter pilot who regarded his job almost as a personal crusade. From the start, NASA had been a civilian organisation but many of its staff had a military background, as was reflected in the command and control structure adopted in Mission Control. This was also apparent in the sense of self-discipline fostered by Gilruth, which extended to unwritten rules on beards and long hair. No-one's hair was more military than Gene's. Kranz was regarded by Kraft as 'sometimes too militaristic, but so quick and smart that it was sometimes scary to remember that he was human'.[6] Kranz's military bearing largely stemmed from his perception that NASA was defending the frontline in the Cold War, and that as a 'Cold War warrior' he was flying the flag as much as anyone in uniform. A loving family man who was prone to tears of emotion during the highs and lows of his work, Kranz was warm and easy-going. Wearing a white waistcoat embroidered with silver thread, made by his wife in honour of the mission, at 2.30pm Gene slipped into Charlesworth's seat. 'A position in Mission Control was the next best thing to being in the spaceship,' Kranz later wrote.[7] In a surprise addition to the flight-plan, he was soon to get an unexpected glimpse of space-flight for himself.

Armstrong: 'If you'd like to delay PTC [passive thermal control] for ten minutes or so, we can shoot you some TV of a seven-eights Earth.'

Houston: 'Apollo 11, Houston. We're ready at Goldstone for the TV. It'll be recorded at Goldstone and then replayed back over here, Neil, any time you want to turn her on, we're ready. Over.'

Having completed TLI, retrieved the LM and abandoned the third stage, the crew had entered a period of relative calm. The risk of the spacecraft suddenly losing pressure had decreased and the astronauts were finally able to remove their bulky pressure-suits along with the uncomfortable urine-collection and fecal-containment devices. The struggle to fold the suits, stuff them into bags and stow them under a couch 'brought about a good deal of confusion', Buzz said, 'with parts and pieces floating about the cabin as we tried to keep logistics under control'.[8] They pulled on two-piece, Teflon-fabric flight-suits over their underwear before replacing the spacecraft's carbon dioxide filter and tending to other routine tasks, including navigation checks, urine dumps and computer updates. Ten and a half hours into the mission, they were ready to try out the television equipment.

Collins: 'OK, Houston. You suppose you could turn the Earth a little bit so we can get a little bit more than just water?'

Houston: 'Roger, 11. I don't think we got much control over that. Looks like you'll have to settle for the water.'

Armstrong: 'Roger. We're seeing the centre of the Earth as viewed from the spacecraft in the eastern Pacific Ocean. We have not been able to visually pick up the Hawaiian Island chain, but we can clearly see the western coast of North America. The United States, the San Joaquin Valley, the High Sierras, Baja California, and Mexico down as far as Acapulco, and the Yucatán Peninsula; and you can see on through Central America to the northern coast of South America, Venezuela and Colombia. I'm not sure you'll be able to see all that on your screen down there.'

Houston: 'Roger, Neil. We just wanted a narrative such that we can – when we get the playback, we can sort of correlate what we're seeing. Thank you very much.'

Collins: 'I haven't seen anything but the DSKY [computer] so far.'

Houston: 'Looks like they're hogging the window.'

Armstrong zoomed in on the Earth, the last refuge of colour in a lonely expanse of black emptiness. Already the planet barely filled his window. As the Earth gradually grew smaller, it gave the crew their only sense of movement, yet this was so slow that Aldrin felt 'we could not immediately detect the fact that the Earth was shrinking as we sped away from it'.[9] With nothing else outside the window to indicate speed it was hard to appreciate that they were moving at all, as was apparent in the TV pictures sent back from more than 50,900 miles away. The colour footage, lasting a little over 16 minutes, was received by NASA's

Goldstone communications station in California before being passed to Mission Control an hour later. From there it was fed to the TV networks.

( )

After returning to Houston from the Cape aboard a NASA aircraft, Janet Armstrong slipped through the huddle of reporters outside her home and quickly switched on the squawk box and the TV. She was just in time to catch the Apollo 11 broadcast. Since the TV transmission had not been included in the flight-plan, NASA was taken by surprise and did not alert the wives. Of the three of them, only Janet caught Neil's images of Earth. For the vast majority of people watching across the nation this was their first opportunity to see anything of the mission for themselves. For the families of the crew, it was hard to believe that after the months of preparation the flight was actually happening. Janet knew that Neil was finally getting a chance to lay to rest his frustration following Gemini 8. Walking on the Moon was not a driving motivation for Armstrong; for the test pilot fascinated by flying machines since childhood, this mission was principally about the pioneering descent to the surface. For Neil, for Janet and for their children, this was the culmination of everything that had shaped their lives over the last 13 years, since the days when Janet had let the Sun heat tubs of water outside their remote cabin as the only way to bathe Ricky.[10] They were still working on the plumbing when Karen was born in 1959.[11]

In June 1961, Janet had taken the children to Seattle where Armstrong was working with Boeing on a NASA project. While visiting a park, two-year-old Karen was running through the grass when she tripped and fell. 'We went immediately home,' Janet said. 'She had a little nosebleed with it, and we thought maybe she'd had a little concussion. By that evening we noticed that her eyes weren't operating properly.' Over time, it became clear that Karen was getting progressively worse; she continued to fall over and her eyes were almost constantly crossed. By the time Janet took her to hospital her eyes had begun to roll and her speech had become affected. Karen was diagnosed as suffering from a malignant tumour growing within the middle part of her brain stem. For seven weeks X-rays were used to try to reduce the tumour, though they disrupted her sense of balance so that Karen could no longer stand. 'She was the sweetest thing. She never, ever complained,' Janet later said.

That summer Neil took two weeks off work so that he and Janet could stay with Karen round the clock while also taking care of four-year-old Ricky. The treatment seemed to work and Karen began to show signs of improvement. She learned to crawl again, and by playing with her Ricky helped her regain a sense of balance. 'It was Ricky who told me, in October, that something was the matter with Karen again,' Janet said. By this time the little girl's body was too weak to take any further treatment and it was decided that she would be happier at home. 'She made it through Christmas,' Janet remembered. 'It seems like the day Christmas was over, she just went downhill ... it just overcame her.' Karen died at her home in the California hills on 28 January 1962, Neil and Janet's sixth wedding anniversary. She was a little less than three years old.[12]

Neil's boss at Edwards, Joe Walker, had lost a two-year-old son in 1958. His wife Grace later described how those who live with the threat of death and danger try to deal with grief: 'I would say it's a pilot thing. Most of them act pretty stoic. They would say they had an "okay flight" and then they would go into the bathroom and vomit. I think Joe was a little more supportive for me than Neil was for Janet. Now I say that not as a criticism, but just the way Neil was – he was very tight emotionally.'[13] Neil's sister June remembered things differently: 'Somehow he felt responsible for her death ... in terms of "is there some gene in my body that made the difference?" ... I thought his heart would break.'[14]

Neil threw himself into new challenges at work. Three weeks after Karen's funeral John Glenn orbited the Earth, and that spring

Neil decided his future lay in space-flight, although the extent to which Karen's death influenced his decision is hard to estimate.[15] In the years that followed he talked of Karen so infrequently in public that many of his colleagues did not know that he had ever had a daughter. When the family moved to Houston many of their possessions remained in storage, and only some of the most important items were unpacked – including photos of Karen.

In 1964, many of these pictures were destroyed when a fire ripped through the Armstrongs' home in the early hours of 24 April. Struggling to get through to the local fire department, Janet rushed out into the garden and screamed for help from their neighbours. The family lived next door to Ed White, who was a year away from his pioneering space walk. Ed and his wife Pat had grown close to the Armstrongs; the wives saw much of each other and the Whites' children had an open invitation to play in the Armstrongs' pool. While Janet rushed out of the house, Neil went to get their ten-month-old baby, Mark. Meanwhile Ed flew downstairs, and after grabbing a garden hose he started to tackle the flames. He took the baby from Neil and handed him over the back fence to Pat, allowing Neil to rush back into the house in search of Ricky. By this point, with the walls glowing red and the glass cracking in the windows, Janet had to hose down the hot concrete floor just to be able to stand on it. Pressing a wet towel over his face, Neil held his breath and fought his way back into the burning building. 'When you take a whiff of that thick smoke, it's terrible,' he said. Desperately, he tried to reach Ricky's room while fearing what he might find there; he later described this as the longest journey of his life. Fortunately, Ricky was unhurt. Scrabbling the boy into his arms, Neil put the towel over his son's face and raced outside where Ed was still fighting the flames. Together the two men pushed the family's cars out of the garage, then returned to tackle the fire. Ed was as strong as an ox and without his help things could have been far more serious. The Armstrongs stayed with the Whites for a few days while they assessed the damage and listed their lost possessions. The blaze, caused by an electrical fault, consumed so much of the house it took six months to rebuild it.[16]

During this time, Neil continued to work on the Gemini programme. He initially served as the Gemini 5 backup commander before flying aboard Gemini 8, a mission that ultimately won him praise from many in the Manned Spacecraft Center. While some of his peers questioned the action he took, robust opinions were part and parcel of life in the Astronaut Office. In Armstrong's case the negative comments were not taken seriously by those in authority: two days after he landed he was named as the backup commander of Gemini 11. Chris Kraft believed that 'Armstrong's touch was as fine as any astronaut'.[17] The Gemini 8 problems began just as Gene Kranz was settling in during a shift handover in Mission Control. 'I was damned impressed with Neil,' Kranz later said. For him, fault lay with the organisation as a whole rather than with the mission commander. 'We failed to realise that when two spacecraft are docked they must be considered as one,' Kranz noted – a lesson he came to view as one of the most valuable of the entire Gemini programme.[18]

During this period Neil also supported the fledgling Apollo programme, the components of which were being developed at various sites around the country. While Mercury and Gemini used converted military missiles to take men into space, Apollo would rely on von Braun's Saturn booster, the first large launch vehicle designed and built by NASA. Assembled by the Marshall Space Flight Center, the new rocket was powered by a cluster of eight modified engines taken from the Jupiter booster. It successfully completed its maiden flight on 27 October 1961. In the first of ten successful launches, the 162-foot-tall Saturn I flew for eight minutes, reaching more than 3,600mph.[19] A month later, the contract to build the command and service modules was awarded to North American Aviation, who had built the X-15. North American's work was to be managed by the Manned Spacecraft Center, which would also oversee designs for the lunar module, submitted by the Grumman Corporation. Due to the protracted row over lunar orbit rendezvous, Grumman was not selected until November 1962.[20]

With the major Apollo development now work in progress, by 1963 the spiralling costs of the programme were causing concern for President Kennedy, whose personal interest in space was less than whole-hearted. Looking for ways of cutting the budget, in June he approached the Russian leader Nikita Khrushchev, according to his son Sergei, with a view to sharing a 'joint venture' in space exploration. At the time the Russians were leading the way in space technology and rejected Kennedy's proposal. In the autumn of 1963, this time armed with the promise of funds from Congress, Kennedy tried again. On 20 September he addressed the General Assembly of the United Nations, saying, 'there is room for new co-operation, for further joint efforts in the regulation and exploration of space. I include among these possibilities a joint expedition to the Moon. Space offers no problems of sovereignty.'[21] This time the Russians were more receptive to the idea, although some in Kennedy's own team were less committed. 'I didn't know what the president was planning,' Gilruth later said.[22] On 21 November, Kennedy joined Gilruth in Houston on an inspection of the Manned Spacecraft Center, still under construction. The site had been selected for political reasons involving Albert Thomas, a local Congressman. That night, at a dinner in honour of Thomas, Kennedy said, 'Next month, when the US fires the world's biggest booster, lifting the heaviest payroll into … that is, payload …' The president paused. 'It will be the heaviest payroll, too,' he grinned.[23] He was never to witness it himself, of course. Thomas was still with the presidential party when Kennedy was assassinated in Dallas the following day.

Kennedy's death was almost as significant for NASA's efforts to reach the Moon as his initial speech to Congress. Beyond the questions and controversies surrounding his murder, America moved quickly to honour the memory of its fallen president. In 1963, Florida's Cape Canaveral was renamed Cape Kennedy and NASA's Launch Operations Center became the Kennedy Space

Center. Kennedy's lunar ambitions lay at the heart of the legacy of a president who had become the most talked-about man on the planet. NASA could not let him down.

Lyndon Johnson, who at the end of the 1950s had done so much to bolster America's position in space, took over the presidency, and after being re-elected in 1964 he continued to support NASA's ambitions. Under Johnson, Gemini achieved its objectives and America took a lead in the space race. He even felt comfortable enough to join the Russians in supporting a treaty preventing any country claiming sovereignty over the Moon. In fact he had no choice. Military action in Vietnam was escalating, and in order to pay for it Johnson had to curb the soaring costs of space exploration. Soviet and American presentations on the use of space were given to the United Nations in June 1966, and these were later merged into an agreement that became known as the Outer Space Treaty.[24] Outlawing any military posturing in space, the treaty also promoted goodwill on the ground by requiring the safe return of any astronaut or cosmonaut who landed in what might otherwise be considered hostile territory. On Friday 27 January 1967, the agreement was simultaneously signed in London, Moscow and Washington.

A ceremony in the East Room at the White House was attended by Vice-President Hubert Humphrey and Secretary of State Dean Rusk, along with the ambassadors of Russia and Britain, together with other international VIPs and a handful of astronauts, including Armstrong.[25] At 5.15pm, President Johnson began the formal part of the proceedings with a speech in which he declared that the treaty would preserve peace in space. He added, 'It means that astronaut and cosmonaut will meet someday on the surface of the Moon as brothers and not as warriors for competing nationalities or ideologies.'[26] Whether there would be cosmonauts there to greet them or not, Johnson was optimistic Americans would indeed walk on the Moon.

He could afford to be. A new type of spacecraft, capable of a lunar mission, was scheduled to launch in three weeks' time, and even as Johnson spoke three astronauts were down at the Cape testing its systems. Sitting in the middle seat of the prototype command module was Ed White, preparing for his second flight into space. On his left sat the mission commander, Gus Grissom, who had flown the second Mercury flight and later led the first Gemini mission. The third member of the team was new recruit Roger Chaffee. Together, the men were checking the spacecraft's electrical systems in preparation for a 14-day test-flight. The biggest manned spacecraft NASA had yet built, the command module contained many more systems than Gemini; its development had been repeatedly held back by its complexity. In the weeks before the test, Grissom had grown frustrated with the delays and technical problems, particularly those disrupting the communications system which was prone to interference from static. That morning, Joe Shea, the manager of the Apollo Spacecraft Program Office, had tried to persuade Grissom that the problem was under control. But according to Deke Slayton, Gus wasn't convinced. 'If you think the son of a bitch is working,' Grissom reportedly told Shea, 'why don't you get your ass in the cabin with us and see what it sounds like.' Declining Gus's invitation, Shea joined Deke in a concrete blockhouse 1,600 feet from launch-pad 34, where the spacecraft sat on top of its empty Saturn IB rocket.[27]

The so-called 'plugs out test' involved an assessment of the spacecraft under its own electrical power. This was to be done under simulated launch conditions, which meant the cabin would be filled with 100 per cent oxygen. The crew, wearing pressure-suits, were strapped into their couches at 1pm, and after technicians resolved a problem with the life-support system they closed the spacecraft's elaborate hatch. Consisting of three separate layers, it couldn't be removed in less than 60 seconds. Once sealed shut, the cabin was flooded with oxygen until the pressure reached 16.7psi – 10 per cent higher than normal conditions at sea level. As a simulated countdown began, the astronauts tried to talk to the operations room. Later they would be in direct contact with Mission Control, 900 miles away, but with static clogging the line Gus was having trouble talking to anyone. 'If I can't talk with you only five miles away,' he snapped, 'how can we talk to you from space?'[28] The problem seemed to clear up, but at 6.20pm, ten minutes from zero, communications failed again, and as dusk descended the countdown was put on hold.

At the White House, the treaty had been signed and Johnson and his guests were attending a reception in the Green Room.[29] While Armstrong mingled with the crowd, Grissom and his crew struggled to complete their tests. They had been sitting in their spacecraft for more than five hours and in that time oxygen had permeated everything inside the cabin. The polyurethane foam covering the floor absorbed oxygen like a sponge, as did the 34 feet of Velcro which was stuck on the walls to secure objects in weightlessness. Elsewhere lay flammable bags, netting restraints, logbooks and more than 15 miles of wiring, much of which had lost its protective layer of Teflon insulation after engineers had worn it away while repeatedly working inside the cabin.

At 6.30pm, defective wiring short-circuited under Gus's couch, producing a spark that quickly developed into a fire. In an oxygen-rich environment, Velcro explodes once ignited; even a solid bar of aluminium burns like wood. As flames raced up the left-hand wall of the cabin, medical telemetry showed that Ed's pulse suddenly jumped. Grissom cried 'Fire!' on the radio; then Chaffee said, 'We've got a fire in the cockpit,' swiftly echoed by White.

With flames consuming the oxygen relief valve, making it impossible to depressurise the cabin, Gus released the straps of his harness and moved over to help Ed with the hatch. Seconds after Grissom's cry had alerted those outside, a pad technician watching a television monitor believed he saw Ed reach over his left shoulder and bang the hatch window with his gloved hand. Fuelled by the oxygen, the foam, the Velcro, sheets of paper and other materials, the fire leapt across the hatch window, burning with increasing intensity. As flames destroyed the life-support system, a flammable solution of glycol cooling-fluid sprayed across the cabin, producing thick clouds of toxic gas once ignited. While Grissom and White struggled with the hatch, Roger Chaffee – who was furthest from the seat of the fire – stayed where he was and tried to maintain contact with the outside world. 'We've got a bad fire – let's get out. We're burning up,' cried Chaffee, followed by an unidentifiable scream that froze the blood of all who heard it. Then, less than 17 seconds after the first cry was heard, came silence.

As the temperature inside the cabin reached 2,500°F, the rising pressure tore open the hull of the command module, releasing sheets of flame and preventing any immediate efforts to attempt a rescue. For five minutes no-one could get near the inferno. Eventually, wearing gas masks and fighting their way forward using fire extinguishers, technicians were able to get close enough to open the hatch. Among the first to look inside was Deke, who had rushed over from the blockhouse. He described the scene as 'devastating … the crew had obviously been trying to get out … [the] bodies were piled in front of the seal in the hatch'. Asphyxiated, and suffering third-degree burns, Grissom, White and Chaffee had fallen into unconsciousness long before anyone had been able to reach them.[30]

News of the fatal tragedy quickly spread. While Deke was inspecting the cabin, Neil was in a taxi returning to his hotel. By the time he got to his room, at around 7.15pm, a message was waiting for him requesting him to call the Manned Spacecraft Center. In Houston, the Astronaut Office asked Janet to go to Pat White's house and keep away from the television until someone could get over to her.[31] That evening Neil and fellow astronauts Gordon Cooper, Dick Gordon and Jim Lovell[32] broke open a bottle of Scotch as they discussed the loss of their friends. For Neil, 'it really hurt to lose them in a ground test … it happened because we didn't do the right thing somehow. That's doubly, doubly traumatic.'[33]

While Roger was new to NASA, Gus was known by everyone. But it was the loss of Ed that Armstrong found particularly hard. Many years later, in reference to the 1964 house fire, Neil said, 'Ed was able to help me save the situation, but I was not in a position to be able to help him.' Ed White was buried at West Point on 31 January, and both Armstrong and Aldrin were among the pallbearers. For Neil, the event was especially difficult: it was five years to the day since Karen's funeral.

Chapter 6

GROUNDED IN SAFETY

Flying through a vacuum in a pressurised spacecraft involves risks that can never be eliminated, no matter how well the vehicle is tested. Of the two million parts in the command module, the thrusters, life-support system, electrical power, water supply and navigation systems could all perform flawlessly throughout the mission – but if the parachutes failed to open minutes before landing, the crew faced serious injury or worse. No spacecraft was more dangerous than a prototype, a fact not lost on Gus Grissom, who once said, 'If we die, we want people to accept it. We are in a risky business and we hope that if anything happens to us it will not delay the programme. The conquest of space is worth the risk of life.'[1]

In the autumn of 1966, Grissom had been battling with the problems plaguing his command module, which was a basic 'Block I' design, an early version of the vehicle that would be flying to the Moon, the 'Block II'. At the same time, Michael Collins was working on another Block I command module, serial number 014. Following the cancellation of 014 at the end of the year, Collins and his crew were reshuffled in a move that had far-reaching implications for all involved.

With the crew in need of a new command module pilot, they were joined by Bill Anders. But Anders, who had not yet flown in space, was considered too inexperienced to be placed in charge of the command module – on a mission to the Moon he would have to operate alone while his two crew-mates departed aboard the lunar lander. To avoid this, a swap needed to be made. Anders became the lunar module pilot, and the command module role went to Collins. In this position Michael began to acquire a depth of experience that later came to be recognised and respected by his peers. 'Years later,' Collins wrote, 'I have answered a thousand times the question "How did you and Armstrong and Aldrin decide who was going to stay in the command module and who was going to walk on the Moon?" I have answered it a hundred ways, none of them completely honest, but then it's so hard to say, "Listen, lady, when they cancelled 014 I lost my chance."'[2]

The fire changed everything. During the subsequent investigation, the Apollo programme stalled as NASA and North American Aviation swapped accusations. The contractors pointed to the pressure they'd been under to complete the spacecraft quickly; in return, NASA attacked what it perceived as North American's lax procedures and shoddy workmanship.[3] 'Everybody was going around pointing fingers at everybody else,' Director of Flight Crew Operations Deke Slayton said.[4] There was truth on both sides. The official report, released on Friday 5 April 1967, blamed faulty wiring, and although it wasn't able to identify the precise source of the spark, it established where the fire had begun. It also found hundreds of failures in the design and construction of the spacecraft, and recommended 11 major hardware and operational changes.[5] As well as a crisis in confidence, the Apollo programme faced other equally serious difficulties. The lunar module was behind schedule, the Saturn's second stage was in Gene Kranz's words 'an engineering and production nightmare',[6] and awkward questions were being asked in Congress. 'We were going too fast,'[7] Deke later conceded. Michael Collins asked himself, 'Would one disaster follow another, just as airplane accidents seemed to occur in clusters ... how could NASA get going again?'[8]

The return to work was led by Slayton. On the Monday after the report was released,[9] Deke called NASA's most experienced astronauts into his office. 'Eighteen of us returned to Houston from our various training activities around the country,' Buzz remembered. Without any elaborate preamble, Deke simply announced that 'the guys who are going to fly the first lunar missions are the guys in this room'.[10] Five manned flights were scheduled, labelled C, D, E, F and G. The first would be led by Mercury veteran Wally Schirra, who would test-fly the Block II command module. Then Jim McDivitt (the commander who had attempted the first Gemini rendezvous) would test both the command and lunar modules in low Earth orbit. The E mission would repeat these tests in deep space, 4,000 miles from Earth. This flight would be commanded by Frank Borman, who had helped investigate the fire. Borman's crew included Michael Collins, while the backup crew consisted of Neil Armstrong, Buzz Aldrin and Jim Lovell. After Borman's flight, the F mission would stage a full dress rehearsal of the landing, while the G crew would make the first attempt to reach the lunar surface.

None of these flights was to be known as Apollo 1, the name being reserved in memory of Grissom, White and Chaffee. Under a revised schedule, drawn up after the fire, there was to be no Apollo 2 or 3, and Apollos 4, 5 and 6 were to be unmanned tests. Schirra's crew would use the call-sign Apollo 7, McDivitt's Apollo 8 and Borman's Apollo 9. In naming the crews, Slayton went no further than the first three flights, leaving everyone to privately rate their chances of flying to the lunar surface. Anyone in a backup crew stood a good chance of joining the first mission to the Moon, and based on Deke's rotation system Pete Conrad looked likely to go first.[11] A veteran of two Gemini flights, Conrad lived the kind of flamboyant lifestyle the press envisaged all astronauts enjoyed. As the Apollo 8 backup commander, he would theoretically skip two missions and then fly Apollo 11. Armstrong looked set to attempt the second landing.

Yet all the missions would be delayed until NASA and North American (known from March as North American Rockwell) settled their differences and produced a reliable spacecraft. The work was managed by George Low, who in 1961 had led the debate on how to reach the Moon, and who now replaced Joe Shea as the manager of the Apollo Spacecraft Program Office. Under Low, 1,341 design alterations[12] were made to the command

Above: One of three X-15 rocket-powered aircraft, carried aloft under the wing of a B-52.

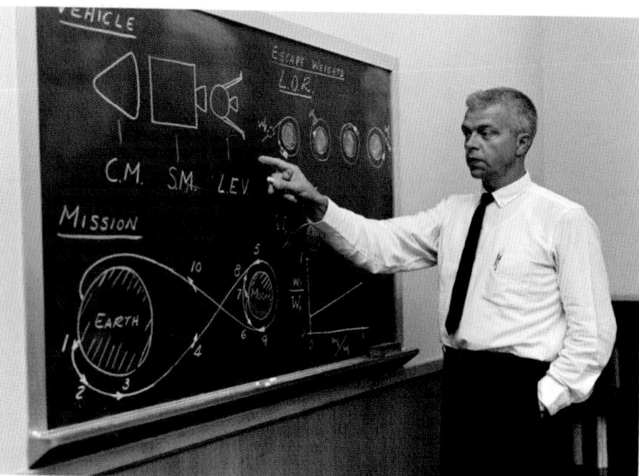

Above: John Houbolt explaining lunar orbital rendezvous. His ideas were initially rejected by NASA but proved vital to the lunar landing.

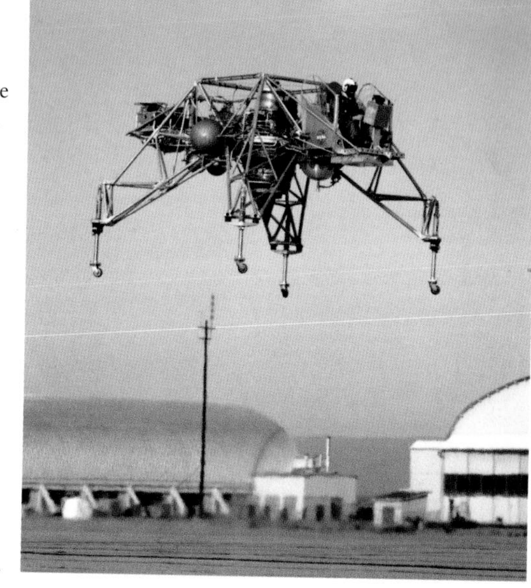

Right: A lunar landing research vehicle at Edwards Air Force Base.

Above: The crew of Apollo 1 (left to right) Gus Grissom, Ed White, and Roger Chaffee, in front of Launch Complex 34, housing their Saturn IB launch vehicle. When a fire broke out during tests the complicated hatch left them unable to escape.

Above: The crew of Apollo 11. From left: Commander, Neil Armstrong; Command Module Pilot, Michael Collins and Lunar Module Pilot, Buzz Aldrin.

Right: The crews of Apollo 10 and Apollo 11 in a debriefing session.

Above: Armstrong in the lunar module simulator at the Kennedy Space Center.

Right: Collins (left) and Deke Slayton, walk away from a T-38 jet, July 1969. As the Director of Flight Crew Operations Slayton was responsible for selecting the crew of each mission.

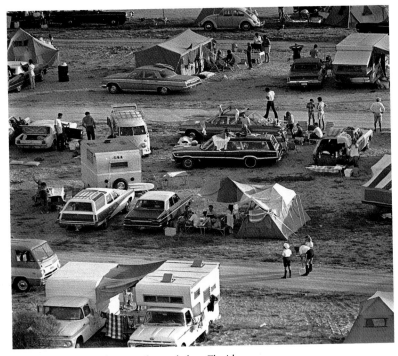

Below: A million sight-seers descended on Florida, camping out on beaches and roads to get a glimpse of the lift-off.

Above: Slayton (right front) reviews charts with Collins (left), Armstrong, and Aldrin (next to Slayton) during breakfast before the launch.

Left: Armstrong checks his communications system before boarding Apollo 11.

Below: Collins prior to launch.

Left: Aldrin prepares himself for the mission.

Above: Armstrong waves to well-wishers in the Manned Spacecraft Operations Building, Kennedy Space Center.

Left: High above the Florida landscape, the crew enter the spacecraft through the tiny white room resting against the command module.

The swing arms move away and a plume of flame signals the lift-off of Apollo 11.

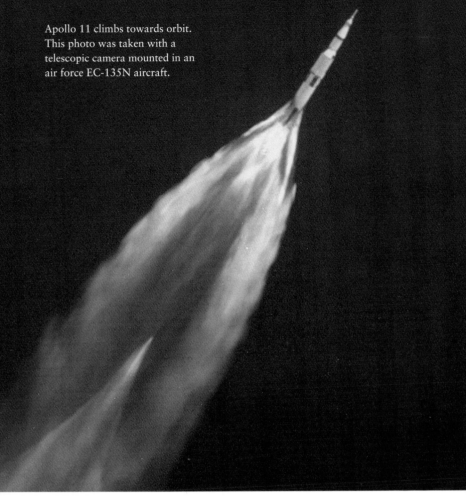

Apollo 11 climbs towards orbit. This photo was taken with a telescopic camera mounted in an air force EC-135N aircraft.

Left: Officials relax in the Launch Control Center following lift-off. Second from left is Dr. Wernher von Braun, looking at George Mueller who stands beside Lt. Gen. Samuel Phillips, Director of the Apollo Programme.

module at a cost of $75 million,[13] including new wiring and better safety systems. The over-complicated hatch that had sealed the fate of the Apollo 1 crew was replaced with a simpler design which could be opened in less than ten seconds. Much of the aluminium tubing was replaced with steel, emergency oxygen masks were installed, the cooling system was equipped with non-flammable liquid, the communications system was modified, and flammable materials were replaced. The amount of Velcro was also reduced, and a decision was made to discontinue the use of 100 per cent oxygen while a spacecraft was on the ground. At launch, the astronauts would breathe oxygen through their enclosed suits, but the cabin itself would be filled with 60 per cent oxygen and 40 per cent nitrogen.[14] In later years, many believed that without the improvements prompted by the fire, NASA may never have reached the Moon in time.

With demands for safety and reliability underpinning the redevelopment work, confidence slowly returned, and NASA began to move forward. To help everyone release some steam, a party was organised by Pat Collins, Joan Aldrin and Deke's wife Marge. Despite the fact that they underestimated the cost, forcing Deke to fork out $200, in Buzz's estimation the party was a great success since it generated 'enough arguments and gossip to get everyone going again'.[15]

Still, the pressure continued. The Block II spacecraft wasn't going to be ready until at least the summer of 1968, leaving just a year and a half to make Kennedy's deadline. Meanwhile, George Mueller, the head of the Office of Manned Space Flight, pushed Wernher von Braun into testing the new Saturn V rocket as quickly as possible. The safest thing to do would have been to separately test-fly each stage of the booster. But under a principle known as 'all-up testing'[16] it was decided to fly the entire rocket in a single unmanned mission. Apollo 4 – the first Saturn V – bellowed into the sky above the Cape on 9 November 1967, its awesome power astounding those who saw it. The sound of the five F-1 engines tore corrugated metal sheets from the roof of the press stands, and brought ceiling tiles down upon Walter Cronkite in the CBS newsroom.[17] Michael Collins felt that 'this machine suddenly reaches out and grabs you, and shakes, and as it crackles and roars, suddenly you realise the meaning of 7.5 million pounds of thrust'.[18] After much soul-searching, NASA had returned to space.

Next to launch, nearly a year after the fire, was Apollo 5. On 22 January 1968, an unmanned lunar module was lifted into orbit by the Saturn IB that was to have been used by Grissom's crew. Operated by controllers on the ground, Grumman's ungainly assembly of metal, foil and glass fired its engines in a near-perfect simulation of a lunar mission. Ten weeks later, on 4 April, Apollo 6, the second unmanned test of the Saturn V, launched. Carrying a greater load than Apollo 4, the rocket suffered dangerous vibrations that caused some structural damage. Two of the five engines on the second stage shut down early, and the third-stage engine failed to ignite a second time, preventing a simulation of TLI. There was talk of using the next available Saturn V to mount another unmanned test, but under continuing time pressures it was decided to correct the problems and stick with the programme as planned.

The unmanned tests completed, by the autumn of 1968 Schirra's crew was ready to test-fly the Block II command module. They would be launched into orbit aboard a Saturn IB, since the next Saturn V was reserved for the first manned test of the lunar module. But the LM's software and electrical systems were behind schedule[19] and the spacecraft was not yet cleared for manned flight. McDivitt would have to wait, and so would the missions lined up behind him.

Without a LM, George Low and Chris Kraft began to look at how they might maintain momentum once Schirra had flown. There was no sense in sending McDivitt into space for the sake of it – he and his crew had been training for their mission for months. While they waited, it was decided that another crew should fly ahead of them. Next on the list was Borman, who was training for a flight into deep space for a second test of the LM. Again, without a LM there was little point going to an empty point in deep space and no point at all in repeating Schirra's mission into Earth orbit. For Low and Kraft, only one option was left: Borman's crew would be launched on a course that would take America to the Moon months earlier than planned. By July 1968, Borman, Collins and Anders looked set to be sent on a daring trip taking the new command module into deep space, in the first manned mission of the Saturn V. All-up testing was being pushed to the limit.

()

Apollo 11's Block II command module had been named *Columbia* following a suggestion by Julian Scheer, NASA's head of public affairs. It was a name that resonated with the *Columbiad*, the fictional cannon that launched a spacecraft from Florida in Jules Verne's novel *From the Earth to the Moon*. The name also had associations with American history, not least Columbus, and to Collins it fitted the bill perfectly.[20]

Whenever Michael had seen *Columbia* on the shop floor at North American Rockwell, it was always resting with the top of the cone pointing up. *Columbia* had a ceiling and walls and not much in the way of floor-space. During the weightless conditions of space-flight, however, to Collins the spacecraft seemed strangely unfamiliar as if its parts had been 'stuck together at different angles'. The crew could rest as easily on the ceiling as they could on the floor, so that *Columbia* seemed more roomy than it had ever done before. Michael found that his legs had a habit of heading up into the ceiling and curling around the tunnel, which took some getting used to.[21] With a living space roughly the same size as a people carrier, *Columbia* was to serve as a bedroom, bathroom, office, observatory, dining room and recreation area for three men for more than a week.

The space was divided into two by a seven-foot-wide display panel, which incorporated a cut-away section in the middle allowing access from the forward compartment down to the lower equipment bay. In the equipment bay lay the spacecraft's computer, along with communications hardware, some of the food supplies and the waste storage facilities. Five additional storage areas, tucked into corners of both sections of the cabin, held the rest of the food along with other supplies including a medical kit, clothing, tools, survival aids, sanitary kits, camera equipment, storage bags, sleep restraint ropes, spacesuit maintenance kits and a fire extinguisher. The spacecraft carried two copies of the flight-plan (each weighing a couple of pounds) together with a further 20lb of other data and documentation. The paperwork alone required an additional 5,000lb of propellant at launch. *Columbia* also contained spare storage capacity, sufficient to accommodate two boxes of lunar rocks.

By keeping the same hours as everyone at home – throughout the flight they set their watches to Houston time – the crew were able to reduce disruption to their sense of time and maintain a consistent sleep pattern. At 7.20am on the morning of the second day, biomedical telemetry suggested that they were already up although they had not yet been contacted by Mission Control. The spacecraft was now more than 93,000 miles from Earth and travelling at little more than 3,800mph. The press and popular fiction had long imagined space-flight to be a relaxing journey towards the stars, with ample time to look out of the window and ponder the mysteries of the universe – and for once they weren't far wrong. During the Gemini programme, the reality had been very different. Working hard on experiments, the crews had been kept busy amid cramped conditions while repeatedly orbiting the Earth. For those who imagined space-flight to be a trip into the unknown, with enough time for a quick visit to an unexplored destination, Apollo 11 met all the criteria.

For most of its journey to the Moon the vehicle was exposed to the Sun, with the risk that while one side baked in temperatures exceeding 250°F, the opposite side would be left to freeze at minus 250°. To protect it from these extremes, the spacecraft remained in a vertical position and gently rotated as it continued towards its destination. By completing one revolution every 20 minutes in a procedure known as passive thermal control (PTC), the Sun's heat could be evenly distributed around the vehicle. Apollo 11 was coasting for most of the trip so there was no need to make sure the service module's engine was pointing in the right direction. Collins had first established PTC shortly before settling down for the night. Now, as the crew took down the metal shades that kept the sunlight at bay, the Moon, the Sun and the Earth rotated past their windows as the spacecraft maintained a steady roll, much like a chicken on a spit. It was a practice the astronauts called 'barbecue mode'. Inside the cabin, the temperature hovered around 70°F.

To freshen up, the crew cleaned their teeth with edible toothpaste, shaved using cream from a tube, and washed with wet towels and tissues. The use of water had to be carefully controlled since it floated freely and could come into contact with electrical equipment. It was even difficult to stop water floating off their faces while they washed. By prior arrangement, Michael took on the brunt of the routine chores in order to allow Neil and Buzz a chance to rest ahead of the lunar landing. From a locker in the left-hand side of the lower equipment bay, Collins retrieved three pre-prepared bags of freeze-dried coffee, containing cream and sugar according to each man's tastes. Attaching the bags to a hot water gun he filled them up, kneaded them, passed out two and began sucking on a tube in the third. Apollo 11 carried scores of packets of food and drink, including chicken soup, ham and potatoes, and turkey with gravy, as well as Buzz's favourite, prawn cocktails (the prawns were individually chosen to ensure they were small enough to be squeezed from the bag). Buzz also liked the soup, and the cheese and meat spreads, but he regarded most of the food as bland.[22]

'Meal A, Day Two', for which an hour was allocated, included fruit cocktail, sausage patties, toasted cinnamon bread cubes and a grapefruit drink. Lunch that day would consist of frankfurters and apple sauce followed by chocolate pudding. While the frankfurters were listed as 'wet-pack' food, the other items were freeze-dried and needed to be rehydrated. After water was added, and the packet kneaded, a corner was cut off and the food was then squirted directly into the crewman's mouth. As well as the hot water gun, there was also a cold water gun; both were attached to long flexible tubes.[23] Germicide pills were added to used food bags to prevent fermentation, and once discarded they were stored in waste disposal compartments. Throughout the two months before the launch the meals were tested by Collins, who expressed his opinions of frankfurters and other simplistic space fare in expansive gastronomic terms, ranging from 'a gustatory delight' to 'the perfect blend of subtle spices'.[24]

After a few brief exchanges with Mission Control regarding the flight-plan, at 23 hours and 14 minutes into the mission, CapCom Bruce McCandless read the morning's news:

> Washington UPI: Vice President Spiro T. Agnew has called for putting a man on Mars by the year 2000, but Democratic leaders replied that priority must go to needs on Earth. Agnew, ranking government official at the Apollo 11 blast-off Wednesday, apparently was speaking for himself and not necessarily for the Nixon administration ... Laredo, Texas, AP: Immigration officials in Nuevo Laredo announced Wednesday that hippies will be refused tourist cards to enter Mexico unless they take a bath and get haircuts ... By United Press International: Initial reaction to President Nixon's granting of a holiday Monday to Federal employees so they can observe a national day of participation in the Apollo 11 Moon landing mission mostly was one of surprise. Rodney Bidner, Associated Press, London AP: Europe is Moon struck by the Apollo 11 mission. Newspapers throughout the continent fill their pages with pictures of the Saturn V rocket blasting off to forge Earth's first link with its natural satellite ... Hempstead, New York: Joe Namath officially

> reported to the New York Jets training camp at Hofstra University Wednesday following a closed door meeting with his teammates over his differences with pro-football Commissioner Peter Rozelle. London UPI: The House of Lords was assured Wednesday that a midget American submarine would not 'damage or assault' the Loch Ness monster. Lord Nomay said he wanted to be sure anyone operating a submarine in the Loch 'would not subject any creatures that might inhabit it to damage or assault'. He asked that the submarine's plan to take a tissue sample with a retrievable dart from any monster it finds can be done without damage and disturbance. He was told it was impossible to say if the 1876 Cruelty to Animals Act would be violated unless and until the monster was found. Over.

Once McCandless had finished, Collins got ready to give fresh navigation details to the computer, a task that required the suspension of PTC. From the point of view of the crew, the Moon was approaching the Sun's position in the sky and soon it would become impossible to see.

Flying towards a moving target that was nearly 240,000 miles away and could not be seen would have been impossible without Apollo's guidance computer. A pilot flying an aircraft uses the Earth as a guide: the planet's magnetic field provides a reference point for the compass, landmarks come and go, and height can be gauged as a specific distance above the ground. In weightlessness, words like 'up' have no meaning, altitude is an empty concept, and a compass is useless. Deprived of familiar points of reference, NASA made up its own, using three imaginary lines drawn through space at right angles to one another. Between them, these lines provided an interpretation of up/down, left/right and ahead/behind. The specific positions of the 'lines' varied during successive stages of the mission (for example, the references used on the way to the Moon were swapped for a different set on the way home), but all were variations on a theme.

Using software written by the Massachusetts Institute of Technology, *Columbia*'s computer was operated by two identical keyboards, one on the main control panel and the other in the wall of the lower equipment bay. In each position, a few basic command buttons and a number-pad were fitted next to a small black display screen showing green digits – a colour combination computer displays were to maintain for the next 20 years. Together, the display and keyboard were known as the DSKY, pronounced 'disky'. Also in the lower equipment bay, beside the DSKY, a telescope and sextant were built into the wall of the spacecraft, each providing a close-up glimpse of the universe outside. Both instruments were hooked up to the computer and could be used to locate any of the 37 stars the astronauts had been trained to find. Being so far away, the stars appeared to be static and so provided a fixed source of information. When one of them was identified in the cross-hairs of the sextant, a button was pressed, allowing the computer to remember its position. By checking the location of two or three specific stars, the computer could be told about the position of the three imaginary lines in use at that particular time.

To help it remember where these lines were, the computer then aligned a device known as the inertial platform, which served as a constant source of reference. Mounted between three gimbals and supported by gyroscopes, the platform remained in a precise position for hours at a time, even when the spacecraft was rolling in PTC. Over time, however, it tended to drift, which meant that it had to be checked and corrected once or twice a day. To do this, Collins would stop PTC, put a patch over one eye, bend down to look through the sextant and search once again for the relevant stars. Occasionally he would need to act quickly, particularly when the platform suddenly lost its sense of direction. This sometimes happened when two of the three gimbals began moving in the same direction, a condition known as gimbal-lock.

Once the computer knew where the three lines were (which

in NASA-speak were together known as the REFSMMAT), it was ready for a final nugget of information. For a driver on a motorway one of the three lines might represent the direction of travel, another might be a vertical line rising up through the roof and the third would be the horizontal horizon. Even so, it's only when he knows that he's doing 80mph, 20 miles north of London, that he truly understands where he is. The specific details of the spacecraft's speed and position, in relation to the lines, were sent to the computer from the ground, in a chunk of data known as the state vector. Now the computer had everything it needed to tell the crew where they were at any time.

The fact that the computer was directly linked to the command module's optical instruments, as well as other parts of the spacecraft, meant it could be described as the world's first embedded system. It relied on a 36KB memory[25] – tiny by today's standards, but modern machines are only as advanced as they are partly because of NASA's driving demand during the early 1960s for small, reliable computers. Until Collins learned to build a love-hate relationship with the dark arts of MIT's software, in the months before the mission the guidance system almost drove him to despair. 'You know we have this crazy computer,' he wrote, 'and we talk to it and it talks to us. We tell it what to do and it spits out answers and requests, and it complains quite a bit if we give it the wrong information.'[26]

The computer program that reset the inertial platform was known as P52. Collins performed this while still in Earth orbit, repeating the exercise a few hours later. Now, just over an hour after waking, he was ready to complete the operation again. Before he started, he first had to fly the spacecraft into a position that would allow him to see the specific stars he needed. Designed with the direct assistance of astronauts, all of whom were pilots, the command module was flown in a way that replicated an aircraft. Astronauts referred to up/down movements as pitch, left/right as yaw, and rotations to one side or another as rolling. Such manoeuvres, initiated by the spacecraft's thrusters, were monitored by the computer and displayed to the crew on the main panel in front of the couches. In fact the computer itself could command the thrusters to operate, via a program serving as a digital autopilot. For the P52 operation, Mission Control worked out the degree of pitch, roll and yaw that would be needed to get into the right position and then the figures were radioed up to the spacecraft. In his reply to Houston, Collins reported the number of hours each man had slept.

'Roger. OK. We note the battery charge as soon as we get around to it, and the attitude for the P52 optics cal[ibration]: roll 330.5, pitch 086.3, and yaw all zeros. The attitude for the P23 as in the flight-plan is OK; and I copy your battery charge. Crew status report as follows. Sleep Armstrong: 7, Collins: 7, Aldrin: 5.5. And we've completed the post-sleep checklist. Standing by for a consumable update. Over.'

While Collins looked at the details of the P23 program, a navigation experiment, Armstrong took another call from Jim Lovell.

Houston: 'Is the commander aboard?'

Armstrong: 'This is the commander.'

Houston: 'I was a little worried. This is the backup commander still standing by. You haven't given me the word yet. Are you go?'

Armstrong: 'You've lost your chance to take this one, Jim.'

Houston: 'OK. I concede.'

Once Collins had finished working on the navigation exercises, he returned to the business of flying the spacecraft. From the moment TLI ended until the point they entered lunar orbit, the service module engine was tested once and then virtually ignored. Although Earth's gravity was slowing them down, they would soon gain speed once they became vulnerable to the gravity of the Moon. In the meantime, nobody needed to do much actual flying. An exception came at 26 hours and 44 minutes when Collins fired the service module engine for three seconds in order to refine the spacecraft's trajectory. Once the burn was completed he reinstated PTC, and as he did so the spacecraft passed the halfway point between the Earth and the Moon. Because they were still slowing down, it was a statistic that meant little in terms of journey time.

As well as navigation tasks, other chores also had to be performed at regular intervals, including purging the fuel cells contained in the service module. The electricity required to run the spacecraft's computer, lights, instruments and other systems was supplied by three fuel cells, each of which generated power by combining hydrogen and oxygen. When the gases came together they produced water. Since electrons in the gases contained more energy than those in the water, the process released excess energy, about 50 per cent of which could be captured and converted into electricity. Compared to batteries, fuel cells produced several times as much energy per equivalent unit of weight, and better still the water they generated was drinkable.[27] Since weight was an important factor, doing away with the need to carry enough batteries and water to last the journey was of great value to the mission planners. In fact so much water was produced, the crew were obliged to dump the excess into space, a routine task that had to be done carefully in order to avoid creating any unwanted momentum. A device attached to the water gun was designed to reduce the hydrogen in the water before the astronauts drank it, but it wasn't always effective and left the crew with wind. At one point the problem got so bad that according to Buzz it was suggested they shut down their thrusters 'and do the job ourselves'.[28]

As Collins went about his work, he exchanged banter with Houston, where Jim Lovell was still at the CapCom position.

Lovell: 'I said it's a lot bigger than the last vehicle that Buzz and I were in.'

Collins: 'Oh, yes. It's been nice. I've been very busy so far. I'm looking forward to taking the afternoon off. I've been cooking, and sweeping, and almost sewing, and you know, the usual little housekeeping things.'

Lovell: 'It was very convenient the way they put the food preparation system right next to the NAV station.'

Armstrong: 'Everything is right next to everything in this vehicle.'

Given the lack of room, nothing triggered as much interest among space fans on the ground as the toilet arrangements. Since there wasn't a toilet, weightlessness made the arrangements primitive, difficult and public. The urine transfer system involved an astronaut peeing into a bag via an interchangeable device that was colour-coded per crewman. In weightlessness it was a difficult process, and spills were frequent. When the bag was periodically vented overboard, the urine formed a vapour around the spacecraft,[29] glinting in the sunlight as if a new constellation had been created. This made it difficult to pick out genuine stars, so a P52 could not be performed immediately after a urine dump.

It was the arduous ordeal of defecation that really tested the men's resolve. In a process that took up to an hour, the astronaut would make himself comfortable in the lower equipment bay. While his colleagues two or three yards away contemplated the meaning of life, he would take up a position with a bag, part of which was designed to fit over the hand like a glove. At the bottom of the bag a pocket contained tissue wipes, and at the top a wide lip incorporated a tape that sealed against the buttocks. Afterwards a germicidal liquid would be added to prevent bacteria developing, then once the bag had been sealed the astronaut was required to knead it in order to provide the desired degree of 'faeces stabilisation'. In case all of this wasn't humiliating enough, the bag was then stowed in empty food containers for post-flight analysis. Such bags would be used a total of five times on Apollo 11. The flap at the back of the underwear created an opening that was too small to seal the bag accurately and 'misses' were a common problem on most Apollo flights. Odours were difficult to control, as Jim Lovell discovered during Gemini 7, which he described as '14 days in a men's room'.

The P23 experiment and household tasks took up most of Michael's morning. After lunch, waste water was dumped and the lithium hydroxide filter – which removed carbon dioxide from the atmosphere – was changed. The crew were then ready to test the TV camera in preparation for a scheduled broadcast. After stopping PTC in order to send a continuous signal, at 6.32pm, 34 hours into the mission, the astronauts began the show. With the spacecraft now moving at 3,000mph, Collins focused on the Earth, 130,000 miles away, before handing the camera to Buzz who filmed his crew-mates in the lower equipment bay.

Collins: 'I would have put on a coat and tie if I'd known about this ahead of time.'

Houston: 'Is Buzz holding your cue cards for you? Over.'

Collins: 'Cue cards have a no. We have no intentions of competing with the professionals, believe me. We are very comfortable up here, though. We do have a happy home. There's plenty of room for the three of us and I think we're all learning to find our favourite little corner to sit in. Zero g is very comfortable, but after a while you get to the point where you sort of get tired of rattling around and banging off the ceiling and the floor and the side, so you tend to find a little corner somewhere and put your knees up or something like that to wedge yourself in, and that seems more at home.'

Houston: 'Roger. Looks like Neil is coming in five-by there, 11. Mike, see you in the background. It's a real good picture we're getting here of Commander Armstrong.'

Collins: 'Yes, Neil's standing on his head again. He's trying to make me nervous.'

With their flight-suits opened at the neck, white boots protecting their feet and communication wires taped over one ear, the men appeared comfortable and at ease. Buzz aimed the camera at a star-chart hanging over one of the windows while giving the audience an explanation of some its mysteries. Armstrong, taking the camera, then filmed Buzz exercising before inviting the audience over to a locker containing a variety of food. Michael pulled out a pack of chicken stew as an example of the menu on offer. Although *Columbia*'s interior was well lit, the lighting was uneven and left many dark nooks and crannies. To look through the food locker Michael needed to use a small torch. At launch, when the crew had been wearing their pressure-suits while strapped into their couches, they had been hemmed in by the grey instrument panels and barely had room to move. Most of the windows had been covered by a protective shroud, and sitting in a gloomy half-light they had been confronted by a vast array of instruments and switches. Now, with the windows uncovered, sunlight flooded the cabin, bouncing off the men's white flight-suits and the bright surfaces of the storage lockers. What had once appeared to be no more than a means of getting from A to B now looked like a bright living space. As the men freely floated about their new home, *Columbia* had the sterile look of a clean, state-of-the-art spacecraft. The era of cramped capsules had been replaced by a taste of the future.

( )

Apollo 11 was spared the sense of trepidation that had accompanied the Block II command module's first outing into deep space. With the LM running behind schedule, Frank Borman's flight was changed to include a pass around the Moon. Then it was changed again, allowing Borman to spend hours in lunar orbit. At the time, Collins believed it was 'rather far-out'[30] to contemplate such ideas before the first Apollo flight had even flown.

While preparing for the mission, in July 1968, Michael had begun to notice something strange. During handball games his legs didn't seem to be functioning normally, his knee would sometimes give way while walking downstairs, and hot and cold water produced abnormal nerve reactions. Finally he turned himself in to the NASA flight surgeon, knowing that as a pilot there were 'only two ways he [could] walk out: on flying status or grounded'.[31] He was referred to a Houston neurologist who found that a bony growth in Michael's neck, between the fifth and sixth vertebrae, was pushing against his spinal cord. It was agreed that he needed surgery, despite the implications of the decision to operate. Collins would have to give up his seat on Borman's mission and accept that he was grounded.

Chapter 7
RISKS AND RISKY REMEDIES

Kennedy had said America should commit itself to putting a man on the Moon 'before this decade is out'. There was some discussion as to whether his choice of words demanded the landing be made by 1969 or by 1970. Either way, although it was a challenging deadline, the end of the decade was at least easy to predict.

The Russians, however, remained an unknown quantity. By late 1968, suspicions were growing that they were about to send men into lunar orbit. NASA's slow but sure approach to the redevelopment of the command module threatened to come at a cost as once again there arose the spectre of being beaten into second place. In 1957, the Russians had launched the first satellite; they had put the first man into space in 1961; they sent a woman into space in 1963 and pulled off the world's first EVA in 1965. But in January 1966, the death of chief designer Sergei Korolev temporarily grounded their space programme. For more than a year Russia suspended its flights, and some in America began to suggest that the space-race was no more than a self-inflicted struggle against time.[1]

During this period the Russians were quietly preparing to return to space. They worked in such secrecy that when cosmonaut Vladimir Komarov launched on 23 April 1967 – beginning Russia's first manned orbital flight in two years – the mission came as a surprise even to Komarov's wife, Valentina. His spacecraft, Soyuz 1, quickly developed technical problems, and when it became clear that he might not survive re-entry Valentina was rushed into the control centre. She was allowed to bid her husband farewell, their final moments of anguish ending only when Komarov, unable to bear any more, asked her to go home.[2]

After re-entering the atmosphere, the spacecraft's parachutes failed to open and Soyuz 1 plummeted into the steppes before bursting into flames. Komarov took the unenviable title of becoming the first man to die during a mission. His loss was a devastating setback to Russia's space programme. Coming three months after the Apollo 1 fire, it led to a similar period of delay to that experienced by NASA. Not until the autumn of 1968 was Moscow ready to send men back into space – the same time as Houston. The space-race was very definitely back on.

On 18 September, Zond 5, an unmanned probe, flew around the far side of the Moon, carrying turtles, meal-worms and other species. Harking back to the days of Laika, when the Russians sent a dog into space before sending a man, Zond 5 appeared to be a prelude to something more ambitious. CIA warnings, presented to NASA's senior chiefs, suggested Russia was developing a giant lunar rocket,[3] these reports fuelling fears that Moscow was about to launch a manned attempt on the Moon. Even if cosmonauts were simply sent on a pass around the far side, this would still be enough to claim that men had been to Earth's nearest neighbour. For NASA, the years of hard work, the loss of the Apollo 1 crew and all the billions of dollars were overshadowed by the prospect of Moscow beating them to it, again. On 26 October, cosmonaut Georgi Beregovoi blasted into Earth orbit aboard Soyuz 3, intending to dock with the unmanned Soyuz 2 which had been launched the previous day. On the face of it, it was a bold mission with objectives that were more adventurous than those of Apollo 7 – which had launched two weeks earlier, on 11 October. Schirra's crew did little more than orbit the Earth. Soyuz 3, however, completed a successful rendezvous and even attempted a docking.

But while Beregovoi's flight essentially resembled a Gemini mission, by demonstrating the reliability of the Block II command module, Apollo 7 took NASA into a new arena of opportunity. Spending 11 days in space, Schirra proved the vehicle was capable of flying to the Moon and back. In fact the hardware out-performed the crew. The astronauts operated a 'watch' system so that one man was awake at any time, but his movements made it difficult for the other two to sleep. Tired and suffering colds, the crew became tetchy and hard to handle. Despite enjoying luxuries unheard of on Gemini, including hot meals and enough room to move about, the astronauts bickered with Mission Control so often that none of them was permitted to fly in space again.

Equipped with a safe spacecraft and a capable rocket, NASA was ready to combine the two in a mission that promised to take the space-race close to the finishing line. As a result of McDivitt's flight being delayed by the problems affecting the lunar module, the flight schedule was rewritten and the next crew pulled forward. In August Frank Borman, a broad-shouldered air force fighter pilot capable of making tough decisions quicker than anybody else, was given command of a daring mission to the Moon.[4] The two remaining seats went to Bill Anders and Jim Lovell (who had replaced Collins). Borman's backup crew was also pulled forward, so that Neil Armstrong, Buzz Aldrin and Lovell's replacement Fred Haise found themselves supporting Apollo 8 instead of 9. This meant they now had an unexpected shot at flying Apollo 11. Aldrin became the backup command module pilot, with Haise training to fly the lunar module.[5]

Although the Houston neurologist who diagnosed Michael's problem had been unable to confirm its cause, Collins suspected that his life as a fighter pilot had finally caught up with him. While stationed in France he had ejected from an F-86, and he wondered whether this may have triggered the weakness in his neck. The neurologist suggested a straightforward operation to remove the offending section of bone. But the air force, still technically Michael's employers, insisted that if he hoped to fly again he would need something more substantial. Michael realised he had no choice but to agree to an operation that would remove the bone spur and then fuse two vertebrae together with a piece of bone from his hip.

Checking into an air force hospital on 21 July, Michael felt himself to have been 'dropped like a hot potato' from Borman's crew.[6] After surgery he endured many weeks of frustrating uncertainty as he waited to find out whether the operation had been a success. By the autumn of 1968 he was back at work. But he was still grounded, and although offered a post at headquarters he got the impression it was a job being offered to an ex-astronaut, and turned it down.[7] If he was to get back into space, Collins knew he needed to stay in Houston. While working with Lovell on preparations for Apollo 8, Michael tried to get back to a physical condition that would allow him to fly. For this mission it was too late; 'those bastards Borman and Slayton' had given his seat away and they weren't about to change their minds.[8] 'I don't think Mike has completely forgiven me yet,' Borman said recently, 'because I think he thought he could have come back. But the mission was more important than anybody.'[9]

While Borman, Lovell and Anders continued with their training, some within NASA struggled to accept that the target they had worked so hard to reach was finally within their grasp. Since 1961, NASA had been looking at the Moon through a shop window, wondering about the cash, the technology and the depth of willpower required to touch what seemed like forbidden treasure. Now that it was actually within their reach, a sense of nervous caution set in. On Sunday 10 November, less than six weeks before the launch of Apollo 8, George Mueller, Chris Kraft, Deke Slayton, George Low and other NASA managers met representatives of more than a dozen contractors to decide whether to commit to putting men into lunar orbit. Amid lingering apprehension, the managers adopted a veneer of confidence in giving the mission the go-ahead.[10] The decision came not a moment too soon. On the same day, the Russians launched another unmanned probe on a mission to the Moon, raising fresh fears of cosmonauts making the trip before Christmas. NASA could beat them to it, if only they could hold their nerve.

A rocket no-one had flown before was to be sent into deep space, on a course dependent on pinpoint mathematical calculations while carrying a spacecraft tested only once in flight. It was a mission so risky there was no point pretending to the press it was anything less. Three days before the launch, the Apollo programme's head of safety, Jerry Lederer, said that Apollo 8 had 5,600,000 parts and even if all functioned with 99.9 per cent reliability 'we could expect 5,600 defects'.[11] Borman wasted no time in dismissing such worries. Believing 'the mission was more important than our lives, than our families', he declared that he had 'no hesitancy about the hardware'.[12] For him the flight was no less than a potential Cold War victory. It was his to be won; 'that's what we were there for,' he said.[13] Privately, one of Frank's teenage sons told his mother, 'You know, Dad's lucky, he gets to choose the way he's going to die. You and I aren't going to have that privilege.'[14]

At lift-off, on the morning of 21 December 1968, Collins was confined to Mission Control. As the launch CapCom he was prepared to call an immediate abort should anything go seriously wrong. 'With 5,600 things about to break,' he wrote, 'we would have plenty to talk about.'[15] The tension eased once the crew reached space, but a hushed sense of apprehension returned to Mission Control when Collins gave them permission to blast out of Earth orbit. In doing so they became the first people to slip beyond the cradle of the Earth and venture out into the open void. Throughout the history of manned space-flight only 24 people have ever gone further than Earth orbit, all of them Apollo astronauts – led by Borman, Lovell and Anders.

For the first time, human beings would be travelling through the potentially harmful radiation belts that stretched out around the Earth. The Van Allen belts posed no great risk to people passing through them quickly, nevertheless all Apollo astronauts wore dosimeters which displayed a measure of the radiation they encountered.[16] Updates were regularly given to Mission Control where they were monitored by the flight surgeon. A day into the mission senior doctors were asked to attend a private meeting, together with Michael Collins and a handful of flight controllers.[17] Borman had suddenly become ill. Dragging himself into the lower equipment bay, Frank had thrown up and then suffered diarrhoea, leaving particles of vomit and faeces floating about the cabin. They had to be chased down by Anders and Lovell using paper towels, as if swotting a swarm of insects. 'Basically it was a mess in the spacecraft,' Anders later remembered.[18] With the world watching such a prominent mission, Borman was reluctant to share publicly details of his illness. He had agreed to provide a short summary on tape, knowing this could be transmitted to the ground using a discrete telemetry channel.

Uncertain of the extent of the problem, flight managers were left wondering whether they would have to announce that the mission was in trouble before the crew were even halfway to the Moon. In a private meeting in Mission Control, the doctors and managers contacted the spacecraft. Borman, by now much recovered, blamed a sleeping pill he had taken a few hours into the flight, but rather than radiation or a reaction to pills it was later established that NASA had encountered its first case of space sickness. The Mercury and Gemini cabins had been so cramped that an astronaut was unable to move about properly. But in the relatively spacious command module there was plenty of room to float around in weightlessness. In doing so, the fluids in the inner ear sloshed about and for some people this induced an illness that lasted a day or so until their body acclimatised to the conditions of space-flight. Neither Lovell nor Anders was ill, and once it was realised that Borman was on the mend the decision was made to allow the mission to continue.

As the backup commander, Armstrong was in the Mission Operations Control Room, watching events. It was here that, on the day after Borman's illness, Deke found him and asked him to step into an office.[19] In his usual direct manner Slayton offered Neil command of Apollo 11. He couldn't confirm the mission's objective since Apollo 8 had yet to be completed, and the critical tests to be carried out by 9 and 10 would have to be successful before a landing could be attempted. Not only was Slayton uncertain about Armstrong's mission, even the choice of crew remained open. By rights Aldrin and Haise could expect to be selected, but Deke had concerns about Buzz, and he wasn't alone. Buzz himself wrote that comments he made during the preparations for Apollo 8 riled Borman so much that, in front of Armstrong, 'Frank shot back that he didn't need any suggestions from me that would screw up his flight'.[20] Deke told Neil that Buzz 'wasn't necessarily so easy to work with', adding that he could make Jim Lovell available if that's what Neil wanted.[21] Currently flying as the Apollo 8 command module pilot (or CMP), Lovell would be well placed to perform the same role on Apollo 11.[22]

But Deke had another suggestion. X-rays had shown that Michael Collins, also a CMP, had made a complete recovery. He was back on flying status and itching to get back into rotation, and Slayton felt he deserved to be given a flight at the earliest opportunity – if Armstrong agreed. Asking for time to consider his choices, Neil slept on it before going back to Deke the following day.[23] He knew that seniority in an Apollo crew ran from the commander to the command module pilot, and then to the lunar module pilot. On paper Buzz ought to fly as the CMP, but while Armstrong wanted Collins to serve on the crew he didn't want to relegate him to third position. Since Collins was a command module specialist it made sense to keep him in this role. Nor did Neil feel he could offer the third seat to Lovell since his Gemini and Apollo flights qualified him for his own command. Aldrin had trained as a lunar module pilot prior to the Apollo 8–Apollo 9 swap and could reasonably be asked to do the job again. Besides, Neil had been working with Buzz for months on Apollo 8 and felt that 'everything seem[ed] to be going all right'.[24] Armstrong rated Aldrin's flying skills, noting that 'Buzz and I had both flown in Korea', and he appreciated the fact that Buzz's intellect, creative thinking and willingness to make suggestions made him a 'fine person to work with'.[25] Neil had always stepped aside from the politics endemic in the Astronaut Office and was not about to start delving into personality conflicts now. In looking at Buzz he saw a man of ability; 'I'm not sure I recognised at that point in time what might be considered eccentricities,' Neil later said.[26] As far as he was concerned, Collins would be the CMP and Aldrin the lunar module pilot, and in accepting his decisions Deke bumped Fred Haise into a place on the backup crew.

While Armstrong was weighing up his options, Apollo 8 entered lunar orbit. In passing behind the Moon the crew found themselves at a point further from home than had ever been experienced before by man.

Ever since John Houbolt had persuaded NASA to adopt the strategy of lunar orbit rendezvous it had been decided that a flight to the Moon would involve two spacecraft. It was assumed from an early point in the planning that should certain emergencies develop in the command module, the crew could use the lunar module as a lifeboat. Without a heat-shield the LM could never survive re-entry into the atmosphere. But equipped with a powerful engine, an independent set of thrusters and its own supplies of oxygen and electricity, it could provide a shelter in the event of a serious problem. The theory was later proved in practice when an explosion drained life from the command module during Apollo 13. The spacecraft was left with only enough power to carry the crew through the atmosphere, so for the four-day journey back to Earth the astronauts took refuge in their LM. The crew of Apollo 8 didn't have a lunar module, and were taking a gamble with every minute they remained in space.

( )

The fragile lunar module was only of use if it survived the rigours of being hurled into space while squashed inside its adapter. Apollo 11's LM had been extracted from its container a little over four hours into the mission, but by the morning of the third day of the flight no-one had yet been inside to see what condition it was in. Opening the way into the lunar module was not an easy process, since an elaborate probe and drogue docking assembly lay in the middle of the tunnel connecting the LM with the command module. The crew completed a round of household tasks (including a waste-water dump and a P52 exercise) before preparing for the afternoon's TV broadcast – during which Aldrin would finally get a chance to assess the lander. Before the mission began, he had fought for an inspection of the LM to be included in the flight-plan at the earliest opportunity. If there was a problem, he wanted to know about it before they entered lunar orbit. At 55 hours into the flight, Neil examined the probe and drogue before Collins dismantled it, clearing the way into the LM. It was 3.32pm in Houston on Friday 18 July. The crew had been awake for seven hours and so far the third day had been relatively quiet. They were now 175,000 miles away from the Earth and travelling at less than 2,200mph.

Once the probe and drogue were removed, Buzz floated into the dimly lit tunnel and gingerly opened the LM's hatch. As it pushed gently inward, he could see that sunshine was filtering through the thin, silver-coloured window-shades, the light bouncing off a stray washer that was floating near the ceiling. Shooting TV pictures as he went, Buzz took a while to get his bearings inside a spacecraft he only knew from an Earth-bound perspective. The hot, cramped cabin was very different from the roomy command module, and was dusty enough to make Buzz cough. The white ceiling fittings, bathed in sunlight, reflected light on to the scores of switches and gauges set in the grey instrument panels. While the command module, like any home, was littered with personal possessions and equipment, the LM contained neatly packed white bags that gave it a sterile atmosphere. It was as if the cockpit were waiting in storage until whenever it might be needed. Although many of the gauges were already displaying meaningful information, the spacecraft looked less than ready for the monumental journey it would be making in a couple of days' time. Allowing the world its first glimpse of the vehicle that was going to go all the way to the Moon, Buzz panned round the cabin until he was looking back into the tunnel. 'Hey, that's a great shot right there,' said CapCom Charlie Duke, 'guess that's Neil and Mike. Better be, anyway.'

Travelling through the dark void of space, the gold exterior surfaces of the lunar module reflected sunrays so brightly that when peering through *Columbia*'s sextant it was sometimes difficult to look for stars.[27] Now, gazing through the LM's windows, for the first time Buzz was able to see the command module's polished surface, gleaming brightly in the sunshine. 'I can see the hatch and all the EVA handrails,' he said, 'first time we've seen the silvery outside of the command module.' Aldrin then pointed the camera back inside the LM, where dust and particles of paint floating above the instrument consoles also looked silver as they shimmered in the sunlight. Since the cockpit was not fitted with chairs, Buzz attached cables to clips on his waist to secure himself in position.

Aldrin: 'The restraints in here do a pretty good job of pulling my pants down.'

Duke: 'Roger. We haven't quite got that before the fifty million TV audience, yet.' A few minutes later, looking at Armstrong in the tunnel, Charlie added, 'Neil, at this attitude you look like you're about 12 feet long.'

Armstrong: 'It seems like I always find myself upside-down in whatever I'm doing around here.'

As he took the TV audience on a tour of the cabin, Buzz believed that the LM was in a good condition. He and Neil wouldn't know for certain until a short time before they were ready to begin the landing. As well as looking at the controls, Buzz also checked some of the equipment that would be needed on the Moon. 'We're giving you a picture now of the floor of the cabin,' he told Mission Control. 'I think you can see one of the two portable life-support system backpacks here in the centre, and on each side we have the two helmet visors.'

()

Buzz had first discovered he was to walk on the Moon on Monday 6 January 1969, 10 days after the safe return of Apollo 8.[28] He and Michael were called into Deke's office, where Neil was already waiting. 'You're *it*,' Slayton told them. He added it was 'conceivable' that Apollo 11 may be the first mission to attempt a landing, as was to be reflected in their training.[29] However, it was also possible that Apollo 9, McDivitt's delayed test-flight of the LM, could be further postponed, which would force NASA to give the landing to Apollo 10 in order to meet the deadline. This would involve an all-out dash for the surface, without first completing a dress rehearsal. Such a bold step would echo the ambitious decision to send Borman to the Moon earlier than planned.

In later years it would be suggested that NASA had carefully hand-picked the crew of Apollo 11, deliberately choosing a civilian commander in order to disassociate itself with the war in Vietnam. But Deke always insisted the men were picked only on the basis that it was their turn to fly next. 'There isn't any big magic selection that goes on for each mission,' he once explained.[30] In fact Deke had long hoped that the first man to walk on the Moon would be one of the Mercury Seven. Before the Apollo 1 fire, this had been agreed with headquarters and with Bob Gilruth, the director of the Manned Spacecraft Center. The obvious choice had been Gus Grissom, but after the loss of his close friend Slayton went back to the system of rotation.[31]

For Deke, the selection process was about the mission as much as about the astronauts. In putting a crew together he looked for three compatible men whose skills complemented one another and who were eligible to fly based on the length of time they had been waiting for a flight. In sending men into space, Slayton took mental stability for granted; gung-ho mavericks, awkward personalities and oddballs likely to reach for the hatch had already been weeded out during the selection process. Believing that all astronauts should be capable of flying any flight, Deke didn't fret about who was best psychologically equipped for any particular role.[32] Once he had put a crew together, the names were sent to Gilruth for approval before being passed to headquarters where they were usually rubber-stamped by George Mueller, the head of manned space-flight. The power Deke held over people's careers was extensive. Chris Kraft, for one, thought it was excessive. Kraft wrote that Deke 'seldom had to justify his actions to Gilruth or anyone else'.[33]

Despite Deke's words of caution about Apollo 11's objective, as Buzz took in the news he was filled with excitement. For the sake of form he knew he had to mask his reaction behind a 'façade of business as usual'.[34] Nevertheless he couldn't wait to tell Joan. The Aldrins' washing machine had broken down, and Buzz later remembered that on the way back from the laundrette, 'driving home in a car jammed full of wet laundry, I told my wife I was going to land on the Moon'. He described Joan as becoming 'half hysterical, partly out of pride, but mostly out of fear'.[35] Three days later an official announcement named the crew of Apollo 11, and subsequent headlines dubbed them the 'Moon Team'.[36] Slayton later told the press that they would be the first crew to concentrate on a landing, and confirmed that the backup crew was to be commanded by Jim Lovell, with Bill Anders training as the CMP and Fred Haise serving as the lunar module pilot.

For Michael Collins, it was the opportunity he feared would never come, and he relished the chance to fly with Neil and Buzz. He had much respect for both men, whom he regarded as 'smart as hell ... competent and experienced'.[37] Michael had first met Neil in 1962, when each was attempting to become an astronaut, and at the time he considered Armstrong to have the strongest background of the six civilians hoping to be taken on. The fact that Neil was selected, whereas he himself was not, came as no great surprise to Collins when he took into account their relative levels of test-flight experience. 'I like him,' Michael said later, 'but I don't know what to make of him, or how to get to know him better.'[38] He considered that while Neil was patient with 'processes', sometimes he could be impatient with people when they didn't meet his standards.[39]

When Collins returned to Houston in 1963, he met Aldrin who in later years he considered to be more approachable than the reticent Neil. Indeed, Michael admitted it was actually he who tried to keep Buzz at arm's length. 'I have the feeling that he would probe me for weaknesses, and that makes me uncomfortable,' he wrote.[40] For his part, Aldrin admired Neil and Michael but didn't feel especially close to either of them. He later recalled that in 1963 there 'wasn't anything that particularly drew me to Mike'.[41] He first met Neil at Ed White's house (possibly in 1964) and later remembered that at the time Neil was roller-skating around the front yard. He discovered him to be 'reserved, deep and thoughtful' and subsequently found that occasionally he could also be stubborn.[42]

Within the Astronaut Office, all three men were regarded as competent and well suited to the mission. Whether their peers universally considered them to be the best three to do the job is unlikely, given the competitive nature of most astronauts, but Deke had made his decision and no-one was going to change his mind.

For all three men, landing on the Moon was one thing; doing it first was something else. There was no doubt that the later, more adventurous flights would attract considerably less press attention than the tentative first attempt, which would be carried out under international scrutiny.[43] Buzz privately discussed with Joan the idea of flying on a different mission, but he knew there was no chance of raising the matter with anyone else. To do so would amount to 'sacrilege', risking the removal of all three men from the mission and seriously prejudicing Aldrin's chances of ever flying again. He felt that 'I was part of the crew and I couldn't let anyone down by my individual concerns'.[44] Yet subsequent events suggest this was not the whole story.

Kennedy had called for a man to land on the Moon and then come home again. There had been no mention of anybody shimmying down a ladder, let alone skipping about on the surface scooping up boxes of dust. But it had come to be assumed that at least one man would venture out on to the lunar plain. Initially it was thought that only one member of the crew would leave the spacecraft, following the precedent set during the Gemini programme. However, a number of experiments were being assembled for the first lunar EVA. There would be little time to set them up and it was realised that two men would be needed to complete the work. On this basis, both Neil and Buzz would step on to the surface.

What the press wanted to know, just a day after the crew's names were officially released, was which of them would go first.[45] Following the example set by Ed White, the EVA was traditionally performed by the second crewman while the commander flew the spacecraft. Buzz had shown that this strategy was successful and that key objectives could be achieved by the junior man operating on his own. If he were to receive assistance from Neil while on the Moon, then so much the better. Early paperwork showed that Buzz was indeed slated to become the first man to step on to the surface, and the press were advised accordingly. Reporters were told by George Mueller that Aldrin would be first.[46]

By March, Buzz began to hear on the Houston grapevine that maybe Neil would go first. Aldrin has suggested that his initial reaction to this news was one of puzzlement. But when it appeared that Neil was being considered ahead of Buzz because he was a civilian, Aldrin grew angry. He felt that 'the implication was that the military service was ... some sort of warmonger'; besides, he knew that 'Neil had learned to fly in the service, just as I had'.[47] As far as Buzz was concerned there were no differences between them and therefore he had as much right to go first as anyone. As Chris Kraft remembered it, 'Buzz Aldrin desperately wanted that honour and wasn't quiet in letting it be known'.[48] Buzz has said that he wanted to take some of the burden off Neil, who would have to cope with leading the EVA in addition to accomplishing the landing. Aldrin recently explained that 'My objective was to try and even out the training workload and follow the precedent that had been set in all space walks up to that time.'[49]

His frustration about who was to be first was fanned by his father's expectations. The family was already in turmoil. The previous May, Buzz's mother had taken an overdose of sleeping pills. She had done this once before, and it had been considered an accident. This time, she had been found by Gene Aldrin and rushed to hospital. The second time may also have been an accident, but Buzz had his doubts. His maternal grandfather had taken his own life and Buzz was aware his mother no longer had a strong will to live. 'When my mother took her life about a year before my Apollo flight,' he said, 'certainly it was a very sad situation, but there wasn't at that point anything I could really do about it except move on and understand that those things happen.'[50] At the family's request the death certificate referred to cardiac arrest, and for years Buzz and his sisters said little about their deeper suspicions.[51]

In early 1969, Gene Aldrin threw himself into the row over who would be first to walk on the Moon. In a phone-call to his father, Buzz persuaded him not to intervene via high-level friends.[52] Slayton wasn't sure the message had got through. 'From the moment Buzz joined NASA,' Deke wrote, 'his old man was trying to pull strings to get him assigned to a flight.' Now, once again he discovered that Aldrin senior had 'got into the act'.[53] Buzz himself declared that amid all the distracting gossip and speculation he simply wanted to know who it was going to be.

The problem began to gnaw at him. Buzz mulled it over for a few days but decided that the issue was 'potentially too explosive for even the subtlest manoeuvring'. Then he went directly to Neil.[54] Armstrong fudged the issue for a minute or two before coolly telling Buzz he didn't want to rule himself out. Deke had warned Neil about Buzz, and now Armstrong found himself caught up in the kind of political wrangling he had traditionally shied away from. Deke himself told Buzz that it would probably be Neil first since he was the more senior of the two. Armstrong was the commander of the mission and had been in NASA for longer.[55] In search of support, Buzz raised the issue with other astronauts, including Michael Collins, who recalled that 'I quickly turned him off. I had enough problems without getting into the middle of that one.'[56]

Subtle diplomacy was tricky. The alternative was to be direct, but this way of doing things had led to problems with Houston's managers during Buzz's campaign for a Gemini flight, and more recently with Neil. Nevertheless Aldrin decided that being direct was worth the risk, and this time he would go to George Low, the most senior Apollo manager in Houston.

Chapter 8
A TISSUE-PAPER SPACECRAFT

While inspecting the lunar module during the third day of the flight, Buzz picked his way carefully about the cramped cabin. Plumbing and bundles of wiring lay exposed on the floor, and in places the walls were no thicker than a couple of layers of aluminium. Fragile as it was, the LM remains unique in being the world's only manned spacecraft capable of a powered landing, whether on the Moon or anywhere else.[1] The Mercury capsule, the Gemini spacecraft, even the Apollo command module were designed simply to fall into water, slowed only by parachutes. The Russians also used parachutes, although their spacecraft came down over land. In touching down on the Moon, which does not have an atmosphere, parachutes would be useless. If the LM were to survive unscathed, a gentle, powered descent was critical.

As he went about his work, Buzz continued to report on what he was doing for the benefit of CapCom Charlie Duke and those watching on television.

Aldrin: 'Like old home week, Charlie, to get back in the LM again.'

Mission Control: 'Roger. Must be some experience. Is Collins going to go in and look around?'

Armstrong: 'We're willing to let him go but he hasn't come up with the price of the ticket yet.'

Mission Control: 'Roger. I'd advise him to keep his hands off the switches.'

Collins: 'If I can get him to keep his hands off my DSKY, it'd be a fair swap.'

The TV broadcast, which NASA regarded as the clearest yet

sent from space, lasted a little over an hour and a half.[2] During that time Apollo 11 coasted more than 3,000 miles.

Once Buzz returned to the command module, the hatch was closed and the LM was sealed shut once again. The crew then completed a round of their routine chores before sitting down to dinner, accompanied by music. Both Armstrong and Collins had taken selections on cassettes which they listened to on a portable tape recorder; Buzz had decided he would be content with whatever they chose.

Once the spacecraft had been put into a PTC roll, Aldrin looked out at the heavens rotating slowly past the windows. Suddenly, there out in space was an object that was reflecting light and which almost appeared to be shadowing them. After Buzz pointed it out to Neil and Michael the three of them gathered at the windows, each waiting for the object to swing into view as the spacecraft gently rolled on its axis. Buzz got down into the lower equipment bay and took a closer look through the sextant and telescope, but all he could say for certain was that the object sometimes appeared to be L-shaped. As flying objects go it was definitely unidentified. In Buzz's words, they 'sure as hell were not going to talk about it to the ground' for fear of the curiosity and even concern it would raise. Someone might even suggest that the mission should be cancelled since aliens were apparently going along for the ride. 'We didn't want to do anything that gave the UFO nuts any ammunition,' Aldrin later said.[3]

The crew had already bid goodnight to Houston, but after thinking over his choice of words, Neil contacted Mission Control.

Armstrong: 'Houston, Apollo 11.'

Mission Control: 'Go ahead, 11. Over.'

Armstrong: 'Do you have any idea where the S-IVB [third stage] is with respect to us?'

Mission Control: 'Stand by.'

Mission Control: 'Apollo 11, Houston. The S-IVB is about 6,000 nautical miles from you now. Over.'

Armstrong: 'OK. Thank you.'

With the third stage eliminated, the men began to discuss other possible explanations. Sometimes the mysterious object looked like a hollow cylinder, at other times it resembled two connected rings. 'It certainly seemed to be within our vicinity and of a very sizeable dimension,' Buzz later remembered.[4]

( )

When Buzz approached George Low in March, seeking an answer to the 'first out of the hatch' question, Aldrin insisted it would be in the best interest of 'morale and training' if the decision were made quickly.[5] Buzz asked whether Neil's civilian status gave him an advantage, but Low told him it was irrelevant.[6]

Buzz was right in arguing that the matter needed to be settled soon, since Aldrin and Armstrong had to begin training for the EVA. For the moment they continued to work with the lunar module. Both had served on the backup crew for Apollo 8 and were already familiar with the LM. But the spacecraft's operational performance was largely untested and there was still much to learn. As part of their training, Armstrong and Aldrin occasionally visited Grumman's plant at Bethpage on Long Island, New York, to monitor the development of LM-5, the lunar module they would fly to the Moon.

After winning the $388 million contract to build a lunar lander in November 1962, Grumman quickly came up against a range of formidable problems. Immersed in a multitude of competing demands, the LM was to become one of the most challenging components of the entire Apollo programme. The painstaking search for solutions was led by Tom Kelly, a likeable engineer from New York. Supported by a team of 100 technicians, Kelly had been working on ideas for a lander even before Kennedy had laid down his challenge in 1961. Early on, he realised the vehicle would need to be small and light yet rugged enough to withstand the launch into Earth orbit and the three-day journey through space.

Kelly's work was to be overseen by the Apollo Spacecraft Program Office in Houston. Already the head of the Apollo office, Charles Frick, was embroiled in difficulties over the command module with his counterpart at North American Aviation. When he saw them 'screaming and cursing at each other' Chris Kraft could barely believe it.[7] Kraft had heard the relationship was troubled but after shifting his attention from Gemini to the lunar missions, he saw for himself that 'bad vibes from Apollo were everywhere'.[8] Kraft found that lessons learned during Gemini were being ignored both inside NASA and beyond. He believed the Apollo office had begun to adopt a stubborn sense of independence, and worse, this was filtering down to North American. Soon he began to suspect Grumman was slipping in the same direction.

The lander would be carried into space by the powerful Saturn V rocket, which could lift a 125-ton payload into Earth orbit. But this distance was less than 1 per cent of Apollo 11's journey to the Moon. After carrying the spacecraft into orbit, the booster's final stage would then re-ignite for the relatively short TLI burn. There was only so much fuel the third stage could carry and during TLI this would be quickly spent. Yet within this small amount of time the stage would have to push the fully laden spacecraft fast enough to send it all the way to the Moon. These limitations meant that at launch the rocket's payload – the spacecraft at the top of the stack – could not weigh more than 50 tons. The sturdy command module, robust enough to survive re-entry, weighed more than six tons, the service module behind it weighed almost 26, and the lunar module would have to carry at least 12 tons of fuel for its round trip to the surface. After equipment, consumables for the crew and scientific experiments had been taken into account, Kelly was told that the lander itself could not weigh more than four tons. The restriction was marginally increased during the spacecraft's development, but from the start the entire project was characterised by a perpetual struggle to save weight. The Saturn's constraints had an impact on almost every element of the LM's design. Failure to accept them would end any hope of a lunar landing before Apollo 11 even left Earth.[9]

Despite its lightweight structure, the spacecraft would have to be strong enough to survive a rough landing on uneven and dusty ground. Its critical systems would have to cope with a hostile environment beyond all hope of assistance, and it would have to be able to successfully launch from the lunar surface on its first attempt. When Apollo 11 lifted off from Cape Kennedy, 463 people sitting nearby guided the launch process and thousands of specialists were ready to resolve any last-minute problems. When the lander launched from the Moon, its two-man crew would be on their own.

In developing what Grumman initially called the lunar excursion module (LEM), Kelly's team proposed a two-stage spacecraft. The bottom half, the descent stage, contained the descent engine and associated fuel tanks. Delivering 10,000lb of thrust, the descent engine was the first large rocket motor that could be throttled up or down. This meant that the spacecraft could be flown at a decreasing speed as it slowly approached the surface. The descent would be partially controlled by a computer, allowing maximum fuel efficiency – which was critical since the LEM was carrying the slimmest margin of propellants. Only in the final stage of the descent would the spacecraft be flown manually.

Most of the top half of the vehicle, the ascent stage, was taken up by the cockpit, though it too had an engine. After the EVA, the astronauts would return to the cabin and when ready they would ignite four explosive bolts that would sever umbilical cables connecting the two sections of the spacecraft. They would then fire the ascent engine. The ascent stage would blast off from the Moon, and on returning to lunar orbit the crew would search for the command module, as envisaged in the original proposal for lunar orbit rendezvous. Armstrong and Aldrin would then rejoin Collins for the journey home.

In an emergency on the way down to the Moon, the crew could jettison the descent stage and use the ascent engine to quickly climb back up into space. Since emergencies in a lightweight spacecraft flying close to the rocky surface of the Moon could potentially be disastrous, the two engines needed to be as reliable as possible. Both were hypergolic, in that each used two types of propellant which ignited simply when allowed to mix. Neither relied on complicated moving parts such as pumps or igniters, therefore they were less likely to go wrong than traditional types of engine. The LEM's 16 thrusters, arranged in four groups of four around the ascent stage, also used hypergolic propellants.

Kelly's team originally put seats in the spacecraft, in common with almost every other flying machine. The crew were to look out of four large windows that were made of extremely thick glass and embedded in a heavy supporting structure.[10] But this design came to be regarded as too heavy and two smaller triangular windows were fitted instead. These made it harder to see from the seats so bar-stools and metal cage-like structures were considered, until 1964, when two Houston engineers suggested Kelly would save further weight by removing the seats altogether. Standing during the short flight, the astronauts would be closer to the window than if they were seated, giving them a better view. 'Trolley-car configuration' astronaut Pete Conrad called it, thinking of a driver standing at his wheel. The crew would be held in place by Velcro strips securing their feet to the floor and by cables attached at the waist that were held under tension by a system of pulleys.

Now that the astronauts would be standing, the floor-space could be reduced until it was just three and a half feet deep. Looking towards the back wall, the space behind the crew positions was largely taken up by equipment casings that protruded into the cockpit. A unit on the left contained the environmental control system, while the floor in the middle of this area was raised to knee height to accommodate the ascent engine. Squeezed into the tiny ceiling above lay the hatch leading up into the command module. Despite the technological breakthroughs in the LEM's design, there was no escaping the thought that man was going to the Moon in a cabin the size of a broom cupboard. It was even equipped with a small vacuum cleaner to deal with the lunar dust.

For many months the spacecraft's torturous development process was delayed by problems, including engine instability, battery faults and leaks from lightweight pipes – and all the while the weight kept creeping up. In 1965, Houston asked for the limit of the LEM's load to be marginally raised. Headquarters consented, but Kelly knew much still needed to be done to keep within the restrictions. Grumman launched 'Operation Scrape' in an attempt to shave as much material from the structure as possible. This was followed by the Super Weight Improvement Program, implemented by a crack team of weight-saving experts personally led by Kelly. 'At one time we were paying about $10,000 an ounce to take weight off,' astronaut Jim McDivitt later recalled. Among other things, these campaigns led to a decision to scrap the panels protecting the vehicle from the Sun's heat and replace them with Kapton. Specifically developed for the LEM, Kapton – a golden, plastic foil – became one of its characteristic features. Crinkled by hand in order to reduce the transmission of heat, the foil was visible only on the descent stage since the upper half of the spacecraft was cloaked in a layer of aluminium plates, designed to dissipate the impact of micrometeoroids. The cockpit was pressurised, but as an added layer of protection during the descent the crew would wear pressure-suits.

Challenging as Kelly's work was, the complicated, occasionally delicate relationship with NASA made things harder still. In Houston, Frick had been replaced by Joe Shea, but old attitudes lingered on. The Apollo office and Grumman were failing to see eye to eye over a multitude of issues, and trust and understanding were beginning to fray at the edges. Chris Kraft later wrote that both Grumman and North American were failing to give technical information and diagrams to astronauts and flight controllers. He also believed the contractors were ignoring their obligation to attend meetings focusing on mission control procedures. Kraft's problems were compounded by internal wrangling within the Manned Spacecraft Center, yet throughout the bickering Kelly had to stay focused on the matter in hand.[11]

The lander needed to be capable of more than simply transporting men to the Moon. After reaching the surface, it would have to shelter its crew from a hostile environment and provide them with somewhere to eat, sleep and prepare for an EVA. The batteries, the environmental control and waste management systems, the oxygen and water supplies and the radio-transmitters all had to perform to high minimum standards in a vehicle that had been repeatedly stripped of anything deemed too heavy. Only lightweight wiring was used, there was no facility for hot water (and therefore hot meals), and even toothbrushes were cut from the checklist.

The spacecraft required an extensive set of gauges and controls, and reducing their weight was hard. The instrument panels were illuminated by electroluminescence, a new technique using phosphors instead of conventional light bulbs. (This proved so popular with the astronauts involved in the design of the LEM that it was adopted in the command module.) In the vehicle's final form, the left-hand wall contained banks of indicator lights which produced a gentle orange glow. Standing beside them, the commander would control the descent engine by gripping a throttle with his left hand, and the thrusters by holding a joystick with his right. In the centre panels between the two crewmen's positions, the gauges included a DSKY. The computer would be largely operated by the lunar module pilot, whose title was misleading since the spacecraft would actually be flown by the commander while the pilot monitored the instruments. Beneath the DSKY, a rectangular hatch opened on to a small platform known as the porch, while up above a telescope protruded into the cabin. Sections of the ceiling were covered with netting, to secure papers and other lightweight materials. Compartments for heavier items were built in to the lower sections of the walls and protected by white beta-cloth, a fireproof fabric.

Since the final phases of the landing would be controlled manually, the instruments' reliability was essential. Redundancy was built into the cabin layout with some controls duplicated on each side of the cockpit. The LEM had two computers, which worked independently of each other. The primary guidance and navigation system (PGNS, pronounced 'pings') relied on an inertial platform similar to its counterpart in the command module. The abort guidance system (AGS) consisted of a separate computer that gathered information from an independent set of movement sensors. Both computers could be updated either manually or by accepting data sent directly from Earth. They could also receive information from the LEM's two radar systems. A landing radar would begin to calculate the spacecraft's altitude once the crew had descended to below 40,000 feet. After the trip to the surface, a rendezvous radar would help the LEM find the command module from a distance of 400 miles. It could also be used in an emergency should the descent be aborted. Connecting the two radars to the guidance and navigation system proved to be one of the most complicated tasks in the development of the LEM. Equally challenging were the engines, which in 1966 were still beset by problems. That year, headquarters decided the word 'excursion' made the whole project sound like a holiday trip and it was decided the spacecraft should simply be called the lunar module.[12]

The astronauts would initially rely on the LM's life-support system, before switching over to the oxygen stored in their backpacks while preparing to open the hatch. This was originally round but was later changed to match the shape of the backpack, making it easier for the crew to leave the spacecraft. The hatch opened inwards and swung to the right so that whoever was to go first would need to be standing on the left. One plan envisaged the astronauts clambering down to the surface using a rope ladder, but this was later replaced with a real ladder, secured to one of the spacecraft's legs. While stowed aboard the Saturn the four legs were folded. Extended shortly before the descent, they contained crushable aluminium honeycomb to absorb the shock of the landing. Each was fitted with a round landing pad, beneath three of which dangled a six-foot-long probe designed to trigger a blue contact light in the cabin upon touching the surface.[13] Armstrong feared that a fourth probe, directly below the ladder, might be bent dangerously upwards during the landing and he had it removed.

By early 1968 the finished product was finally ready to be tested.[14] The world's only true spacecraft, the lander was designed purely for flight in a vacuum, and was not fitted with a heat-shield. Nor was it aerodynamic. The propellant tanks for the ascent engine were contained in awkward external bulges, as if they had been bolted on at the last minute. Although it contained more than a million parts, from the outside the LM looked as if it had been thrown together by the winner of a children's competition. Adorned with thrusters, radars, transmitters and probes, its odd-shaped body, two bug-eye windows and four spindly legs gave it an almost sinister appearance. Michael Collins likened the LM to an enormous praying mantis, and he wasn't alone in mocking its odd appearance. Volkswagen used a picture of it in a Beetle advert, beside the line 'It's ugly, but it gets you there'.[15] By the end of the programme 3,000 engineers were working for Tom Kelly, and although much of the spacecraft was eventually developed by committee, in later years he came to be known as the 'Father of the LM'.

Despite continuing concerns about the ascent engine, the first finished spacecraft, LM-1, was transferred to the Cape in preparation for Apollo 5, the unmanned test-flight of 22 January 1968. The Launch Control Center insisted that all rockets should carry a destruct mechanism in case anything went wrong. But the prospect of such a device inadvertently exploding while the crew were wandering about on the Moon led Houston to resist the Cape's demands, and eventually the rule was relaxed. Although

Apollo 5 successfully achieved its objectives, the instability of the ascent engine continued to raise concerns that were not resolved until June 1968. Meanwhile, fears about the safety of the docking mechanism, allowing the LM to connect to the command module, dragged on into early 1969, further postponing Jim McDivitt's long-delayed mission. (A second unmanned flight, involving LM-2, was cancelled. Today, LM-2, the only intact lunar module to survive, can be seen at the Smithsonian Institution in Washington.)

Noted for his thoroughness and attention to detail, McDivitt, a former air force pilot, had been training to fly the LM since 1966. Regarded by Michael Collins as 'one of the best. Smart, pleasant, gregarious, hard-working, religious', McDivitt was one of the more conservative members of the Astronaut Office, certainly compared to his relatively free-thinking lunar module pilot Rusty Schweickart.[16] Supported by command module pilot Dave Scott (Armstrong's dependable partner during Gemini 8), together they would be responsible for demonstrating the reliability of the final link in Apollo's chain of rocket stages and spacecraft modules. Manned missions had verified the safety of the rest of the hardware, but only the LM could carry astronauts the final few miles to the lunar surface. Already its development had put NASA behind schedule. Now, if McDivitt failed to prove the lander was up to the job, the challenge of reaching the Moon by the end of the decade could easily slip beyond reach. 'We were all cognisant of the time pressure,' McDivitt later said.

On 3 March 1969, the fourth Saturn V lifted off from the Cape, carrying with it Grumman's hopes of taking America to the Moon within the next nine months. For the first time, the complete Apollo package would test the sequence of manoeuvres required for a lunar mission, short of the landing itself. Launch flight director Gene Kranz subsequently wrote that the 'Apollo 9 mission was sheer exhilaration for both the astronauts and Mission Control'.[17] For McDivitt, here was a rare chance to fly a spacecraft that was radically different to anything anyone had flown before. Operating LM-3 in Earth orbit, he and Schweickart planned to fly many miles away from the command module before returning for the critical rendezvous manoeuvre. For the first time since the rendezvous between Gemini 6 and Gemini 7 two spacecraft would be operating simultaneously, and to ease communications the crew were allowed to name their vehicles. The LM was given the call-sign *Spider* and the command module was named *Gumdrop*.

As Dave Scott prepared for the delicate task of using the command module to extract the LM from its container, he discovered that at this crucial point in the mission some of his thrusters weren't working. Flight controllers found the crew had accidentally pushed a switch, and through patient diligence they were able to correct the problem and keep the mission on track. Scott gingerly retracted the LM before taking the two spacecraft through a series of manoeuvres. The initial tests were due to include an EVA. Schweickart planned to leave the LM, and by using handrails mounted on its hull he intended to climb over to the command module. This would test an emergency procedure that could be used in the event of an unsuccessful docking. But after he suddenly vomited twice, plans for the space walk were scaled down to something less ambitious. Schweickart eventually performed a small EVA on the porch of the LM, testing the portable life-support system that would be worn on the Moon. At the same time Scott leant out of the command module hatch, and since both men were able to reach the handrails they successfully demonstrated that they could cross over in an emergency.

The next task for their 'tissue-paper spacecraft', as McDivitt called it, was to separate from *Gumdrop* and begin to pull away.[18] For him and Schweickart there was more at stake than Kennedy's deadline. Failure to find the command module would be fatal, as without a heat-shield the LM would never survive re-entry. 'When ... we finally pulled away from the docking mechanism,' McDivitt later recalled, 'I'm sure it was in Rusty's mind, I know darn well it was in my mind [that] we better get back to this place or we're going to be toast, and I really mean toast.' After covering more than 100 miles, they simulated an abort by ditching the descent stage and firing the ascent engine. McDivitt greatly enjoyed flying the ascent stage and found that its slender mass had the agility of a fighter jet. Waiting for his crew-mates to return, Scott eventually saw a vibrant pyrotechnic display cutting through the darkness as *Spider*'s thrusters kept the LM on course for the rendezvous. The subsequent docking finally secured confidence in Grumman's claims to be able to bring men home from the Moon. 'We had a certain set of objectives, almost all of which were essential to the next mission,' McDivitt later said. 'We accomplished them, what more could we do? We were happy.' Chris Kraft recalled, 'I went home that night knowing that we could actually do this thing.'[19]

Despite the challenges, Kelly had produced a space-worthy vehicle that had performed up to expectation. Now NASA could push ahead with the next mission, this time testing the LM just a few miles above the lunar surface. George Mueller, the head of the Office of Manned Space Flight, even suggested that Apollo 10 should be given the landing, arguing that in making a low-level pass above the Moon the crew would be taking a great risk without much to show for it. But Mission Control wasn't ready for such a demanding flight and Mueller's demands were resisted. The debate was settled when it was established that Apollo 10's lunar module, LM-4, was too heavy to leave the surface safely. Apollo 10 would carry out the practice run while LM-5 would be made ready for the landing.[20] Like its predecessors, LM-5 had suffered its fair share of problems – a window had blown out during a test, and fittings were replaced after cracks were discovered – but eventually the final component of Apollo 11 was declared ready for launch. Fully laden, LM-5 would weigh just short of 17 tons. If allowed to stand on its legs while full of fuel it would collapse under its own weight, even in the minimal gravity of the Moon.[21] Only after burning a sufficient quantity of propellant would the spacecraft actually be able to land.

With the safe return of Apollo 9, and a decision made about Apollo 10, Armstrong, Aldrin and Collins began to feel a little clearer about their own mission.[22] Unresolved issues were suddenly met with a new sense of urgency, not least the question of who would be first to walk on the surface. After Buzz had approached Deke in search of a Gemini flight, he had been deemed to be brash. Since then, in terms of intellectual ability, rendezvous expertise and EVA experience, Aldrin had proved himself to be one of the leading astronauts. While some questioned the way he had pursued the 'first out' issue, no-one could deny that it needed to be settled. His opinions could easily have been brushed aside but in fact they were addressed in a top-level meeting. Chris Kraft, the director of flight operations, Bob Gilruth, the director of the Manned Spacecraft Center, George Low, the Apollo office manager, and Deke Slayton, the director of flight crew operations, knew that whoever they selected would go down in history.[23] Overnight they would become, in Kraft's words, 'an American hero ... beyond any soldier or politician or inventor'. Kraft was clear: 'It should be Neil Armstrong.'[24]

While Aldrin's talents were admired, the managers were not so much concerned with technical ability as with who would best serve as a representative of NASA. Three of them plumped for Neil, only Deke reserved judgement, but he was outvoted and the decision was carried.[25] On 14 April, at a press conference in Houston, Low announced that 'plans called for Mr Armstrong to be the first man out after the Moon landing'.[26] Deke explained to Buzz that in addition to Neil's seniority, Armstrong ought to leave first since Buzz would be hemmed in by the inward-opening hatch.[27] Aldrin later suggested that this technical explanation was plausible and he was happy to accept it. But Michael Collins remembered that 'Buzz's attitude took a noticeable turn in the direction of gloom and introspection shortly thereafter'.[28] With the question finally settled, the training regime could be amended and the crew once again could focus on the mission.

The question of how someone might train to land on the Moon was raised almost as soon as Kennedy had finished talking to Congress.[29] The people best placed to provide answers were experienced test pilots. Men like Armstrong had spent years learning about the principles of aerodynamics and other key elements of flight – but none of this knowledge would be of much use in a vacuum. Working with data gathered from X-15 flights, and not much else, they would have to start virtually from scratch. A NASA study group, set up in 1961 at Edwards Air Force Base, took on the difficult and dangerous task of building a flying machine that could simulate flight in lunar gravity, which is just one-sixth that of Earth's.[30] Initially, Armstrong was the team's only test pilot.[31] Ironically, he found himself working on the problems that would be faced by whoever came to fly the first mission to the Moon. By chance, Bell Aerosystems in New York were working on the same idea and together the two groups agreed on a basic design that looked as if a jet engine had been dropped into a pile of scaffolding.[32]

Officially described as the lunar landing research vehicle (the LLRV), the machine was popularly known as the 'Flying Bedstead' due to its strange appearance. Armstrong considered it to be 'unconventional, sometimes contrary, and always ugly'.[33] After leaving Edwards, Neil continued to monitor the development of the LLRV. While working on simulators and other NASA training facilities he ensured the two machines Bell sent to Edwards in 1964 met Houston's requirements.[34] After the vehicle climbed to around 500 feet, the jet engine was throttled back until it supported five-sixths of the LLRV's weight. Once in 'lunar mode', the machine used a pair of throttleable thrusters to carry the remaining weight and simultaneously manage the rate of descent. A further 16 thrusters controlled roll, pitch and yaw, hissing as they fired jets of gas in short, sharp bursts. The machine had none of the controllable surfaces found on an aircraft, it was hard to fly, and the pilot was not enclosed in a cabin but found himself sitting in an ejection seat that was precariously perched on a platform.

Dangerous as it was, the LLRV was regarded as a prototype lunar lander, and its value as such was quickly recognised.

While the LLRV was still being developed, Deke Slayton looked at alternative ways of teaching astronauts how to fly to the Moon. As well as operating in an unfamiliar gravity field, the lunar lander would have other characteristics that would be new to a jet pilot. Since it would be able to fly slowly above the ground without stalling, and would even be able to hover, Deke encouraged the men to learn to fly helicopters. Although they could replicate lunar descent trajectories, including hovering, helicopters could not simulate lunar gravity – something Armstrong knew had already been concluded while he was still at Edwards.[35] The Lunar Landing Research Facility in Langley, Virginia, however, offered a closer taste of the real thing. The facility used cables and rigging to carry five-sixths of the weight of a replica lander that was suspended from an A-frame structure, 260 feet tall. Safer than a genuine flying machine, it allowed pilots to try things nobody would attempt in an LLRV. But its action was limited and ultimately so too was its value as an effective preparation for lunar flight. In some ways the closest comparison to the LM was an electronic simulator built by Grumman, which closely matched the interior of the spacecraft. Although it couldn't leave the ground, it was essential in developing an astronaut's familiarity with the LM's computers, radars and propulsion systems. Unlike the LLRV, the simulator offered only virtual risks, in that if anything went wrong the crew could simply switch it off and start again. Ultimately the best way to prepare for a trip to the surface of the Moon was to spend time using all of the available resources.

In early 1966 it was decided that the LLRV was of such value that three more would be built.[36] The original two were sent from Edwards to Ellington Air Force Base, Houston, and all five were to be known as lunar landing training vehicles (LLTVs). The LLTV was to be given a more powerful jet engine, upgraded electronics, longer endurance in 'lunar mode' and a cabin that more closely resembled the cockpit of the LM (including the instruments).[37] Beginning in the summer of 1966, a few months after his Gemini 8 flight, Armstrong periodically worked with Bell on the development of the LLTV, but it wasn't until March 1967 that he got his first chance to try it.[38] After an initial test-flight, he didn't fly it again until the following year.

Dangerous as it was, Bill Anders believed that of all the astronauts Neil was particularly suited to machines that were difficult to handle because 'if it required something counter-intuitive or otherwise against the grain, he figured it out'.[39] On 6 May 1968, Armstrong had been airborne for five minutes when the vehicle began to tilt sharply while he was just 200 feet above the ground. Unable to recover, by the time he had dropped to 100 feet the machine was tilting over so far he risked being propelled into the ground by his ejection seat. With less than a second to spare the seat rocketed him clear of the LLTV, and dangling beneath his parachute he hit the ground in front of groups of shocked onlookers.[40]

( )

Aboard the command module at the end of the third day the crew were beginning to set switches in the correct position, place blinds over the windows and turn down the cabin lights. During each rest period one man slept in a couch, with a lightweight headset taped to his ear in case Houston needed to call and a seatbelt fastened across his lap to stop him drifting into the instrument panel. The others used sleep restraints, which resembled light sleeping bags and were made of a mesh fabric with a zip down the middle. These were anchored beneath the two side couches where there was plenty of room to stretch out, the men's feet reaching towards the lower equipment bay.

They had not reached any firm conclusion about the unidentified object accompanying them at a distance of 100 miles or so. They presumed it was either debris from the spacecraft, or else one of the four panels that had enclosed the LM within its container.[41] It was not the first mystery the crew had encountered during the mission. Buzz later recalled that while trying to doze at the start of the second night he had seen 'little flashes inside the darkened cabin, spaced a couple of minutes apart'.[42] On two further occasions he saw 'double flashes, at points separated by maybe a foot'. Buzz believed something was penetrating the spacecraft, causing an 'emission' as it entered. He thought the second flash might occur when the object, whatever it was, struck part of the cabin. He realised that whatever was causing the flashes was coming from the direction of the Sun, and said as much to the others. Armstrong also saw flashes of light, counting more than 50 while looking into the spacecraft's interior over the course of an hour.[43]

Bill Anders, who flew to the Moon with Apollo 8 and who had a degree in nuclear engineering, later suggested the flashes may have been caused by 'cosmic radiation'.[44] Radiation had long been a major concern for the Apollo mission planners, and flights were timed to avoid dangerous periods of solar activity. NASA's efforts to predict solar storms were proving to be successful. But the flight surgeons remained wary, and at the end of each day the crew dutifully reported their personal radiation measurements. It was later believed the flashes were taking place not inside the spacecraft but inside the eyeball, although their precise nature remains subject to speculation.

At 61 hours and 40 minutes into the mission, the astronauts were settling down for the night. They were now 186,400 miles from Earth and travelling at little more than 2,000mph. At this point, the spacecraft coasted out of the Earth's gravitational influence and slipped into the Moon's, although no physical evidence of this was felt by the crew. After Apollo 8 had reached this neutral point in space, flight controller Philip Shaffer told the press that in working out where the spacecraft was, Houston's computers were no longer using the Earth as a frame of reference but the Moon instead. On paper this meant the position of the spacecraft appeared to jump by several miles, and some reporters mistakenly wondered whether the astronauts had felt a jolt.[45] Aboard Apollo 11, the crew were still unable to see their destination. They would nevertheless become aware of its presence as it pulled them towards it at a steadily increasing speed. Neil, Michael and Buzz were now held within the grip of the Moon – and come what may, they would soon be dragged towards its mysterious far side.

Chapter 9
INTO THE DARKNESS

Piercing sunlight flared through each of the command module's five windows as the spacecraft slowly rolled on its axis at the start of the fourth day. The crew experienced a gentle sense of momentum as the sunshine meandered through the cabin, slowly drifting across the glass on the instrument gauges and bouncing off the transparent breakfast bags. Sunlight and the Earth were largely all the men had seen through the windows since day two. They had been able to identify specific stars when working on the P52 computer program but familiar constellations had been obliterated by sunshine. Today would be different. While they ate, a cold gloom shrouded the spacecraft, and the sun's rays receeded before being snuffed out altogether. The crew had coasted so close to their destination that, silently and without warning, they passed into the shadow of the Moon and perpetual day was exchanged for night. 'I feel that all of us are aware that the honeymoon is over,' wrote Collins. 'We are about to lay our little pink bodies on the line.'[1] In a few hours Michael would climb into the left-hand couch, and once they reached the far side of the Moon he would fly them into lunar orbit. He hadn't slept particularly well and feared that the pressure of the work ahead was threatening to overtake them.[2]

Blocking the Sun's glare, the hostile surface of the Moon loomed towards them, filling their windows with an alien landscape that stretched for hundreds of miles. Much of the surface lay hidden in shadow, the darkness merging with the black sky above. 'We are able to see stars again and recognise constellations for the first time,' Armstrong told Houston. Away from the filtering effects of Earth's atmosphere, the stars didn't twinkle but stood out as static pinpricks of light. Whereas previous manned missions had been confined to Earth orbit, Neil was commanding the first flight to a specific destination – and now, suddenly, here it was, a little more than 11,000 miles away. As Earth's oceans reflected sunshine back out into space, pools of cool blue light were cast upon the lunar surface, illuminating it as if it were an empty stage lit for a sinister night scene. Earthshine is three times brighter than moonshine, and to Michael it revealed the 'most awesome sphere I have ever seen'.[3] When the crew switched off the interior lamps to photograph the stunning view outside they found the light was bright enough to read by.

By putting the Moon between themselves and the Sun, the men had arranged their own solar eclipse. Although the Sun itself lay hidden from view, its atmosphere of hot gases could be seen streaming away from the edges of the lunar surface. Beyond the swathes of shadow, the Moon's entire circumference was crowned by a spectacular reddish-golden light. The ring of fiery colours was impossible to see from Earth with such clarity. Backlit by the Sun, the Moon took on a distinctly three-dimensional appearance. The crew could clearly see that it was no longer the romantic disc they had known since childhood but had become a giant rocky sphere, foreboding and unwelcoming, and apparently not much into romance after all. Lifeless plains lay at the foot of arid mountain chains. Here and there channels cut through great seas of dust, and everywhere craters of all sizes indicated an ancient landscape that had been bombarded by meteoroids for years beyond imagining.

Aldrin: 'It's quite an eerie sight. There is a very marked three-dimensional aspect of having the Sun's corona coming from behind the Moon the way it is.'

Houston: 'Roger.'

Aldrin: 'And it looks as though – I guess what's giving it that three-dimensional effect is the Earthshine. I can see Tycho fairly clearly – at least if I'm right side up, I believe it's Tycho – in Earthshine. And, of course, I can see the sky is lit all the way around the Moon, even on the limb of it where there's no Earthshine or sunshine.'

Now that they had travelled so close to the Moon, spectacular features such as the crater Tycho were particularly impressive. The Moon too had come quite a way, travelling nearly 200,000 miles since the mission began. While orbiting its bigger partner, the Moon simultaneously rotates so that it permanently presents the same side to Earth. While the near side has been studied by astronomers over many centuries, the far side has barely been examined at all. (Although it's sometimes erroneously described as the dark side, the truth is the Moon does not have a permanent 'dark side' any more than the Earth does.) Flying through darkness, Apollo 11 was being pulled towards the unmapped regions of the far side that were awaiting them 'over the hill'.

()

It remained an uncertain journey. Lunar gravity includes mysterious pockets of energy which are strong enough to affect the orbit of unmanned probes. It was known that these patches of super gravity were associated with the flat lunar 'seas', where the interior rock was more dense than surrounding areas.[4] These concentrations of mass (known as 'mascons') posed risks that were hard to calculate. Apollo 8 had investigated their impact on an orbiting spacecraft, but without a lunar module the crew had been forced to leave many questions unanswered.[5] Would the LM be pulled off course at a critical moment during the landing? What effect would the mascons have on the rendezvous with the command module? Apollo 9 had proved the LM worked well in the benign conditions above the Earth. But it was hoped that by flying the spacecraft above the Moon, Apollo 10 would discover how it would react to lunar gravity. Accurate information was essential to those planning a future landing, among them Armstrong – who wanted to know as much about mascons as possible.[6]

McDivitt had encountered minor problems with his LM, as was to be expected with any prototype spacecraft. Modifications, and not an inconsiderable amount of faith, were adopted before the lander was permitted to venture into the potential dangers of lunar gravity. By the time Apollo 10 was ready to fly, there were just seven months left before Kennedy's deadline. In taking the complete Apollo system to the Moon for the first time, commander Tom Stafford, command module pilot John Young and lunar module pilot Gene Cernan were to put the 'tissue-paper' vehicle through a demanding series of tests, nearly a quarter of a million miles away from Earth. 'What do you tell your six-year-old daughter?' Cernan later asked. 'I don't know, I just tried to find a way that wouldn't disappoint her if I didn't come home.'

After launching on 18 May 1969, the Apollo 10 crew became the first astronauts to broadcast live, colour TV pictures from space. Later, inspecting the pressurised cabin of the lightweight LM, Young couldn't believe how far the hatch bowed out into the vacuum.[7] On 22 May, Young remained aboard the command module (named *Charlie Brown*) while his crew-mates sealed themselves into the lander. Stafford and Cernan – who together had come close to disaster during the Gemini 9 EVA – then separated ('undocked', as NASA described it) from the command module at the start of their exploratory flight towards the probable landing ground. Within two hours Stafford and Cernan had flown the LM, call-sign *Snoopy*, down to a height of just 47,000 feet, or eight miles, above the surface.

In a viewing gallery overlooking the Mission Operations Control Room, senior NASA officials listened in as the LM made two low-level passes over the Sea of Tranquility. Flying almost precisely the same track across the lunar surface that Apollo 11 would take, Stafford and Cernan studied the proposed touchdown site, tested the landing radar and photographed distinctive landmarks.[8] Soaring above cliffs 4,000 feet high, Cernan excitedly called, 'We is go and we is down among 'em.'[9] Later he added, 'I almost felt like I had to pick up my feet, to keep them from dragging on the top of those mountain tops ... we really came in low and fast.'[10] Both he and Stafford were amazed by the towering highlands and the spectacular craters. 'I've got Censorinus right here, bigger 'n shit!' exclaimed Stafford. In Mission Control, Chris Kraft cast a nervous eye back towards the viewing gallery. 'Son of a bitch ... son of a bitch,' said Cernan as craters sped beneath them, each bigger than the last.[11]

Stafford and Cernan had been advised to keep the rendezvous radar on all the time in case they should quickly need to find the command module. It sent a continuous stream of data to the spacecraft's computer, and after completing their objectives the crew prepared to follow its lead back to Young. Suddenly *Snoopy* started bucking around the sky, wildly throwing itself about before rolling hard to the left. For eight long seconds the LM was out of control. 'Son of a bitch,' blurted Cernan over his open microphone, 'what the hell happened?' Stafford quickly jettisoned the descent stage and by reducing the weight of the spacecraft he found it easier to control the thrusters. Calming *Snoopy*'s erratic behaviour, the crew fired the ascent engine before beginning their search for the command module. After completing the rendezvous, Stafford, Cernan and Young then headed for home. The problem with the LM was later traced to a checklist error in switch settings.[12]

Apollo 10 served as more than a simple rehearsal for the landing. Flight controllers helped to produce the first accurate flightplan for a lunar mission, viable navigation and tracking techniques were developed, and the procedures necessary for each phase of a flight towards the surface were proven in practice. By tracking the rendezvous, Mission Control was able to refine the model of the Moon's uneven gravitational field, thereby easing some of the concerns about mascons. Glitches encountered during the flight exposed weaknesses in the crew's checklists and hardware. These represented the final obstacles that could potentially delay preparations for Apollo 11. It was soon established that none was serious, and two weeks after the Apollo 10 mission ended it was confirmed that the landing was still on track.

For Armstrong, Apollo 10 was critical in providing first-hand experience of the LM's performance in lunar gravity, and he talked in detail to Stafford and Cernan.[13] Also invaluable were the crew's observations of the surface. Stafford, Cernan and Young had laid a path to the Moon that stopped just a few miles short of the proposed landing site. They had 'painted a white line' in the sky, Cernan told the Apollo 11 crew during a post-flight briefing on 3 June.[14] Stafford warned them that while parts of the landing zone looked smooth, other areas, particularly at the western end, were more dangerous than expected.[15] Stafford had seen a large field of boulders in this region, and suggested that if Armstrong's approach were 'long' he might need to abort.[16] The warning was taken only as informal advice; Apollo 11's designated landing site remained unchanged.

NASA's last three missions had been a triumphant success, and now that the Moon was in sight there was none of the hesitancy that had marked the preparations for Apollo 8. Neil, Buzz and Michael were thrust towards the centre of an enormous government organisation whose prime concern was the next manned mission. Now that their flight had been pushed into the spotlight, they found themselves at the head of the queue for the limited training resources.

For Neil, the LLTV continued to be a priority. After his ejection at Ellington Air Force Base in May the previous year, the vehicle had plummeted to the ground before bursting into flames beneath him as he dangled from his parachute. Landing a short distance from the wreckage, he escaped injury, beyond biting his tongue.[17] Word quickly reached the nearby Manned Spacecraft Center, where an hour later Alan Bean overheard a group of fellow astronauts discussing the accident. 'That's bullshit!' Bean exclaimed. 'I just came out of [the] office and Neil's there at his desk ... shuffling some papers.' Running back to the office, Bean checked the story with Armstrong who to Bean's amazement coolly said that, yes, he'd been forced to bail out. 'I did go back to the office,' Neil later confirmed. 'I mean, what are you going to do? It's one of those days when you lose a machine.'[18]

Dangerous as the LLTV was, in Armstrong's opinion it provided the best preparation for flying something as unusual as the LM in the unfamiliar gravity field of the Moon. Bob Gilruth and Chris Kraft were nervous about their astronauts using such an unstable vehicle, but Armstrong and others fought their corner, insisting that the LLTV was the best facility they had for learning to land on the Moon.[19] Since the final phase of the descent would be flown manually, the astronauts felt such practical training was essential. Ground-based simulators were useful up to a point, but at the heart of Neil's mission lay the challenge of a pioneering flight, and only the LLTV could help him properly prepare, both physically and mentally.

For Michael Collins, Apollo 11 presented a different set of challenges. In listing what he considered to be the 11 most dangerous elements of the flight, he found that two (launch and TLI) would be tackled by the whole crew. Another four (descent, landing, EVA and lift-off) would be carried out by Neil and Buzz – but the remaining five were largely down to him. The first was the separation of the command module from the third stage, leading to the docking with the LM. For Michael, perhaps the most daunting aspect of the docking involved the removal of the complicated probe and drogue assembly from the tunnel. The bulky components were awkward to handle, and during training the process was always a tricky manoeuvre. In space he would have to complete the procedure more than once, and if the docking mechanism failed to detach as planned Collins would have to dig out a tool kit and take the whole thing apart. 'I hated that probe,' he later admitted, 'and was half convinced it hated me.'[20]

The second item on Michael's list was lunar orbit insertion, the two-part manoeuvre that would carry them into orbit around the Moon. If he got this wrong he ran the risk of either banishing the crew into deep space or sending them crashing into the surface. The third item was the rendezvous, on which the lives of Armstrong and Aldrin depended. Fourth was the critical burn that would free them from lunar orbit and put them on the journey home. Finally, Collins would have to guide the command module back into the atmosphere at speeds approaching 25,000mph, to plunge into the ocean within reach of the rescue agencies.

Given that there was a chance Neil and Buzz might not return from the Moon, Collins had to know how to accomplish the final tasks on his own. He never gave odds on the possibility of coming home alone, and the subject was barely discussed beyond estimates about how long he could wait in lunar orbit before running low on consumables. The command module could afford to remain in position for two days longer than scheduled, by which time no-one would be in any doubt about the fate of Armstrong and Aldrin since the LM's oxygen and power would last only 24 hours.[21] Neil's personal opinion was that 'on a risk-gain ratio this project would look very favourable compared to those projects that I've been used to in the past 20 years'.[22] Fretting over moral arguments, what-ifs or the implications for the future was not the 'right stuff'. Nevertheless, there was no escaping the reality of the situation. As far as Collins was concerned, 'they know and I know, and Mission Control knows, that there are certain categories of malfunction where I just simply light the motor and come home without them'.[23]

Journalist and speechwriter William Safire was asked to prepare a statement for Nixon that could be used in the event of a disaster. Calling him on behalf of the White House, Frank Borman told Safire, 'You want to be thinking of some alternative posture for the president in the event of mishaps ... like what to do for the widows.' Safire duly wrote a speech in which Nixon would say, 'Fate has ordained that the men who went to the Moon to explore in peace will stay to rest in peace.' Safire also drafted proposals on protocol that might be followed, including the thought that after Nixon had contacted the families, a clergyman should adopt the same procedure as a burial at sea.[24]

Beyond some of the trickiest moments of the trip, Michael was also responsible for keeping the spacecraft on track throughout the flight. This involved learning the intricacies of the guidance and navigation system, particularly the computer. Permanently cosseted and frequently tetchy, the computer nestled at the centre of the system like a giant queen bee, its 'operator error' warning light frequently stinging Collins as he struggled with the complexity buzzing at his fingertips. Only by spending hours in the simulator did he begin to master it. Of the three command module simulators available, the machine in Houston was mostly used for research and Michael principally used the two at the Cape. But from the moment his training began in January he had trouble getting access to any of them. Until March, priority went to the Apollo 9 crew and their backups, with the Apollo 10 prime and backup crews next in line. Collins was part of the fifth flight in the queue. He, Neil and Buzz were only given top priority once Apollo 10 was ready to fly, by which time there were just two months until they themselves were due to launch.

To enter the simulator, Michael climbed a carpeted staircase up to a hatch 15 feet above the ground. Built by North American, inside it closely replicated the command module, complete with images of constellations, the Moon and the Earth visible through the windows.[25] Technical equipment and machinery were housed in more than a dozen odd-shaped boxes mounted on the shell of the simulator, each the size of a washing machine. From the outside it looked such a jumble of parts that when John Young first saw it he dubbed it the Great Train Wreck.[26] The instrument displays were driven by a mainframe computer, controlled by a team of instructors whose task it was to prepare Collins for any eventuality. As virtual lunar and command modules attempted to rendezvous beside a virtual Moon, the computer kept track of Michael's progress. If the LM failed to reach the surface, or if it got there early or late, or was delayed in its journey back to the command module, the rendezvous would shift from a textbook manoeuvre into one of a number of emergency procedures. Sometimes the command module would need to remain in a high, slow orbit to meet its errant partner while in other situations it would have to fly low and fast. Nevertheless, Collins could only go so far in mounting a rescue attempt. There would be no point in retrieving Neil and Buzz only to find there wasn't enough fuel to get home.[27] Collins practised 18 different options, and at the end of each session the instructors told him whether the rendezvous had succeeded before he had run out of time, fuel or both.[28]

The crew had to complete many mandatory simulations involving Mission Control before they could be said to be ready. With the flight fast approaching, the mission managers began to fear they might not make it.[29] The 16 July launch date had been dictated by the need for the Sun to be in the best position to provide ideal lighting conditions during the landing. If necessary, lift-off could be pushed back a month as similar conditions would return in mid-August. But no-one wanted to ask for a delay, and to Deke's occasional questions about progress Michael gave reassuring answers. Privately, however, when they became the next crew to fly Collins felt that they still had a year's work ahead of them.[30]

Now with free access to the simulator, Michael anxiously sought to get to grips with his rendezvous procedures, entering notes, diagrams and instructions in the 'Solo Book' he would rely on once Neil and Buzz had departed. For each rendezvous option, a checklist had to be written detailing the sequence to be followed when pushing switches and using the computer. In focusing on the most likely scenarios, Michael struggled to find the time to master some of the more obscure alternatives, and as May slipped into June he stayed at the Cape for days at a time, working in the simulator. After each session he would wander over to the instructors and check the 'Collins looks good' light they had fitted to their huge bank of consoles. Usually it was glowing cheerfully. If not, he would switch it on himself.[31] The instructors' computer, updated after the McDivitt and Stafford missions, had the final say over everything – until it broke down and stranded everyone in a bout of frustration while an army of technicians battled away at the problem. Sometimes Michael would spend hours going through the early orbital procedures only for the rendezvous itself to be suddenly scrubbed by the computer 'bombing out'.[32]

With many of the mandatory training exercises still to be completed, Collins yearned to tuck himself away in the simulator every day. But managers, memos and phone messages persistently demanded his attention. NASA's Langley centre – home of the Lunar Landing Research Facility, dangling from its A-frame – invited Collins to fly a full-size replica of the command module that was suspended from wires. Time also needed to be set aside for the centrifuge at the Manned Spacecraft Center (MSC), and for fitting the pressure-suits in Delaware. Publicity photos had to be taken, meetings had to be attended (in various corners of the country), long-lost relatives chasing tickets to the launch had to be answered, and the family in Houston couldn't be ignored. With the training regime pushing ahead at full steam, the only lingering doubt was whether everyone would be ready. In the first weeks of June, Deke asked Neil, Buzz and Mike whether another month would be necessary but each of them stuck to the launch date.

On 17 June, Sam Phillips, the director of the Apollo programme, led a nine-hour flight readiness review at the MSC. Among other things, this focused on whether an attempt to land should continue if communications with Earth were disrupted. The exchange of information was essential. Mission Control managers, led by Chris Kraft, knew that in the event of a crash they would need to have enough data to be able to reconstruct what went wrong. At the end of the meeting, Phillips announced that the preparations were on target and he permitted Apollo 11 to proceed as planned. Collins was elated. Technicians at the Cape could now begin loading the spacecraft with hypergolic fuels. These were so corrosive that if the launch were delayed to August, any last-minute hardware failures could lead to serious problems. The fuel tanks would have to be drained and parts of the vehicle would have to be sent away to be repaired, and no-one knew how long this process might take.[33]

The debate about aborting the landing if communications were seriously interrupted rumbled on for weeks. Flight director Gene Kranz was asked to write down agreements on the subject, to be added to the rest of the rules for the mission. Writing mission rules was one of the first jobs Kranz had performed while working on the Mercury programme. In meetings held before each flight, Chris Kraft had tried to identify areas of uncertainty so that solutions could be agreed, which were then written down by an assistant. The assistant – Kranz – produced lists of all the agreed decisions, a task he was appointed to two weeks after joining NASA. Looking him in the eye, Kraft had muttered, 'Everyone else is tied up. You're all I've got.'[34] At other times, on the instructions of his indomitable boss, Kranz ignored the agreed decision and wrote down what Kraft told him to.[35] He put everything in an easily digested format, listing potential problems alongside the appropriate action to be taken.

The list of rules used during the Mercury programme was 30 pages long. By Apollo 11 it was up to 330.[36] The first complete version was published on 16 May, and while some rules were virtually written in blood ('if data from the landing radar is not available before the LM descends to 10,000 feet, the landing must be aborted'), others gave the crew room for manoeuvre.[37] Each flight controller would only allow a critical phase of the mission to begin if he were sure that the vehicle was measuring up to the rules. If everything was satisfactory, he would say so to the flight director. With a lot of information to be passed to one man by many controllers in a short time, the only way to do this quickly was to offer a simple yes or no – which in NASA jargon became 'go' or 'no go'. Even this could be confusing. After landing on the Moon, did 'go' mean 'OK' or did it mean 'leave'? To prevent the spacecraft launching unnecessarily just seconds after touching down, go/no go would become stay/no stay. The mission rules were supplemented by the flight-plan and associated checklists which together detailed everything that would or could happen throughout the trip. Individual controllers also prepared their own personal books. Kranz was so worried about losing his that he made them instantly recognisable by plastering them with pictures of women from the swimsuit edition of *Sports Illustrated*.[38]

Following lessons learned during training, new rules were added every week based on agreements between flight controllers, engineers, managers and astronauts. Kranz found that Buzz, who reminded him of an eccentric teacher, 'generally dominat[ed] the crew side of the conversations'.[39] He admired Aldrin's intricate grasp of rendezvous trajectories as he gave his forthright opinions to the 'trench', the front-row controllers whom Kranz knew to be a pretty forthright bunch themselves. Neil was more the quiet observer, 'but when you looked at his eyes,' Kranz later said, 'you knew that he was the commander and had all the pieces assembled in his mind.' According to Kranz, the astronaut who spent the most time getting to know the key people in the Mission Operations Control Room was Mike Collins, whom Kranz regarded as 'steady, dependable' with 'a reputation as being extremely competent in his judgement'.[40] Working alone throughout much of his training, Mike knew that during the mission the flight controllers would be looking over his shoulder, and he was grateful for their support.

Communication between Collins and the ground, like most components of manned space-flight, relied on procedures developed during Mercury. At launch, messages sent to the crew were transmitted directly from the Cape. But since radio signals travel in a straight line, communications would stop the moment the rocket went over the horizon, less than ten minutes after lift-off. There would be no telemetry from the booster, nor from the spacecraft it was carrying, and Houston would not know whether it was safe to let the crew head towards the Moon. During Mercury an additional transmitter was built on Bermuda, in British territory. But since a rocket travelled round the Earth in an hour and a half it would not be within reach of a single transmitter for very long. A chain of tracking stations was needed around the world.

In seeking to build transmitters at sites across three continents, Kraft and his colleagues suddenly found themselves embroiled in international politics. Dealing with the Brits was one thing, but installing tracking stations with space age telemetry facilities in remote corners of Africa was something else. Seven sites involved the State Department in 'serious diplomatic discussion', as Kraft put it, while two others were in the middle of oceans, and for these NASA needed help from the navy.[41] Some of the locations were so remote Kraft felt that 'the word primitive was the accurate description'.[42] According to Gene Kranz, late one night in 1962 flight controller Charles 'Skinny' Lewis was driving the two members of his team back to their quarters on Zanzibar when he saw a roadblock made of burning oil drums 'manned by natives not in uniform'[43]. Lewis, a former tank commander who before joining NASA had never left America, accelerated towards the barrier and escaped by smashing his way through the blazing obstacles.

By the late 1960s, the tracking stations had been substantially developed and brought within the control of NASA's Manned Space Flight Network. The MSFN permitted a permanent link between Houston and Apollo 11 through a worldwide chain of 17 ground stations, supported by four specially adapted ships and up to eight aircraft. Eight of the ground stations were equipped with 30-foot antennas, capable of tracking the spacecraft in Earth orbit and for some distance beyond. Once the crew had reached an altitude of 10,000 miles, communications would be provided by the more powerful 85-foot antennas installed at Madrid, Canberra in Australia and Goldstone in California. These used a system known as S-band, a single signal capable of simultaneously carrying tracking data, telemetry, voice and television. The spacecraft responded by bouncing the signal back, which helped the ground keep track of its position. As the Earth spun on its axis, at least one of the three powerful antennas would be in sight of the Moon throughout the mission, with each station handing control to the next to maintain a continuous connection.

Voice signals, tracking data and telemetry were passed to Houston via NASA's Communications Network, which linked the ground stations and other facilities through two million miles of landlines and undersea cables. Relying on six intermediate switching centres around the world, and two communications satellites, the network included redundant signal routes to increase reliability. Some remote switching points were triggered automatically whenever the CapCom began to speak. Each time he pressed his microphone button, it emitted a short beep known as a Quindar tone. This prompted the remote site to begin operating, and gave a distinctive sound to transmissions from Mission Control.

All communications were routed through NASA's Goddard Space Flight Center in Maryland. From there, radio signals were relayed to and from Mission Control, where secure rooms on the ground floor housed the Real Time Computer Complex. Houston's powerful computers monitored launch operations as well as the continuous supply of tracking and telemetry data. The data was recorded, processed and sent upstairs to the Mission Operations Control Room (MOCR), where it was displayed on the controllers' consoles. The flight surgeon might look at Neil's heart-rate while the CapCom talked to Buzz, at the same time a flight controller could follow the spacecraft's position displayed on a wall-sized map, while the man next to him monitored the performance of *Columbia*'s thrusters. Once the LM separated from *Columbia* at the start of the descent, the MSFN would have to supply this information for two spacecraft simultaneously. Reliability was critical since mission rules could lead to an abort if the signal from space failed at key moments during the landing.

Although redundancy and reliability were built into the communication systems, Apollo 10 had still encountered many problems. Course corrections and PTC manoeuvres frequently left the spacecraft's antennas in a position where they were either pointing away from Earth or trying to send a signal through the body of the vehicle. Sometimes John Young in the command module had to ask Houston what the astronauts in the lunar module were trying to tell him. Prior to Apollo 11, these issues were addressed by better co-ordination of both the manoeuvres and the communications demands. To maintain the strongest signal, the crew were trained when and how to swiftly switch antennas.

( )

Armstrong: 'The view of the Moon that we've been having recently is really spectacular. It fills about three-quarters of the hatch window, and of course, we can see the entire circumference, even though part of it is in complete shadow and part of it's in Earthshine. It's a view worth the price of the trip.'

Mission Control: 'Well, there are a lot of us down here that would be willing to come along.'

Collins: 'I hope you get your turn, and soon.'

Armstrong: 'One of these days, we'll be able to bring the whole MOCR along, I hope. Save a lot of antenna switching.'

Mission Control: 'That's jolly.'

Drifting closer to an alien world that was itself moving towards them at more than 2,200mph, the crew were now caught up in a galactic game of chicken. Instead of hopping over the tracks in front of a speeding train, they had to put themselves in a position where the 'train' – here, the size of a small planet – effectively picked them up and carried them along with it. Getting into lunar orbit was fraught with danger. If they did nothing, they would be pulled around the far side and flung back into space towards the Earth on a free flight home, without having to use the big engine at the back of the service module. By burning the engine for precisely six minutes and two seconds they hoped to slow down enough to enter lunar orbit. If the engine failed to ignite, their 'free-return' trajectory gave them a hope of coming back. However, if the braking manoeuvre lasted longer than planned, it might cause the spacecraft to slow so much it would crash into the surface. If the engine stopped early, the crew would be sent off into space at an angle that could be impossible to recover from. Apollo 8 had reduced the risk by breaking the lunar orbit insertion (LOI) manoeuvre into two separate burns. Apollo 11 would do the same.

To successfully perform LOI-1 Michael would have to fire the engine at precisely 75 hours, 49 minutes and 49 seconds into the mission – while they were behind the far side. Radio signals could be sent to and from the spinning spherical Earth via the elaborate network of radio stations, but the spinning spherical Moon didn't have much beyond dust. Radio communications would be unable to curve round to reach the far side, so LOI-1 would have to be done without the support of Mission Control. If it were unsuccessful, Collins would need to urgently establish whether they would be able to get home, and if so how – something he had practised many times in the simulator.

Three hours before ignition, at 9.22am on the morning of Saturday 19 July, a long list of numbers was read up to the spacecraft, giving Michael navigation instructions and details on roll, pitch and yaw. The radio link would break at 12.13pm. A few minutes before losing contact flight director Cliff Charlesworth asked each of his controllers for a go/no go decision on LOI. The spacecraft was now 9,000 miles away from the Moon. With the two fast approaching each other, the distance between them would be covered in less than 12 minutes.

Mission Control: 'Apollo 11, this is Houston. Over.'

Aldrin: 'Roger. Go ahead Houston, Apollo 11.'

Mission Control: '11, this is Houston. You are go for LOI. Over.'

Aldrin: 'Roger. Go for LOI.'

Mission Control: 'Apollo 11, this is Houston. All your systems are looking good going around the corner, and we'll see you on the other side. Over.'

After a flight of nearly 240,000 miles, during which they had made just one course correction (a three-second burn on day two), Armstrong, Aldrin and Collins dodged the leading edge of the Moon by just 309 miles. Having halted PTC, the main engine faced the direction of travel as the spacecraft silently coasted through the darkness at 5,200mph. The crew were now less than eight minutes from LOI. Above them, the stars were beginning to fade as the first rays of sunshine reached over the curved horizon, stretching towards the approaching spacecraft. With two minutes to go they slipped from the gloom into glaring sunlight, and for the first time they could clearly see the heavily cratered landscape, more than 2,000 miles wide.

Collins: 'Yes, the Moon is there, boy – in all its splendour.'

Armstrong: 'Man, it's a—'

Collins: 'Plaster of Paris grey to me.'

Aldrin: 'Man, look at it.'

Armstrong: 'Don't look at it. Here we come up to ignition.'

Aldrin: '8 seconds.'

Collins: 'Stand by for ignition.'

Armstrong: 'Burning.'

Chapter 10

PUSHED TO THE LIMIT

The final say on whether Apollo 11 would launch on schedule was down to the crew as much as anyone, and determined to make the deadline they pushed themselves through their training regime. For six months, Armstrong, Collins and Aldrin regularly spent 14 hours a day, six days a week, preparing to fly to the Moon.[1] With evenings and weekends often devoted to studying, this was the most demanding period of their lives. While Michael got to grips with the computer and the rendezvous procedures, Neil and Buzz worked in the lunar module simulators, particularly Grumman's elaborate replica at the Cape. Like its command module counterpart, the cabin of the LM simulator mirrored the real thing. Hooked up to external computers, the instruments indicated apparent changes in the flight-path as the crew perfected engine burns and other manoeuvres. Initially the practice flights were straightforward and free of problems – 'nominal' in NASA-speak. But like Michael, as their skills developed, Neil and Buzz began to be tested by their instructors.

Shortly after the mission rules were issued on 16 May, the flight controllers were due to begin their own training for the descent to the surface. In a spacecraft, as in an aeroplane, the commander has the final say and the controllers knew that in certain situations Neil might overrule them. To discuss this possibility, Gene Kranz held a meeting with the crew.[2] They were joined by Charlie Duke, an astronaut who had been selected in 1966. Duke, who had yet to fly in space, had served as a CapCom on Apollo 10, doing the job with such a degree of reliability and easy confidence that Armstrong requested he serve as CapCom for the descent. An air force pilot from North Carolina, Duke successfully supported both the flight controllers and the astronauts. To the controllers he represented the accessible side of an overstretched and rapidly tiring crew, who spent much of their time at the Cape. At the same time, he defended the crew's opinions among a tight team of people who had little personal experience of the demands facing the astronauts. Sometimes occupying a precarious position, Duke did a smooth job in extending understanding on both sides.[3]

In his meeting with the crew, Kranz said that if difficulties developed early in the descent Houston would halt the mission and start the rendezvous procedure. Such problems were potentially easier to deal with than emergencies that might occur during the middle of the flight. If the mission needed to be aborted, the descent stage could be jettisoned and an attempt made to return to orbit. But the lunar module had been tested in just two manned missions and both had ditched the descent stage under calm conditions at high altitude. Armstrong considered aborts to be 'not very well understood'. The theory called for the descent engine to be closed, pyrotechnic bolts to be ignited, the descent stage to be jettisoned and the ascent engine to be fired. 'Doing all of that in close proximity to the lunar surface was not something in which I had a great deal of confidence,' he later said.[4] For Kranz, a late abort was like a parachute – only to be used as a last resort after all other options had been tried.[5] Both he and Armstrong believed that if a problem should strike just as the LM was about to land, actually settling down on the surface would be better than attempting a last-minute abort. At least this would provide a full set of technical data that could improve the chances of the next mission.

In the last few hundred feet of the descent, only the crew would know whether it was safe to land. But just how far would they push their luck? Kranz knew that on this issue Armstrong had his own thoughts, 'I just wanted to know what they were'.[6] Neil kept his opinions to himself, and since he was less than forthcoming, Kranz was left to guess what he might do if it were possible but risky to reach the surface. He suspected Armstrong would press on, 'accepting any risk as long as there was even a remote chance to land'.[7] Neil later admitted that he would have been willing to use what he called his 'commander's prerogative' to disregard a mission rule, if he felt that was 'the safest route'.[8] He said that while he would not have continued if there were only a 'remote chance' of landing, he would have pushed on if there were a 'good chance' of settling down safely.[9] Unsure what Armstrong might do in the event of difficulty, Kranz decided he would let the descent continue as long as there was a chance of success.

Such gaps in communication were to be addressed during a formal series of joint simulations involving Neil, Buzz and the flight controllers. These sessions, focusing on the landing, could not begin until late May because of delays in developing software for the LM simulators.[10] Since the final phase of the descent would last just 12 minutes, a number of training 'runs' could be carried out in a single day, under the supervision of the Mission Control Center's Simulation Branch. A handful of simulation supervisors (shortened to 'Sim Supe') took responsibility for various phases of the mission, and between them they trained the prime and backup crews for Apollo 11, as well as four teams of flight controllers. To accommodate everyone, the simulators were run 16 hours a day. With the computers stretched to the limit they frequently broke down – leading to varying degrees of abuse being directed at the technicians.

The Sim Supe for the descent phase was Dick Koos, who – according to Kranz – 'was a thin guy, wore wire-rimmed glasses, expressed himself in incomplete sentences, and seemed unsure of what he was trying to say'.[11] Beyond his understated demeanour lay a talent for dragging astronauts and flight controllers through sweat-drenched training sessions that Kranz said took him and his team to a 'place beyond exhaustion'.[12] Frank Borman later remembered that while his crew were preparing for Apollo 8, 'we were killed more times in simulation than you can shake a stick at'.[13] Armstrong believed 'these were the most extensive simulations I had ever encountered'.[14]

The first few formal sessions were designed primarily to develop everyone's understanding of the landing sequence. At the same time, they also identified points of no-return. At these moments, each controller was required to give a curt 'go' or 'no go' depending on whether he felt confident in letting the mission continue. These early exercises also helped prepare everyone for the fact that the distance between the Moon and the Earth would delay communications. Travelling at the speed of light, radio messages from the Moon take 1.5 seconds to reach Earth, adding at least a three-second delay to any response urgently required from the ground.

As the training progressed, the procedures improved, and new mission rules were agreed before the next round of simulations began. Focusing on aborts, these threatened to take everyone on a steep learning curve. In each simulation, Armstrong and Aldrin worked closely with the controllers on the latest challenge Koos had thrown at everyone. Nobody beyond Koos and his team knew what the next problem would be. In some cases the crew would act quickly without advice from the ground, at other times they urgently needed support. Working in this way the two flight teams became familiar with each other, and all the while Koos continually tried to expose the fault lines between them. Sometimes Collins would be involved, for example when the LM crew and the ground controllers practised the rendezvous procedure. Everybody knew what was at stake. The simulations consequently became as realistic and as demanding as possible, with Koos raising the tension in every successive session. Trajectory problems, electrical failures, emergency launches, master alarms and data dropouts – anything was possible. 'Nothing is sacred; no quarter is given and none asked,' Kranz later wrote.[15]

After each round of simulations, Neil and Buzz spent time on their own, refining their procedures and leaving the flight controllers to do the same. The mission rules would then be updated, and the next series of exercises would begin. Once again Koos would scatter catastrophes about, daring the crew and controllers to take on his mischievous team of instructors. After particularly difficult sessions, the flight controllers would conduct a soul-searching inquisition into what had gone wrong. Especially challenging was the 'dead-man's box', the region between the surface and a few hundred feet above. At this height, the complex relationship between speed, altitude and time made a safe abort impossible.[16] This wasn't lost on Armstrong. With Kranz and his team sitting on a planet far removed from them, Neil knew the final decisions would be down to him. Chris Kraft, the director of flight operations who saw his flight directors as 'God', wondered whether Armstrong would be prepared to accept a higher degree of risk than he was ready to allow.[17]

In mid-June, Kraft brought Neil into Mission Control to go over the rules that had been agreed so far. As far as Kraft was concerned, Houston was running the show and an independent decision by the crew 'wasn't something we encouraged'.[18] Yet Armstrong made no secret of the fact that he would be the man on the spot. Neil, who was first and foremost a test pilot, knew that instruments could sometimes give faulty readings, needlessly causing concern. Unless the spacecraft was actually out of control, what was there to worry about? But inaccurate telemetry sent from space could prompt a controller to mistakenly order a safe flight to be aborted. Neil's opinion on the issue 'led to some heated discussions', Kraft wrote. '"I'm going to be in a better position to know what's happening than the people back in Houston," he said over and over,' Kraft later remembered. 'And I'm not going to tolerate any unnecessary risks,' Kraft retorted, 'that's why we have mission rules.' In the final weeks before the launch, Kraft suspected Armstrong still privately harboured doubts about some of the rules. 'I wondered then if he'd overrule all of us in lunar orbit,' he said.[19]

In addition to his work in the LM simulator, Neil spent a further 34 hours practising descent trajectories, both at the research facility at Langley and in the Lunar Landing Training Vehicle.[20] He continued to believe that the LLTV provided the best training despite his accident in May 1968, which prompted modifications to the machine's control system. But after Houston's chief test pilot Joe Algranti was forced to eject from the improved version in December, Chris Kraft and MSC director Bob Gilruth were ready to bar anyone else from flying it.[21] Once again the astronauts fought back, Armstrong as keen as anyone to fly it. As the next commander to go into space, and the first to attempt a lunar landing, his opinion could not be overlooked. After further modifications, by June 1969 a new LLTV was ready, and Neil was among the first to fly it.[22]

Kraft asked him to justify his use of such a hazardous vehicle.

'It's absolutely essential,' Armstrong told him, 'by far the best training for landing on the Moon.'

'It's dangerous, damn it,' snapped Kraft.

'Yes, it is,' Neil replied. 'I know you're worried, but I have to support it. It's just darned good training.'

Kraft received the same response from other astronauts, so 'with our fingers crossed, we let them keep it', but a compromise was reached in that only the commanders of lunar missions were to fly it.[23] Neil flew the machine a total of 27 times, more than any other astronaut.[24] Buzz never got the chance.

After the flight readiness review of 17 June, Neil, Buzz and Michael transferred to the Cape where they could work at maximum capacity with minimum interference. Having been cleared for launch, Collins moved to Florida 'with my bottle of gin and my bottle of vermouth, and a heavy load removed from either shoulder'.[25] Hidden away on the fourth floor of the Manned Spacecraft Operations Building, the crew were given small, windowless bedrooms that were joined to a shared living room, exercise room, sauna, dining room, kitchen and briefing room. After a hurried breakfast, each morning they would go to the simulators awaiting them in a nearby building and work until lunchtime, when they would attend to piles of sandwiches and phone messages. In returning his calls Michael found that many of the conversations followed a similar theme: '"Oh really, Mrs —, you haven't received an invitation to the launch? Why, I can't understand that, anyone as dedicated to the space program as you have been!" Who the hell is in charge of this anyway,' he would ask himself, 'and why is this broad calling me?'[26] His brief lunch over, Collins would climb back into the couch for the next rendezvous workout, knowing that no matter how rickety the simulator computers were, Neil and Buzz probably had it worse.

Difficulties with the LM simulator, and its connections to Houston, began to put Armstrong and Aldrin behind in their tight training schedule. 'The amount of work seemed endless,' Buzz later wrote, 'and, at times, practically insurmountable.'[27] There was more talk of delaying the launch to August but neither man openly supported the idea. Yet nor did they seem eager to commit to July. Collins wondered whether they needed time simply to complete minor things or whether they were genuinely unprepared. With several mandatory simulations yet to be completed, it was hard to escape a growing sense of pressure as they tried to get everything done. When the hardware was working satisfactorily, Armstrong tried to wring as much as he could from each training session. He had been involved in the design of simulators since his days at Edwards, and knew that by actively encouraging problems there were useful lessons to be learned.[28] Neil wanted to use the LM simulator to do something more than just 'win', as others did. 'They tried to operate perfectly all the time and avoid simulator problems,' he said. 'I did the opposite.'[29] Armstrong knew that the occasional 'crash' would reveal useful information about difficult parts of the trajectory. For Buzz, however, a crash wasn't the kind of thing he felt they should be striving to achieve. Aldrin believed they should be mastering not the simulator but the mission.[30]

Collins recalled that, late one night, Buzz angrily told him they had been replicating a landing when a thruster had stuck open and they had been ordered to abort. Neil did not react immediately, and by the time he tried to take action the computer showed that the LM had already fatally crashed. Michael remembered that Buzz was incensed and, accompanied by a bottle of Scotch, 'kept me up far past my bedtime complaining about it'. Suddenly Neil emerged from his bedroom and entered the debate, at which point Michael crept off to bed, grateful for the fact that in the command module it was just him and the computer, 'and if that son-of-a-bitch mouthed off, I would turn off its power supply'.[31] Buzz found that what he referred to as Armstrong's 'communication reticence' was compounded by his own inability to penetrate it.[32] At breakfast the following morning, Michael noticed that neither of his crew-mates appeared ruffled after what he assumed to have been a 'frank and beneficial discussion, as they say in the State Department'.[33]

Occasionally the three of them would train as a team on the elements of the mission they would perform together, such as the launch. By the end of the training schedule, Neil had accumulated 383 hours in the LM simulator, and a further 164 hours in the command module. Aldrin's figures were even higher, at 411 and 182 respectively. As was to be expected, Collins focused almost exclusively on the command module, spending three times as long as Armstrong in studying as many aspects of the spacecraft as he could.[34]

The final simulation, late on the afternoon of Saturday 5 July, was expected to be a simple confidence-boost for the controllers. Armstrong and Aldrin did not take part and the Mission Control team trained instead with the Apollo 12 backup crew, Dave Scott and Jim Irwin. According to Kranz, things were going smoothly when three minutes into the landing Dick Koos triggered a series of computer alarms that had never been seen before. Steve Bales, the 26-year-old guidance officer, suddenly discovered the LM's computer was reporting a 1201 alarm code. A glossary of the LM software showed that 1201 meant 'executive overflow, no vacant areas' – and Bales realised the computer was overloaded. He had no mission rules on how to react to a 1201 alarm, and as more warnings appeared he called his software expert Jack Garman, who was in one of the backroom offices. Both knew the computer was unable to complete some of its tasks, but Bales couldn't tell which of them were being neglected and he urgently advised Kranz to abandon the landing. Kranz quickly agreed. 'If there was one word guaranteed to get your attention in Mission Control,' he wrote, 'it is the word abort.'[35]

Kranz believed he had given the correct order, but Koos knew otherwise. Whatever the computer's difficulties were, everything else had been working properly. 'This was not an abort. You should have continued the landing,' he told Kranz's team during a subsequent debriefing. Bales was devastated: on the last simulation before launch he had needlessly halted the mission. At first Kranz was angry that they had ended on a failure but he knew the lesson had been necessary.[36] That night Bales investigated the problem, and the following morning he worked with various alarm codes in hastily arranged simulations. He added a new entry to the mission rules book, listing a dozen alarms that could prompt an abort. They did not include 1201. The changes were included in the final edition of the book, which was published just five days before the launch. While the crew were familiar with its key points, no-one could be expected to memorise the whole book, and since they were not required to commit the many alarm codes to memory they were not told about the new rule.[37]

With the training schedule now largely complete, Chris Kraft asked Neil, 'Is there anything we've missed?'

'No, Chris,' Armstrong replied, 'we're ready. It's all done except the countdown.'[38]

Lingering in the back of Kraft's mind, he later wrote, were memories of the conversation about who would have the final say, the astronauts or Mission Control. But by then he knew there was nothing left to be said. 'We had come at last to this point,' he recalled, 'and for a moment I felt my legs shake.'[39]

()

Armstrong: 'Burning; we're looking good.'

Collins: 'Pitch trim is up at 1.5 degrees, cycling about that, which is a little bit off the simulation value. Yaw trim is cycling about zero. Chamber pressure is 95.'

The lunar orbit insertion (LOI) burn began precisely on time. With the service module's engine silently ejecting a bright streak of flame, the spacecraft began to slow and the crew found themselves pushed against their seats as a reassuring sense of gravity briefly replaced weightlessness. When the pressure in the combustion chamber began to rise above its predicted level of 95lb per square inch, the crew realised that the engine was working harder than expected. This meant it would operate for less than the predicted time of six minutes and two seconds, and would be shut down early by the computer. While keeping an eye on the chamber pressure, Collins was also watching the two flight director attitude indicators. Each featured a ball display that allowed the crew to monitor the vehicle's attitude in space.

Collins: 'OK, she's steering like a champ; chamber pressure sneaking up to 100.'

Armstrong: 'We're now predicting 5 seconds early, 05:57.'

Collins: 'Ball number 1 and ball number 2 both right on value. Roll zero, pitch 225, roughly, and yaw 348; and hold.'

Armstrong: '10 seconds.'

Collins: 'OK, 9, 8, 7, 6, 5, 4, 3—'

Armstrong: 'Shutdown.'

The engine cut their speed from 5,600mph to 3,700mph, allowing them to be captured by the Moon's gravity.[40] They had now entered an elliptical orbit, taking them around the Moon on a great oval-shaped path that at its highest point carried them nearly 170 miles above the surface and at its lowest brought them down to 60. During the burn, the computer monitored how far they had drifted in the roll, pitch and yaw axes. They could have easily wandered off course. But the computer had successfully kept them on the straight and narrow, and they had strayed by only one tenth of a foot per second in each axis – something that impressed them all.

Collins: 'Minus 1, minus 1, plus 1. Jesus! I take back any bad things I ever said about MIT – which I never have.'

Armstrong: 'That was a beautiful burn.'

Collins: 'Well, I don't know if we're 60 miles or not, but at least we haven't hit that mother.'

Aldrin: 'Look at that! Look at that, 169.6 by 60.9.'

Collins: 'Beautiful, beautiful, beautiful, beautiful!'

Aldrin: 'What – what'd it say ... 60.2.'

Collins: 'You want to write that down or something? Write it down just for the hell of it, 170 by 60, like gangbusters.'

Aldrin: 'We only missed [the predicted highest orbital point] by a couple of tenths of a mile.'

Collins: 'Hello, Moon; how's the old back side?'

With the burn complete, they were free to look out of the windows at the alien landscape below. In the great void of space here was land – like home. Although baked by the Sun, the barren ground appeared coldly foreboding and anything less like home was hard to imagine. A 'withered, sun-seared peach pit' Michael called it. 'There is no comfort to it ... its invitation is monotonous and meant for geologists only.'[41] Even its colour was hard to judge. Apollo 8 reported the surface to be black-grey-white, while Apollo 10 described it as black-brown-tan-white.[42] Armstrong, Aldrin and Collins had been asked to settle the issue, and to them there appeared to be truth on both sides. The colours varied according to the angle of the Sun. Immediately either side of the region of shadow the ground appeared to be a shade of grey, but once lit by bright sunlight it was more tan, fading to brown and then grey as it shrank into the darkness once more.

Coasting around the remainder of the far side, Neil, Buzz and Michael were still out of radio contact, and for a moment it felt as if the grown-ups had left the building. Free to enjoy the view, the crew looked in amazement at the enormous craters passing beneath them. Their excitement led to unguarded comments that they knew would not be broadcast to the nation – but which were captured by a tape recorder.

Armstrong: 'What a spectacular view!'

Collins: 'God, look at that Moon! Fantastic. Look back there behind us, sure looks like a gigantic crater; look at the mountains going around it. My gosh, they're monsters.'

Armstrong: 'See that real big–'

Collins: 'Yes, there's a moose down here you just wouldn't believe. There's the biggest one yet. God, it's huge! It is enormous! It's so big I can't even get it in the window. You want to look at that? That's the biggest one you ever seen in your life. Neil? God, look at this central mountain peak.'

Armstrong: 'That's kind of a foggy window.'

Collins: 'That's a horrible window. It's too bad we have to shoot through this one, but – oh, boy, you could spend a lifetime just geologising that one crater alone, you know that?'

Armstrong: 'You could.'

Collins: 'That's not how I'd like to spend my lifetime, but – picture that. Beautiful!'

Aldrin: 'Yes, there's a big mother over here, too.'

Collins: 'Come on now, Buzz, don't refer to them as big mothers; give them some scientific name.'

Aldrin: 'It sure looks like a lot of them have slumped down.' [The tops of the craters had collapsed into the pit below.]

Collins: 'A slumping big mother. Well, you see those every once in a while.'

Aldrin: 'Most of them are slumping. The bigger they are, the more they slump – that's a truism, isn't it? That is, the older they get.'

Radio contact with Mission Control was imminent, and not wanting their initial public exchange with Houston to begin with a conversation about ageing mothers, slumped or otherwise, Armstrong changed the subject: 'Well, we're at 180 degrees, and now we're going to want to stop that and start a slow pitch-down.'

()

The far side of the Moon had eluded man's curiosity until October 1959 when the first eye-opening pictures were sent home by a Russian probe. Astronomers were taken aback by the far side's heavily cratered landscapes, devoid of seas and strewn with what Collins later described as an 'uninterrupted jumble of tortured hills'.[43] Anxious to demonstrate prowess in the emerging space-race, in December 1959 NASA commissioned its own series of probes, named Ranger. Rangers 1 and 2, however, never got beyond short-lived low-Earth orbits, and Ranger 3 missed in its attempt to reach the Moon. Ranger 4 suffered electrical failure, 5 also missed, and for good measure also suffered electrical failure, and 6 was disabled at launch; but Ranger 7 proved, five years later, that NASA could also snap pictures of the Moon. Deliberately plunging towards the lunar surface, before it was destroyed on impact Ranger 7 briefly transmitted TV images that were a thousand times sharper than anything that had been seen through a telescope.[44] They revealed not the jagged mountains that appeared in the speculative paintings by Chesley Bonestell, but rolling hills and open spaces. Since boulders littered the ground, it appeared the surface was capable of supporting a spacecraft.

Following Kennedy's challenge to land on the Moon, NASA commissioned the Surveyor series of probes. Designed to carefully examine the nature of the surface, the information they would send home was urgently needed by Tom Kelly's team working on the lunar module. In May 1966, Surveyor 1 gently landed in the Ocean of Storms; equipped with a television camera, it sent back images of a flat area pockmarked by rocks and craters. Surveyor 2 was lost en route to the Moon, but in April 1967 the third Surveyor also successfully landed in the Ocean of Storms. Fitted with a mechanical arm, it managed to dig into the surface, unearthing details about the material below. Surveyor 4 was also lost, but the fifth probe reached the Sea of Tranquility where it investigated the chemical properties of the lunar dust, work that was later extended by Surveyor 6 in the Meridian Bay.

As well as discovering general details about the surface, NASA also needed to identify places that might serve as landing sites for manned missions. The ideal spot would be within easy reach of a spacecraft that was travelling on a free-return trajectory and had little fuel to spare. In practice, this meant finding an area within a narrow band stretching horizontally across much of the middle of the near side of the Moon. The site would have to be away from high hills and deep craters, which might send misleading altitude signals to the landing radar. It would have to be largely smooth and predominantly flat, and would have to receive a consistent level of sunlight in case the launch were delayed. A lunar day lasts two weeks, and during the Moon's lingering dawn the long shadows cast by the Sun made it easier to spot rocks and craters when looking from above. All of this meant that ideally the landing would be attempted just after local sunrise at a suitable site near the eastern half of the equator. This way, as the Sun moved further west, areas in the western region of the equator would become available once the shadows began to shorten at the first location.

Using telescopes, the Apollo Site Selection Board initially produced a list of 30 potential landing grounds. These were to be photographed from a height of 35 miles by the Lunar Orbiter missions, NASA's third series of probes. In August 1966 Lunar Orbiter 1 sent home medium-resolution pictures of nine of the targets. These included an area in the Sea of Tranquility, later labelled Apollo Landing Site 2 (ALS-2). Lunar Orbiter 2 later photographed a further 11 sites, and also sent back high-resolution images of some of the places inspected by its predecessor, among them ALS-2.[45] Some of the pictures were given to the press, and a spectacular image of the crater Copernicus appeared on front pages around the world. Released from the flat pictures taken with telescopes, for the first time the Moon was exposed as a three-dimensional place where towering mountains overshadowed haunting valleys, and empty stretches of wilderness extended for miles in all directions. The photograph gave millions of people a chance to see for themselves what it might be like to study the surface from a pilot's perspective.

Landmarks on routes approaching the most promising landing sites were photographed by Lunar Orbiter 3, and pictures from all three Orbiter missions helped the selection board whittle down the options to five areas. In looking for a flat plain in the east near the equator, the Sea of Tranquility stood out as an obvious candidate, and here two sites were chosen, ALS-1 and ALS-2. The first was inspected by Apollo 8, and Apollo 10 flew over the second, both bringing back pictures that helped the crew of Apollo 11 prepare for their own mission.[46] It was decided that Armstrong and Aldrin would attempt to land at ALS-2, in the south-western part of the Sea of Tranquility. If the flight were delayed, secondary sites further west were located in the Sinus Medii (almost in the centre of the visible face of the Moon) and in the Ocean of Storms.

Meanwhile, having taken the first pictures of the far side of the Moon, the Russians continued to develop their Luna series of probes. In many cases their unmanned spacecraft outperformed America's just as decisively as their manned missions beat NASA's in achieving key objectives. Luna 9 landed on the Moon in January 1966, four months ahead of Surveyor 1. Although cosmonauts were unlikely to reach the surface, some in NASA feared that a Russian probe might still try to retrieve the first samples of lunar rocks. Three days before the launch of Apollo 11, on Sunday 13 July 1969, the Soviet Union announced that Luna 15 had been launched on a mission to the Moon. Amid US fears that Armstrong's crew would have to contend with a chunk of Russian metalwork in their vicinity, there were suggestions that Luna 15 might scoop up some dust and bring it home while Neil and Buzz were still strapping on their boots.

( )

Thirty-four minutes after Mission Control lost contact with the crew, the powerful antenna in Madrid picked up their signal as the spacecraft came within sight of the Earth. It was Houston's first indication that the initial LOI burn had been successful. Many of the features on the desolate far side were unnamed, but now that Apollo 11 was coasting across the near side the crew were passing over more familiar ground. For months, Neil and Buzz had been studying photos of distinctive landmarks they would look out for during critical phases of the descent. Features of the Moon were identified, in Latin, according to rules set out by the International Astronomical Union in 1961. The plains, traditionally described as oceans and seas, were named after states of mind, such as the Sea of Tranquility and the Sea of Crisis. The highlands were named after mountain ranges on Earth, and craters recalled eminent scientists, while some of the smaller features were informally named by the two previous Apollo missions.[47]

Armstrong: 'Apollo 11 is getting its first view of the landing approach. This time we are going over the Taruntius crater, and the pictures and maps brought back by Apollo 8 and 10 have given us a very good preview of what to look at here. It looks very much like the pictures, but like the difference between watching a real football game and watching it on TV. There's no substitute for actually being here.'

Soaring 127 miles above the surface, the feature Neil particularly wanted to see was the landing ground. Eleven miles long and three wide, it was still officially identified as ALS-2, but the astronauts had come to refer to it using the baseball term 'home plate'. Half the Moon was bathed in sunshine, but for the moment the landing site lay just beyond the terminator, the line dividing sunlight and darkness. Dawn would not reveal it until the following day. Until then Armstrong would have to content himself with studying the approach route, including the hill Jim Lovell had named after his wife.

Aldrin: 'We're going over Mount Marilyn at the present time, and its ignition point.'

Mission Control: 'Roger. Thank you. And our preliminary

tracking data for the first few minutes shows you in a 61.6 by 169.5 orbit. Over.'

Aldrin: 'Roger.'

Mission Control: 'And Jim is smiling.'

Armstrong: 'Currently going over Maskelyne. And Boot Hill, Duke Island, Sidewinder, looking at Maskelyne-W, that's the yaw round checkpoint. Just coming into the terminator.'

And with that, the crew flew back into the Moon's shadow, knowing that somewhere down in the darkness ALS-2 was awaiting them.

While coasting through dark skies, at around 1.50pm they tried to answer questions about the surface until Neil reminded Mission Control that they were tucking into lunch. He wanted to focus on the next major task on the flight-plan, the second lunar orbit insertion burn, but he knew Houston had other ideas.

Mission Control: 'We'd like to know if you're still planning to have the TV up with the beginning of the next pass. Over.'

Armstrong: 'Roger, Houston. We'll try to have it ready.'

Mission Control: 'This is Houston. We are inquiring if it is your plan to. Over.'

Armstrong: 'It never was our plan to; but it's in the flight-plan, so I guess we'll do it.'

Mission Control: 'Houston. Roger. Out.'

While passing behind the far side for the second time, the astronauts set up what Neil once referred to as the 'camera claptrap'. There hadn't been time on the ground to practise using it. 'Neil and Buzz didn't even know how to turn it on or focus it,' Collins recalled, 'and my knowledge of it was pretty sketchy.' Having had a chance to play around with the equipment on the way to the Moon, they were now a little better prepared to start filming the surface. Nevertheless, Michael was mindful of advice he had been given, reminding him that there would be a billion people watching, 'so don't screw it up'.[48]

By the time they swung back into radio contact they were already broadcasting TV pictures. For the first time during the mission, the lunar surface – which for so long had been preoccupying so many minds – suddenly became clearly visible to those on the ground. Impressed by the quality of the images, Bruce McCandless told the crew that Houston was receiving a beautiful colour picture of the Moon's horizon, capped by the empty blackness of space.

Now 92 miles above the hills of Smyth's Sea, Neil, Buzz and Michael once again looked for the approach to the landing site. Collins had noticed that the LM (still docked with the command module) had a tendency to sink down towards the surface and he put this down to the effect of the mysterious mascons. While Buzz described the craters passing beneath them, Mike asked the flight controllers to watch the telemetry so that they could see the effect for themselves.

Travelling east to west, nearly 26 minutes after resuming contact with the ground the spacecraft passed over the triangular shape of Mount Marilyn for the second time. Apollo 11's elliptical orbit meant its altitude was changing all the time, and as they continued towards the landing site the crew were now around 150 miles above the surface.

Aldrin: 'The largest of the craters near the centre of the picture right now is Maskelyne-W. This is a position check during descent at about 3 minutes and 39 seconds, and it's our downrange position check and cross-range position check prior to yawing over face-up to acquire the landing radar. Past this point, we would be unable to see the surface below us until getting very near the landing area.'

Mission Control: 'Roger. I imagine you'll get a real good look at that tomorrow afternoon.'

Then once more the crew plunged back into darkness, the Sun setting in the east behind them.

Switching off the camera, they were now able to focus on LOI-2 – the second lunar orbit insertion burn. This was designed to exchange Apollo 11's elliptical path around the Moon for a more circular orbit. The previous two lunar missions had tried to reach as circular an orbit as possible, only to find that the mascons later pulled them out of position. Apollo 11's burn would take the orbital wobbles into account, allowing them to pull the spacecraft gradually back into a precise orbital path.

After McCandless read up the data they would use to get home if the 17-second burn did not go to plan, Collins completed a P52 exercise to check their position. They then lost contact with Houston at the start of their third orbit. Collins put the spacecraft in the correct attitude to be able to begin the burn, which once again would take place on the far side, beyond assistance from Houston. Again the engine had to fire precisely on time, at 80 hours, 11 minutes and 36 seconds into the mission. It could not be allowed to continue for a second longer than scheduled or else 'we'd be on an impact course with the other side of the Moon', as Buzz put it.[49] Once Michael was ready, at 4.43pm he allowed the burn to begin. The engine started smoothly and the manoeuvre successfully put the spacecraft in a near circular orbit roughly 60 miles above the Moon. Now travelling at a little over 3,600mph, it would complete one circuit every two hours. Michael would stay on this track for the remainder of his time in lunar orbit, and would not fire the engine again until he was ready to begin the journey home.

After making radio contact, the crew let Mission Control know that LOI-2 had gone to plan. In the hours before they went to bed their final task of the day was to prepare for the landing, due to take place the following afternoon. Equipment needed to be transferred into the lunar module which meant that once again they had to open the hatch and remove the docking mechanism. As Buzz began carrying supplies into the LM, he noticed that the terminator had crept back a fraction and that for the first time the landing site was softly emerging from the darkness. He found himself looking down on what he considered to be a beautiful landscape, and he urged Neil and Michael to look for themselves. The area was still streaked by long shadows, and privately Michael thought he couldn't see anywhere smooth enough 'to park a baby buggy, never mind a lunar module'.[50] Even Buzz admitted the whole region looked eerie.

Following a suggestion by Michael, they agreed to stow the docking mechanism in the cabin, rather than secure it back in position. 'I'd rather sleep with the probe and drogue than have to dick with it in the morning,' he said. Replacing the command module hatch, he began to prepare dinner. Meanwhile, Buzz quietly ran through the many procedures they would be following in the morning, leaving Neil to his own thoughts. Procedures could be followed from checklists but some things were left to Armstrong's personal preference, including the first words he would say on the surface.

En route to the Moon, Michael and Buzz had asked Neil what he might say.[51] They were not alone in their curiosity. In late June, George Low, the Apollo programme manager, had asked Armstrong whether he had thought about his choice of words. Neil had replied, 'Sure, George, I've been thinking about it. Tell everybody thanks from all of us. We know how hard everybody's been working.'[52]

Chapter 11

A PLACE IN HISTORY

On 10 July 1969, Frank Borman returned from an official goodwill trip to Russia. Three days later he was still briefing senior politicians in Washington when Chris Kraft urged him to find out what he could about the Luna 15 mission. Borman consulted the National Security Advisor, Henry Kissinger, before using the infamous White House hotline to call the Soviet Academy of Sciences. The following day, telegrams detailing the probe's trajectory and promising that radio interference would not be a problem were sent to the White House and to Borman's home in Houston.[1] In a rare moment of co-operation, the two superpowers were brought a hair's width closer through a spirit of unity fostered by the leaders of their respective space programmes. In space at least, if not elsewhere, the Cold War was showing signs of a thaw.

An atmosphere of mutual respect between astronauts and cosmonauts developed in rare meetings at international air shows. In May 1967, Michael Collins was asked by NASA to attend the Paris Air Show, along with Dave Scott. Besieged by photographers, autograph hunters, security men and tourists, they sat down with cosmonauts Pavel Belyaev and Konstantin Feoktistov. But the formalities evaporated when everyone retreated to the privacy of the Russians' airliner and opened the vodka. The Russians insisted they had no plans for a manned landing on the Moon but admitted that cosmonauts were training to fly helicopters, leading Collins to suspect that secretly their lunar ambitions were far from over.

Compared to NASA's open way of doing things, Collins considered the Russian space programme to be 'hidden from view, secret and mysterious'.[2] This was a widely held opinion.

The Russians never announced flights in advance and disasters were always concealed. News of the loss of cosmonaut Valentin Bondarenko, during a training accident in 1961, did not emerge until the 1980s.[3] Worse, many in NASA believed the Russian space programme to be tinged with a nasty communist way of doing things, including ordering cosmonauts to undertake risky ventures simply to beat the Americans in achieving key objectives. The Russians might have put the first man in space, and the first woman, and carried out the first EVA, but some in NASA wondered just how much risk they were accepting along the way. There were indeed occasions when cosmonauts were sent on missions against their better judgement. Unknown to NASA, Vladimir Komarov had raised concerns about the many technical problems with Soyuz 1, before it claimed his life in April 1967.[4] Yet the fact that the Russians were sometimes getting ahead of themselves, and consequently taking unnecessary risks, did not prove that NASA occupied the moral high ground. It was the Americans who had publicly set a deadline, forcing developments to move forward so quickly that while the Russians lost one man during a mission NASA lost three on the ground. A month after Komarov died, Collins, Scott, Belyaev and Feoktistov drank to an end to accidents.

By 1968, the CIA was warning NASA's leadership of a giant rocket being secretly built by the Russians.[5] It appeared that Moscow was preparing to send men to the Moon, in an attempt to beat the Americans once again and steal the ultimate prize laid down by Kennedy. In fact Kennedy, as we have seen, had invited Khrushchev to take part in a joint expedition to the lunar surface. Although the Russians were receptive to the president's UN speech, they were never to find out what he had in mind.[6] After Kennedy's assassination Khrushchev was persuaded to go it alone, and he secretly set in motion the necessary preparations – as Collins had suspected. A top priority was a powerful rocket to rival the Saturn V, and by February 1969 the Russians were ready to test their N-1 booster. Although big enough to impress the

CIA, the N-1 lacked the Saturn's reliability and exploded just over a minute into its flight. On 3 July, just two weeks before the launch of Apollo 11, a second N-1 blew up, the huge explosion destroying its launch-pad at the Baikonur Cosmodrome in Kazakhstan and bringing an end to any realistic hope of a Russian manned mission to the Moon. No announcement was made of the disaster and the world did not learn of it for some months to come.[7]

In the struggle for ideological supremacy, America made much of its self-appointed role as the guardian of freedom and democracy. In this spirit, NASA claimed that unlike the menacing Russians it was freely allowing the world to see every triumph and tragedy. In 1957, Vanguard TV3 was set to become America's first satellite. But when it got no further than four feet from the ground, TV networks were allowed to continue their live footage of the unfolding disaster. Similarly, in January 1967, news of the Apollo 1 fire was quickly passed to the press. This policy of making the agency publicly available was to have far-reaching consequences for many of its personnel and their families. Unlike their Russian counterparts, who largely remained anonymous, America's astronauts were living in a country where Hollywood and rock 'n' roll created new heroes every week. Alongside movie stars and music legends, spacemen were offered up to an admiring public by reporters who described them as dashing adventurers. Astronauts were the real-life embodiment of the space-travelling supermen of science fiction, the type of guys who would readily throw you a smile and a salute on their way to ridding exciting new worlds of bug-eyed monsters. The public didn't care about orbital mechanics and P52 platform alignments, they wanted to know what astronauts had for breakfast. Some liked the attention. Others, among them Neil Armstrong, enjoyed press adulation as much as engine failure and considered this aspect of the job a necessary evil.

There was a feeling within NASA that, as a government agency spending billions of public dollars, the public were owed something in return. This led to astronauts being despatched to dinners and local functions across the country. Before his Gemini mission, Michael Collins was sent to a Boy Scouts event in Ohio. He always found such PR work difficult, but on that occasion his dismay was outweighed by the Boy Scouts' own disappointment after they discovered he had not yet flown in space. 'Aren't any of the real astronauts coming?' one of them wanted to know.[8] Once in training for a flight, the men were spared such duties.

Initially, the Mercury Seven found it hard to cope with the flood of requests for interviews, but help came in the form of a controversial contract tying the men exclusively to *Life* magazine. In return for an annual sum, divided equally among the astronauts, the men gave their stories to *Life* in an arrangement that allowed them to tell other reporters they were unable to give anything to anyone else. As servicemen, none was highly paid and they found it hard to resist the offer of extra cash. In 1969, Aldrin was still technically in the air force (as was Collins), and he received a modest serviceman's salary of $18,600; Collins received $17,000. The *Life* deal gave him an extra $16,000 per year for his first two years with NASA, although when the number of astronauts later swelled the pot was stretched more thinly.

Armstrong, a civilian employed by NASA since 1955, was earning $30,000 a year, putting him among the highest-paid astronauts.[9] Neil believed that reporters, whether from *Life* or elsewhere, frequently misunderstood the truth. Many wanted to know what thoughts were going through his mind at launch and what it was like to ride a rocket. They wanted answers soaked in emotion, that ideally expressed a philosophical message about voyages to the heavens. Armstrong knew they wanted more than abort modes and guidance programs but felt they were missing the point. No-one was writing poems at lift-off. Even the normally sanguine Collins was frustrated by the myopic press whom he believed had a 'morbid, unhealthy, persistent, prodding, probing pre-occupation with the frills, when the silly bastards didn't even understand how the machines operated'.[10]

It wasn't just the astronauts who were signed to *Life*: the deal also included the personal stories of the men's families. Before a mission, quietly concerned children were asked what they thought about Daddy dying in the depths of space. For an astronaut's wife, life was difficult enough without such questions from the press. Janet Armstrong, Pat Collins and Joan Aldrin had each moved hundreds of miles from relatives and friends to join their husbands in Clear Lake, a distant suburb of Houston. The sprawling Manned Spacecraft Center that dominated their lives was 28 miles from the city centre. With the men spending so much time at work, many astronauts' wives found themselves effectively running one-parent families. Frank Borman later said, 'I was a part-time father ... my input was well-meant and sincere, but it was also too sporadic for me to take much credit for how well they turned out.'[11] Few wives had the time or opportunity to pursue a career of their own, marital difficulties were common, depression was a problem, and more than one of the wives turned to alcohol. 'Of course they were treated like royalty,' Tom Stafford's former wife Faye said of the men, 'it was hard for them to come home. What could ever compete with that? I was lucky if I could come second.'[12] Most of the women had experienced service life, and knew that military families traditionally developed strong networks in support of each other. A similar thing emerged in Houston, with friends and neighbours rallying round to help those involved in a mission. Janet had never been a service wife and chose not to actively participate in wives' clubs.[13] For Joan, the most difficult elements of life during a flight included the daily press conferences she was expected to give. Prior to Gemini 12, *Life* had reserved key stories about the Aldrin home, yet every day she had to find something new for the rest of the press.[14]

This was all the harder since NASA expected wives to play their part without getting in the way. In practice this meant that they were not welcome at launches, nor were they given any official advice or information before the mission. When Neil experienced problems aboard Gemini 8, NASA switched off the squawk box in Janet's home. Desperate for information she went to Mission Control but was refused entry.[15] Joan Aldrin once told Buzz 'no-one tells me anything'. For her, the wives' role was clearly defined: 'Our job is to keep house, take care of children, and not ask questions.'[16] Some felt particularly vulnerable since NASA controlled the world in which they lived yet their exclusive link to the agency was through their husband. After Charlie Bassett's jet crashed into the building containing the Gemini 9 spacecraft, his widow Jeannie felt isolated to the point that she could no longer live in Houston. She remained friends with Joan Aldrin, but Joan told Buzz that 'it was as though she wasn't a part of us any more'.[17] When Buzz confirmed he was going to the Moon, Joan later wrote in her diary, 'I wish [he] were a truck driver, a carpenter, a scientist – anything but what he is. I want him to do what he wants, but I don't want him to.'[18] A few days before the launch of Apollo 11, Pat Collins gave Michael a poem she'd written, which referred to 'nighttime stabs of fear' and 'tears, unbidden, welling'.[19] While their husbands were risking their lives in the name of their country, the wives had to maintain a public façade of excitement and awe, as did their children. Officially, as they were once reminded by George Mueller, the head of the Office of Manned Space Flight, they were proud, thrilled and happy; anything else they might be feeling was best hidden from view.[20]

Nothing was allowed to pierce the wholesome public image of the average astronaut, who occupied a place in the public's consciousness somewhere between a Boy Scout and Buck Rogers. It was an image preserved in print by *Life*, which fostered an impression of clean-cut, contented all-American families. Under the surface, however, the all-too human truth was understood by *Life* writers like Dora Jane Hamblin. Hamblin knew better than most that in space the astronauts were heroes but on the ground they were still men. While life in Houston was based around the family, there was a greater degree of freedom at the Cape. 'There were plenty of pretty women imagining love with a space hero,' Gene Cernan said, and some of the men ensured they didn't have to imagine for very long.[21] If an astronaut wanted to take his wife and children to the Cape, permission had to be obtained from Deke.[22] Hamblin and other reporters saw what was going on but knew that neither the men nor NASA would allow them to say anything. Nothing untoward could be printed without breaching the astronauts' trust, which *Life* had invested so much in acquiring.[23] After spending time with a group of off-duty astronauts, journalist Robert Sherrod saw that in print they 'came out as usual, deodorized, plasticized, and homogenized, without anybody quite intending it that way'.[24]

No mission had ever attracted as much attention from the press as Apollo 11. As the launch date approached, the flight became bigger than NASA. Interest at home and abroad inevitably focused on the men who were going to the Moon, eclipsing the tremendous efforts of people like Bob Gilruth, Chris Kraft and George Low who had been involved in the mission for years. 'We were our nation's envoys,' wrote Collins. 'We would be watched by the world, including the unfriendly parts of it, and we must not fail.'[25] As attention from the press grew more intense, in June Michael was able to escape from life under Houston's magnifying glass by retreating to the Cape, taking Pat and the children with him for the first couple of weeks. What he found particularly difficult was the popular misconception that the mission was already all but done. It seemed the press were encouraging a feeling that the flight would pass without a hitch. Astronauts had already travelled as far as lunar orbit and nothing had gone wrong; next time it would be a simple case of going the extra distance.

The fact that Apollo 11 was a test-flight, which might or might not succeed, seemed to be largely misunderstood. From the word go, Deke and the crew had been working on the basis that the mission had the best shot at completing the first landing, but nothing was certain. Armstrong, Collins and Aldrin were simply first in the queue. Neil himself believed that while they had a 90 per cent chance of making it home, the probability of actually reaching the surface was no more than 50 per cent.[26] As well as overestimating the mission's chance of success, the press also misunderstood the flight's main objective, which was the landing itself. To many, the idea of a gentle landing didn't hold the same level of wonder as walking on the Moon. Bringing flying machines to a stop was something man did on a daily basis. But to walk on another planet was the stuff of dreams, and speculation about what the astronauts might find was rife. While many scientists interested in Apollo 11 were working on phenomena such as radiation, most focused on the geology of the Moon. They saw in the mission a unique opportunity to study a snapshot of the solar system's history, undisturbed by weather or life. In agreeing to place a range of experiments on the Moon, NASA allied itself to the wider scientific community and thereby raised the flight beyond a simple level of oneupmanship with the Russians. But the science was an afterthought. Approval for an experiments package didn't come until 1964, three years after Kennedy's speech, which had been a vision presented by a politician and was more about politics than geology.

Ambitious plans for extensive scientific work could be left to the later Apollo missions. During the first manned flight to the surface, time would be limited and priority would be given to gathering samples of rocks and dust. This meant only a small number of experiments would be carried by Apollo 11. An astronaut's ability to work with tools and scientific equipment was investigated in an area of volcanic rock near Cinder Lake, Arizona. Geologists wearing pressure-suits explored a simulated lunar landscape that had been blasted out of the rock, replicating a Lunar Orbiter picture. The results of these and other tests influenced the design of the experiments that were being considered for the flight. A list of potential experiments was prepared in May 1965, and a month later Houston set up a department to develop those that were to be selected. By 1966 a preliminary timeline for the moonwalk had been put together, suggesting that once the astronauts had collected an initial sample of stones they should deploy the experiments before using tools to gather a broader selection of material.[27]

Two years later, in October 1968, NASA headquarters approved the development of a solar-powered seismometer that would measure meteoroid impacts and 'moonquakes'. To prevent it freezing during the two-week lunar night, the device was equipped with a heater system that incorporated 2.4 ounces of plutonium 238. This represented the first major use of nuclear energy in a manned mission. As well as the seismometer, NASA also commissioned an unpowered laser reflector which would help to improve tracking of the position of the Moon. Together, the two items were known as the Early Apollo Scientific Experiments Package (EASEP). On Earth, the instruments – each the size of a suitcase – weighed a total of 170lb, but in the one-sixth gravity of the Moon it would be easier to carry them from the spacecraft to a suitable point on the surface. As well as the EASEP, the astronauts would be a given a solar wind composition experiment (abbreviated to SWC). This would capture evidence of electrically charged particles emitted by the Sun.[28] In addition to filling two 'sample return containers' and setting up the experiments, Neil and Buzz would also have to put a TV camera into position and erect the US flag. After photographing their work, the surface and the LM, they would have to prepare the containers and the film magazines for flight before returning to the spacecraft. All of this had to be completed within two hours and 40 minutes, with each task given a specific slot in a detailed timeline.[29]

Preparations for the extra-vehicular activity took up less than 14 per cent of the entire training period, and mostly took place at the Manned Spacecraft Center.[30] Fully suited, Neil and Buzz would clamber down from a makeshift LM and set up their various pieces of equipment on an extensive sand tray. Sections of the EVA were also occasionally practised elsewhere, including the pool at Houston's Neutral Buoyancy Facility and the KC-135 'vomit comet', both offering the ability to work in reduced gravity. Lunar gravity was also replicated at Grumman's plant in New York, using a cable and pulley system which Armstrong referred to as the 'Peter Pan rig'. By supporting five-sixths of his weight, the facility gave him the sense of being able to jump very high. 'You also had a feeling that things were happening slowly, which indeed they were,' Armstrong noted. Through such tests, it was established that once they'd readjusted their sense of balance the crew would be able to walk about in search of stones.[31]

Armstrong and Aldrin liked the geology lessons that astronauts had been taking part in since 1964, and both acquired extensive knowledge of the subject.[32] Collins, however, was not a fan, telling Dora Jane Hamblin, 'I hate geology. Maybe that's why they won't let me get out on the Moon.'[33] A final geology field trip was made in February 1969, when Neil and Buzz visited west Texas, accompanied by the press. On 18 June, the day after the flight readiness review approved the launch date, senior NASA managers watched them complete a full run-through of their work on the surface. Amid concerns about what could be expected of them during their search for lunar material, it was agreed that the astronauts would not venture further than around 100 feet from the spacecraft. Armstrong later said, 'If the descent and the final approach to landing were rated a nine on a ten-point scale of difficulty, I would put the surface work down at a two.'[34]

As well as using the simulators at the Cape, and taking part in EVA training in Houston, the crew also spent time at Grumman on Long Island, and at North American Rockwell in Downey, California. They attended computer briefings at the Massachusetts Institute of Technology, and studied stars at the Morehead Planetarium, Chapel Hill, North Carolina, and at the Griffith Planetarium in Los Angeles. In order to travel quickly between these and other places the astronauts were provided with supersonic T-38 jets, the air force's most modern training aircraft. To Collins, the T-38 was one of the joys of the job, particularly when given the chance to talk about it: 'Sure, I left Houston after work, refuelled at El Paso, and landed in LA before sunset. Would have been here sooner except I had to shut down one engine just past Phoenix.'[35] It was not always an easy aircraft to fly. As well as Charlie Bassett and Elliot See, astronauts Ted Freeman and C. C. Williams were also killed in T-38 crashes.

Time also had to be found for non-essential parts of the mission. Collins wrote that during a discussion on ideas for the mission patch, Jim Lovell suggested an eagle. Flicking through a book at home, Collins found a picture of a bald eagle, legs down, coming in for a landing. He traced the image on to tissue paper and added a lunar surface and the words 'Apollo' round the top and 'eleven' round the bottom. Armstrong felt 'eleven' might not be understood abroad, so 'Apollo 11' was added to the top. Collins wanted to introduce an element of peace to the patch but wasn't sure how. A simulator instructor suggested he include an olive branch, which Collins then added to the eagle's beak before submitting the design for approval. NASA headquarters felt that the eagle's claws looked too aggressive, as if the bird were about to seize the Moon for itself. After he moved the olive branch from the beak to the talons, Collins sent the patch back to Washington and this time it was approved. The crew decided not to include their names so that the emblem would be representative of everyone who had worked on the mission. Once the patch was complete, it was a short jump from there to naming the lunar module *Eagle* – the symbol of America serving as an appropriate partner to *Columbia*, which at one stage had almost become the country's name.[36]

In between the training sessions, the crew also needed to assemble their personal preference kits (PPKs). Each consisted of a pouch made of fireproof cloth that was not much bigger than this book. Subject to weight and space restrictions, the men were largely free to take what they wanted, as long as they gave a list of everything to Deke. NASA kept the contents of PPKs confidential, and a degree of mystery still surrounds the kits, including even their number. It appears three were tucked away in a compartment in the command module (weighing up to five pounds each) and another two were in the lunar module (neither heavier than half a pound). A sixth PPK (probably consisting of several small packages, together weighing more than 50lb) was known as the Official Flight Kit, while a seventh was easily accessible and contained frequently used items such as pens, torches and other small objects. The secrecy surrounding the kits stems from the fact that most contained the men's private property, along with mementos passed to them by friends and relatives. A measure of discretion was also required since not everything given to Neil and Buzz would actually go to the surface. Nor would anything given to Mike – unless taken down to the Moon on his behalf. Prior to the mission the men agreed that all personal items taken into space would simply be described as 'carried to the Moon', regardless of which spacecraft the object was actually on.[37]

The three men personally spent $2,700 on 450 silver medallions bearing the Apollo 11 eagle, to be shared between them. They also took with them a commemorative Apollo 11 envelope issued by the US Postal Service, complete with commemorative stamp. Additional Apollo 11 envelopes, signed by the crew, were also carried into space, alongside six-inch flags of the US and other countries. Aboard the LM was an Apollo 1 mission patch, along with two medals honouring Vladimir Komarov and Yuri Gagarin (who had been killed in an air crash in 1968) that were brought back from Russia by Frank Borman. Secured within the command module were two full-size US flags that had flown above Congress before the flight and which were due to be returned to Washington.[38] The men also carried a number of mission patches, three gold olive-branch pins for their wives and other items of jewellery. Buzz took to the Moon a small vial filled with wine and a miniature chalice, photos of his children and a gold bracelet that had belonged to his mother. Mike carried his college ring, together with a gold locket for his daughter Ann, and a gold cross that had been in the family for many years and which was to be given to his daughter Kate. He also carried many small items at the request of other people, including prayers, poems, coins, tie-pins, cufflinks and a hollow bean containing no less than 50 tiny ivory elephants.[39] By special arrangement, Neil took aboard the LM a small section of muslin and a piece of wood from the left propeller of *Flyer*, the Wright Brothers' first successful aircraft. 'Did he take something of Karen with him?' Armstrong's sister June later wondered. 'Oh, I dearly hope so,' she added.[40]

Throughout April, May and June, assembling the PPKs, designing the patch, learning to use the stills, TV and 16mm cameras, and other minor duties had to be squeezed into the relentless training regime. For Neil and Buzz, the hardest time came in early June when difficulties with the simulator were slowing their progress and, according to Janet, sapping morale. Janet recalled that 'Neil used to come home with his face drawn white, and I was worried about him'.[41] But while the wives may have seen the impact the mission was having on the men, according to Collins the crew never discussed among themselves the difficulties facing them. He himself felt subject to an imaginary commandment proclaiming 'thou shalt not screw up', but he had no idea whether Neil and Buzz felt the same way since they rarely talked about anything beyond technical details. 'Amiable strangers,' he later famously called the three of them.[42] To outsiders, Armstrong, Collins and Aldrin seemed unconnected. Guenter Wendt, the technician in charge of the launch-pad, noticed that they always arrived for launch training sessions in separate cars.[43] But beneath the surface, having worked together so closely for so long they were able to read each other's thoughts. By July, Michael believed that they had come to know each other 'by osmosis or some other mysterious transfer process, rather than by direct communication'.[44]

As they got closer to lift-off, the pressure continued to build. When the Apollo 9 crew reached the same point in their preparations, they were physically run down and suffered chest infections that postponed their launch by three days. Apollo 11 could not afford a similar delay since suitable lighting conditions on the Moon would not return for a month. To limit the risk of infection, the men went into quarantine at the Cape, emerging on Saturday 5 July for a press conference in Houston. Extraordinary measures were taken to protect them from any germs carried by the press. Walking into the room, the crew wore gas masks which they removed only once they'd taken their seats within a large three-sided plastic box. Beside them, fans blew air out into the auditorium.[45] Each of them spoke before taking questions. One reporter asked Armstrong whether he believed the Moon would eventually become part of the civilised world; another wanted to know if he feared losing his private life after the mission. To a question about what he would be taking to the Moon, Neil wryly replied, 'If I had a choice, I would take more fuel.' After sitting through an array of arid answers, Norman Mailer wrote that Armstrong 'surrendered words about as happily as a hound allowed meat to be pulled out of his teeth'.

While the reporters vainly searched for drops of emotion as if looking for water on the Moon, a few hundred yards away Gene Kranz and his team were beginning their final training session. The crew later gave many individual interviews before going home at the end of a 14-hour day – unaware of 1201 alarms that could be safely ignored.[46]

After flying back to the Cape on Monday 7 July, the men returned to the simulators, once again living a life of relative isolation. During one flight to Florida, Michael shared a T-38 with Deke Slayton, who mentioned that he had been looking at future missions. As the command module pilot on such a prominent trip, Collins could expect to lead a future flight, giving him a chance to walk on the Moon. Michael told Deke that if Apollo 11 aborted he would be looking to fly again but if all went well this would be his last space-flight. He had come to believe that 'I simply was putting too much of myself into Apollo 11 to consider doing it all over again at a later date; besides, the strain on my wife was not good and should end as soon as possible.'[47]

The mission consumed so much time and energy over so many months that in some respects the astronauts knew more about what was happening on the Moon than on Earth. 'When you're part of the pioneering effort,' Buzz later said, 'there's a focusing of an individual's concentration and level of attention that is at the exclusion of a lot of other things. It's a kind of gun-barrel vision.'[48] They largely remained aloof from developments dominating the news at home and abroad, events that, like their own mission, promised to occupy a place in modern American history. For in 1969 America was a divided country, and there was hope that the flight would restore some of the national pride that had corroded over the previous 18 months.

In January 1968, the Viet Cong's series of successful counter-attacks demonstrated that America was not going to be able to extricate itself from Vietnam any time soon. At home, smouldering resentment over the war was ignited by revelations of a massacre of up to 500 civilians by US soldiers in the village of My Lai. Anti-war protesters were involved in fighting on university campuses and elsewhere across America. For five days in August 1968, demonstrators in Chicago clashed with police in the streets surrounding the Democratic National Convention.

Armstrong, Collins and Aldrin believed they were going to the Moon in the name of America, but for millions of black Americans, many of whom had until recently been confronted by widespread segregation, NASA was almost exclusively white, spectacularly rich, and might as well have been on the Moon already. During the 1968 Olympic Games in Mexico City, sprinters Tommie Smith and John Carlos presented a Black Power salute by raising their gloved fists in the air. They, at least, did not share the notion of a unified America such as might have been felt in Houston. The $24 billion invested in Apollo was said to be benefiting the economy since not a cent of it was spent in space, but critics couldn't help wondering how much of it was being spent in the poorer corners of the nation. The cash largely went to other rich white organisations such as North American Rockwell and

Grumman. NASA was picketed, and there were reports of bomb threats. For much of America, the deluge of fire surrounding the launch of Apollo 6 was overshadowed by the assassination of Dr Martin Luther King on the same day. In Houston, Buzz joined a march in memory of the civil rights leader, accompanied by his church minister, the Reverend Dean Woodruff.

In the midst of the turmoil, for many people a rocket launch, or 'shot' in US terms, was an exhilarating distraction, and of course nothing would represent sparkling success – American success – more than NASA's Moon shot. It was the stuff of fantasy, always a safe refuge when times are bad. It would be a decisive blow against communist Russia, it would remind the rest of the world that America was a force to be reckoned with, and as such it simply had to succeed. It was all down to the 'Moonmen', as the crew were described in the press.[49] The extent of the pressure the men were under was clear to NASA administrator Dr Thomas Paine, who joined them for dinner on Thursday 10 July, just days before the launch. Emphasising that they were not to take undue risks, he told them that if they were unsuccessful they could try again on the next flight. His promise was unrealistic, but it served its purpose in encouraging the men to avoid unnecessary dangers.[50]

That weekend – as thousands of people began partying on the Florida coast, and Chris Kraft and other managers quietly fretted over Luna 15 – a sense that things were finally about to get under way descended on Houston and the Cape. On Monday 14 July, a flight readiness review confirmed the launch would go ahead in two days' time, and at 5pm the extended countdown began.[51] A rising tide of tension threatened to engulf the men at the centre of all the activity. Neil, Michael and Buzz calmly tried to shut out the world's expectations and focus on the task in hand. Janet believed that Neil finally felt ready to attempt the landing. Previously, she had told the press there was no point in worrying about the outcome of the mission because 'It doesn't do any good. They're up there on their own. There isn't anything we can do to help.'[52]

Chapter 12
THE EAGLE HAS WINGS

Groggy after a difficult night's sleep, Michael Collins wondered whether the insistent voice in his ear could possibly be talking to him.

Mission Control: 'Apollo 11, Apollo 11. Good morning from the black team.'

Collins: 'You guys wake up early.'

On the morning of Sunday 20 July, Collins was woken 93 hours and 32 minutes into the mission, at 6.04am. The fifth day of the flight promised to be the most demanding, and none of the crew had slept well. 'The pressure was beginning to build at this point,'[1] Neil later said. After preparing the LM, the two spacecraft would undock. Neil and Buzz would then make the first of two burns, putting them in an elliptical orbit with a lowest point above the Moon of 8.3 miles. At this point, the crew would begin a second burn that would carry them down to the surface. For the moment, the men were just about to begin their tenth orbit around the Moon, and there were just two minutes to go before radio contact was lost.

Mission Control: '11, Houston. Looks like the command module's in good shape. Black team has been watching it real closely for you.'

Collins: 'We sure appreciate that. Because I sure haven't.'

As they passed around the far side Buzz entered the lower equipment bay and began to prepare for the landing that would take place in nine hours' time. He and Neil would remain in their pressure-suits throughout their time aboard *Eagle*, which meant that once again they would have to put on the urine and fecal collection devices. After doing this, Buzz pulled on a set of long johns that contained hundreds of thin plastic tubes. These allowed the underwear to be cooled by water during the arduous work on the surface. He then floated into the LM, making room for Neil to begin the same process, while Mike prepared breakfast.

In Houston, Mission Control's black team were coming to the end of their shift, and nearly two hours after they had woken the crew they began handing over to the white team of Gene Kranz. Carrying a plastic bag, Kranz walked into the Mission Operations Control Room and greeted his controllers as he slowly threaded his way towards his seat. By his own admission he was the most emotional of all the flight directors, and was keenly aware of the historical significance of what he and his men were hoping to do.[2] He hadn't slept well either. Leaving his bag at the flight director's console, Kranz headed out of the MOCR to pass the time of day with the engineers and contractors in the spacecraft analysis room. After chatting to Grumman's Tom Kelly and the president of North American Rockwell, by 8am he had returned to his console. From his bag, Kranz retrieved his white and silver waistcoat. Once he'd slipped it on he was ready to take over.

Aboard *Columbia*, breakfast was taking longer than usual. Tired, busy and preoccupied by the events ahead of them, the men fell out of their mealtime routine. Normally they helped each other prepare the many breakfast bags and packages, but with bits and pieces of their bulky spacesuits taking up precious room it had become difficult to move about. 'The rhythm got slightly out of whack,' Buzz remembered, 'and once we finally got it going properly we all three bemoaned the fact that the simple act of eating was something there was no training for.'[3] After the meal, Buzz – still only wearing his long johns – returned to the LM to begin preparing *Eagle* for flight, a five-hour process. While Aldrin worked through his checklist, Michael helped Neil into his pressure-suit, doing up the inaccessible crotch-to-shoulder zip and checking everything was as it should be. Meanwhile, Mission Control read them the day's news.

> Among the large headlines concerning Apollo this morning, there's one asking that you watch for a lovely girl with a big rabbit. An ancient legend says a beautiful Chinese girl called Chang-o has been living there for 4,000 years. It seems she was banished to the Moon because she stole the pill of immortality from her husband. You might also look for her companion, a large Chinese rabbit, who is easy to spot since he is always standing on his hind feet in the shade of a cinnamon tree. The name of the rabbit is not reported.

'Jesus Christ,' Collins thought to himself. While trying to make coffee and stay on top of the confusion around him he couldn't quite believe he was listening to Houston's thoughts on large Chinese rabbits.[4] 'OK. We'll keep a close eye out for the bunny girl,' he told the ground.

Since the two vehicles would later be undocking, all three men would have to put on their suits, in case either spacecraft suddenly lost pressure, though Michael wouldn't be walking on the Moon and therefore wouldn't need the so-called 'liquid-cooled garment' the others were wearing. After helping Collins into his suit, Armstrong entered the lunar module. Sunlight, streaming through the windows, bounced off the white beta-cloth locker covers, while in front of him the grey instrument panels had come alive in the orange glow emanating from the gauges.

After powering up the inertial platform that fed the primary computer, Neil and Buzz tested communications with Houston. They were about half an hour ahead of the flight-plan. While Collins gave Armstrong details of their position, to be entered into *Eagle*'s guidance system, Buzz returned to *Columbia* to put on his pressure-suit. Once Aldrin floated back into the LM he shut the hatch and for the first time he and Neil were sealed inside the cramped spacecraft that would be their home for the next 30 hours. Michael then installed the probe and drogue docking assembly and secured *Columbia*'s hatch. Now that *Eagle* was powered up and operational, he could open a valve that would allow the tunnel connecting the two spacecraft to empty of oxygen.

Collins: 'OK, I'm ready to go to LM tunnel vent.'

Aldrin: 'You got it all vented now?'

Collins: 'Negative, it's a slow process. I'm on vent, but – it's just going to take a little while here.'

Aldrin: 'Roger. Just give us a call. We're pressing on with some other stuff.'

Now wearing their gloves and 'bubble' helmets, and connected to the life-support system, Neil and Buzz tested the suits' radio connections. They then fired the explosive bolts that unfolded the LM's four legs. Passing across the near side of the Moon on the twelfth orbit, Armstrong and Aldrin began checking the inertial platform and the primary computer. Houston needed to send information using the powerful S-band signal, which could only be done once the LM's most powerful transmitter/receiver – the high-gain antenna – was directly facing Earth. Using controls in the cabin, Buzz tried to rotate it into the correct position but found its signal was blocked by the lunar module itself. For the moment they could only talk to the ground using less powerful omni-directional antennas. Once S-band communications became available, Houston sent navigation data to the abort guidance system (the AGS, serving as the LM's backup computer). After this, Armstrong and Aldrin tested their thrusters, the final major check they needed to perform. In Houston, Kranz had polled his controllers on whether they were happy to proceed with the undocking, and five minutes before the crew went 'over the hill' permission was given to separate.

Mission Control: 'Apollo 11, Houston. We're go for undocking. Over.'

Aldrin: 'Roger. Understand.'

Collins: 'Houston, *Columbia*.'

Mission Control: 'Go ahead, *Columbia*. Over.'

Collins: 'Roger. There will be no television of the undocking.

I have all available windows either full of heads or cameras, and I'm busy with other things.'

Before the mission Collins had admitted that 'I would be either a liar or a fool if I said that I think I have the best of the three seats on Apollo 11... but I'm an integral part of the operation and happy to be going in any capacity.'[5] For the rest of the world, Neil Armstrong and Buzz Aldrin were just names in a newspaper – in Russia, *Pravda* had taken to calling Neil 'the Czar of the Ship' – but for Michael, Neil and Buzz were the only people who had shared everything he had been going through since Christmas. Now that the two of them were about to begin the key part of their mission, the time was fast approaching when he would have to bid them farewell. All that remained to be done was for the command module to be held still while Armstrong punched computer buttons as he finely tuned the AGS.

Collins: 'I have 5 minutes and 15 seconds since we started. Attitude is holding very well.'

Aldrin: 'Roger, Mike. Just hold it a little bit longer.'

Collins: 'No sweat, I can hold it all day. Take your sweet time. How's the czar over there? He's so quiet.'

Armstrong: 'Just hanging on – and punching.'

Collins: 'All I can say is, beware the revolution. You cats take it easy on the lunar surface. If I hear you huffing and puffing, I'm going to start bitching at you.

Aldrin: 'OK Mike.'

After Buzz finished setting up a 16mm film camera in his window, at 12.44pm Michael pushed a button releasing the latches holding the two spacecraft together. Excess oxygen immediately escaped from the tunnel, gently pushing the two spacecraft apart. From that moment Neil and Buzz were flying aboard a vehicle in which it would be impossible to come home.

Mission Control: '*Eagle*, Houston. We see you on the steerable [antenna]. Over.'

Armstrong: 'Roger. *Eagle* is undocked.'

Mission Control: 'Roger. How does it look, Neil?'

Armstrong: 'The *Eagle* has wings.'

Mission Control: 'Roger.'

With the two spacecraft flying in formation, 60 feet apart, Collins took a careful look out of the small window directly in front of the left-hand couch.[6] He had made a trip to the Grumman factory specifically to see what the lunar lander should look like once the legs were properly extended. Now, as Neil slowly rotated the LM, it seemed to Michael that with its legs locked in position *Eagle* was 'the weirdest-looking contraption ever to invade the sky'.[7] A minute before he was due to move off to a greater distance, Collins embroidered the truth a little.

Collins: 'I think you've got a fine-looking flying machine there, *Eagle*, despite the fact you're upside-down.'

Armstrong: 'Somebody's upside-down.'

Armstrong: 'See you later.'

Collins: 'OK, *Eagle*. One minute until ignition. You guys take care.'

Firing his forward thrusters for eight seconds, Michael flew the command module away from the LM; at the same time Neil and Buzz tested the all-important rendezvous radar by locking on to *Columbia*'s transponder. Once *Columbia* was a thousand feet away, Armstrong and Aldrin were ready to begin the first part of the descent to the surface, a manoeuvre known as descent orbit insertion (DOI). To put themselves on the correct approach route, the burn would have to be made while they were out of radio contact with Houston – like so many other key moments of the mission. In igniting their engine on the far side of the Moon, the spacecraft would enter an elliptical orbit. At its lowest point, this would bring *Eagle* down to just 50,000 feet (or 8.3 miles) above a spot 260 miles east of the landing site.[8] One hour and six minutes after undocking, the ground gave permission for DOI, and ten minutes later the two spacecraft slipped out of contact, at the beginning of the fourteenth orbit.

()

On a steaming day in Houston, the crew's homes were crowded with visitors. Through the squawk boxes, everyone had overheard Neil and Buzz preparing the LM – but the technical jargon was sometimes hard to understand. 'Better than 90 per cent of what families could ever hope to hear on this party line was incomprehensible,' Jim Lovell later said.[9] Joan was helped through some of the more complicated things by Apollo 9 veteran Rusty Schweickart. That morning she had attended the Presbyterian church where Buzz was an elder, taking with her their children Michael, Jan and Andy. Reporters had tried to capture a comment as she entered but Joan had waved them away before settling down to listen to a sermon about the 'epitome of the creative ability of man'.[10] She was home by 11.30, and while she waited for the landing to get under way she watched the continuous TV coverage. Friends from church had brought lunch, including a cake with icing in the shape of an American flag beside the words 'we came in peace for all mankind'.[11] At her home in the suburb of El Lago, Janet was also watching the TV coverage, while Bill Anders, a member of the backup crew, tried to answer her questions about the landing. 'What can go wrong and they can still go?' she asked. 'It depends on what went wrong,' Anders told her.[12]

Since the launch, four days earlier, Janet, Joan and Pat had been keeping open house, with a steady stream of friends and relatives bringing them food and other gifts. Among those staying with Joan was Jeannie Bassett, who was helping to look after the children.[13] Entering or leaving the crew's homes meant having to push through throngs of reporters camped outside. On the first day of the flight a photographer had sneaked over Joan's back fence, which had upset her.[14] She very much wanted to give the right image to the press, but on her terms, and on the morning of the second day she made a point of raising the American flag on her front lawn to give them an early picture. Her duties done, she and the children sneaked out of the back of the house and into the car of a waiting friend who whisked them off to a shopping centre 12 miles away.[15] Janet had spent much of the second day clearing leaves from the pool, before settling down to watch the TV broadcast in the evening. Joan also caught the broadcast, she and Jeannie helping the children to identify the voices as the crew described the Earth. 'You'd better watch yourselves, boys – you're going to run out of material,' she joked. 'Especially those three,' quipped somebody in the background. When Pat saw the broadcast she discovered Mike was growing a moustache.[16]

Despite attempts to remain light-hearted, by the third day the pressure was beginning to take its toll. Pat and Janet joined Joan for a pool party, the three of them giving a joint picture for the press. Reporters had managed to put questions to the children after Pat dropped them off at a day camp en route to the party. When six-year-old Michael was asked if his daddy was going to go down in history, he replied, 'Yeah,' but gave as good as he got when he asked, 'What is history?'[17] When Pat went to get her hair done on the morning of the fourth day, three female reporters had managed to get appointments at the same time and at the same place. Later that day, listening to radios and squawk boxes, the wives waited for the men to safely come round from the far side of the Moon after LOI-1. Janet had been briefed by Apollo 10 commander Tom Stafford so that she would feel prepared ahead of the landing. That night, while her family and friends accepted a dinner invitation from next door, Janet stayed at home, preferring to eat alone.[18]

The following morning, Sunday 20 July, the Aldrin family attended the packed service at Webster Presbyterian Church. After the sermon, the Reverend Dean Woodruff broke the Communion bread and held it up for everyone to see, pointing out that a piece was missing. The implication was that it had gone with Buzz. He called on the Aldrin household later that afternoon, listening to the transmissions and sharing the tension during the radio silences.[19] For 48 minutes in every two-hour orbit, the crew were out of contact with the Earth. During their fourteenth circuit of the Moon, Neil and Buzz would theoretically complete the DOI burn. No-one could know for sure until radio contact resumed. At that point, if all had gone to plan, the landing would begin less than 20 minutes later.

In TV studios around the world, anchormen and experts were preparing for what promised to be the most significant moment in television history. There was a sense that humanity was going somewhere radically new. Unlike historical voyages of discovery, this time, through the wonders of television, the explorers were bringing mankind with them. It was a tight squeeze. Diagrams and animations supplied by NASA revealed how the astronauts were standing up in the tiny cabin of the lunar module. After explaining to viewers that there wouldn't be any TV pictures from space until the moonwalk, the networks broadcast the radio messages sent to and from Mission Control.

In the Mission Operations Control Room (MOCR), Kranz and his team were waiting for *Eagle* to resume contact. Kranz felt that the air had started to 'crackle' as anticipation of the coming events took hold of his young flight controllers.[20] Sitting to his left was Charles Lewis who, having survived his brush with the 'natives' on Zanzibar, was now serving as an assistant flight director. Further along the third row was communications officer Ed Fendell, supporting Michael in the command module. According to Kranz, Fendell liked to poke fun at his fellow controllers, but while some found him disruptive, Kranz respected his independence and reliability. Also supporting *Columbia* were John Aaron and Buck Willoughby (call-signs EECOM and GNC), who would be on hand to help Collins should he need to rescue the LM. *Eagle* itself was assisted by most of the rest of the controllers, including Dick Brown, who looked after communications and sat next to Fendell. In front of them, flight surgeon John Zieglschmid sat near to Deke Slayton and CapCom Charlie Duke, while across the aisle to the right were Bob Carlton and Don Puddy. The dry, laconic Carlton (call-sign Control) was monitoring *Eagle*'s navigation, control and propulsion systems, while the quick-witted Puddy (known as TELMU) watched the electrical power and life-support equipment. In the front row sat Steve Bales, the diligent Guido officer, who was looking after the LM's radar and computers and who had requested the extra training sessions to study the alarms. To his left, watching the LM's trajectory, was flight dynamics officer Jay Greene, described by Kranz as a cocky 'pipe-smoking rabble-rouser'. The final members of the slightly rebellious front row were Chuck Deiterich, who would help plot a route home in an emergency, and Gran Paules, who was supporting Bales. Assisted by their backroom colleagues, the white team were monitoring the 270 measurements continuously transmitted by the LM.[21]

Also sitting in the MOCR were astronauts Pete Conrad, Fred Haise, Jim Lovell and Bill Anders, while at the back, in 'management row', were Bob Gilruth, George Low, Chris Kraft and General Sam Phillips, Director of the Apollo Program. Behind the windows of the viewing gallery were more senior NASA figures from than had ever been gathered in one place before. They included administrator Tom Paine, the directors of four space centres (including Wernher von Braun), and astronauts Tom Stafford, Gene Cernan, Jim McDivitt and John Glenn. With them was John Houbolt, the man who had so energetically pushed for lunar orbit rendezvous.

When radio contact was lost prior to the DOI burn, Kranz suddenly became aware of the pressure his young team was under. Their average age was just 26, and some, like Puddy and Bales, had come straight from college. Instructing them to switch from the usual voice loops, he addressed them on a private internal circuit. Cornered in the viewing gallery, the brass were literally cut out of the loop. Later, Kranz remembered that he 'had to tell these kids how proud I was of the work that they had done'. In a stirring, off-the-cuff speech, he reminded them that by landing a man on the Moon they were about to write history. He finished by saying that whatever decisions they chose to make he would stand by them, for 'we came into this room as a team and we will leave as a team'.[22]

The morning's tasks had occasionally felt like a simulation. When Kranz ordered the doors to be locked, no longer was there any doubt that this was the real thing. From now on no-one would be able to enter or leave Mission Control until the crew had either crashed, aborted or landed.[23]

()

Nearly eight minutes after losing contact with the ground, Neil and Buzz ignited the LM's engine for the first time. The DOI manoeuvre began in almost total darkness, only the thinnest rays of the Sun reaching beyond the curve of the Moon. Burning for nearly 30 seconds, the engine produced enough thrust for them to feel its force in their legs. Once the burn was complete, *Eagle* was flying faster and lower than *Columbia*, and descending all the time. By the time they were ready to resume contact with Houston, 40 minutes after DOI, Armstrong and Aldrin were already down to an altitude of 18 miles and coasting at nearly 3,700mph.[24] The LM was in a horizontal position with its engine facing the direction of travel, so that it might have been described as flying backwards. It was also flying windows down. Had they not been in weightlessness, Neil and Buzz would have considered themselves to be travelling feet first and face down. In this attitude they could look down at passing landmarks and use their engine as a brake. With the Sun on its back, *Eagle*'s golden foil glittered brightly against the grey plains below as it swooped low and fast across the surface.

More than 40 miles above, Michael used his sextant to follow its progress. 'The LM is nearly invisible,' he later said, 'and looks like any one of a thousand tiny craters, except that it is moving.'[25] Although he was coasting behind the LM, his higher altitude meant that *Columbia* would peer over the edge of the Moon before *Eagle*, which in turn meant that Collins was the first to get through to Houston. Immediately, Charlie Duke wanted to know about the LM's burn.

Mission Control: '*Columbia*, Houston. Over.'

Collins: 'Houston, *Columbia*. Reading you loud and clear. How me?'

Mission Control: 'Roger. Five-by, Mike. How did it go? Over.'

Collins: 'Listen, babe. Everything's going just swimmingly, beautiful.'

Mission Control: 'Great. We're standing by for *Eagle*.'

Collins: 'OK, he's coming along.'

At 2.48pm, a wave of energy ran through the MOCR as Houston resumed contact with *Eagle*. Just two minutes later, however, the all-important high-gain signal dropped out. While other mission rules dealt with clearly defined problems, the question of whether there was enough telemetry or not was down to Kranz's personal opinion. He felt that of all the rules in the book, 'this is the only one that really bothers me, because it's a pure judgment call'.[26] The link was re-established, but just four minutes later, with *Eagle* now down to around 12.5 miles altitude, the controllers' screens froze once again. In a little over 10 minutes' time, Neil and Buzz were due to begin the powered descent initiation (PDI), their second and final burn. But if the situation didn't improve soon Kranz knew he might have to send them around the Moon on another orbit. After that, if he still wasn't ready to allow the final burn, the LM's dwindling electrical supply would force him to scrub the mission.

With time ticking by, Duke asked for help from Collins.

Mission Control: '*Columbia*, Houston. We've lost *Eagle* again. Have him try the high gain. Over.'

While Neil checked their position relative to objects on the surface, Aldrin monitored the primary and backup computers, and did what he could to maintain communications. He adjusted the position of the high-gain antenna, *Eagle*'s strongest transmitter-receiver, but once again it was trying to send its signal through the body of the spacecraft. With the LM quickly approaching the critical low point in its orbit, all that Buzz picked up was static.

Collins: '*Eagle*, this is *Columbia*. Houston lost you again. They're requesting another try at the high gain.'

Mission Control: '*Eagle*, Houston. We have you now. Do you read? Over?'

Aldrin: 'Loud and clear. I don't know what the problem was there. It [the steerable high-gain antenna] just started oscillating around in yaw. According to the needle, we're picking up a little oscillation right now, as a matter of fact.'

With less than six minutes until the burn, Armstrong was advised to yaw ten degrees right to make communications easier. But again there was no response from *Eagle*. With time running out, Kranz had to decide whether he could let the descent begin. He needed to poll his team on the landing, but waited 40 seconds longer than scheduled before asking them for a judgement based on the most recent information. As he rapidly went through the call-signs, Kranz received a curt 'go' from each man – then Steve Bales reported, 'We're out on our radial velocity, we're halfway to our abort limits.' The spacecraft's rate of descent showed a discrepancy Bales couldn't explain. Jay Greene also noticed that the LM was lower than expected. Despite the references to 'abort' before the burn had even begun, Kranz told Duke, 'CapCom, we're go for powered descent.'

Duke passed on the instruction, but again there was no response. Unable to talk directly to Buzz, Charlie again asked for help from Michael, who was now 120 miles behind *Eagle*.

Mission Control: '*Columbia*, Houston. We've lost them on the high gain again. We recommend they yaw right 10 degrees and reacquire.'

Collins: '*Eagle*, this is *Columbia*. You're go for PDI and they recommend you yaw right 10 degrees and try the high gain again.'

Collins: '*Eagle*, you read *Columbia*?'

Aldrin: 'Roger. We read you.'

Collins: 'OK.'

Mission Control: '*Eagle*, Houston. We read you now. You're go for PDI. Over.'

Aldrin: 'Roger. Understand.'

Coasting over the surface towards the shadows looming up at them from the west, Buzz switched on the 16mm camera in his window, recording their panoramic view of the brightly lit ground passing below. While Michael moved freely around the spacious command module, looking through the sextant and monitoring the flight-plan, Neil and Buzz were held in position by their cables as they checked their position. If they were much higher than 51,000 feet at PDI, they risked running out of fuel.[27] The Manned Space Flight Network was able to give a rough estimate of their altitude but could be up to 10,000 feet off. Neil had to supplement its information with his own calculations.[28] While waiting for ignition, Armstrong noted the speed at which objects on the ground passed along a scale etched on his window. By combining this information with the LM's velocity and orbital period, he was able to do some quick arithmetic to gauge *Eagle*'s altitude.

Satisfied with his calculations, he and Buzz waited for the computer to complete its countdown to ignition – and at 3.05pm Armstrong permitted Aldrin to instruct it to fire the engine. Five seconds later, Neil called 'ignition', simultaneously telling Houston and millions of TV viewers around the world that the final leg of Apollo 11's historic journey had begun.[29]

Up to this point, the fuel in *Eagle*'s tanks had been floating in weightlessness. When the thrust from the engine caused it to settle, Houston had a chance to assess the quantity consumed during the previous burn. But again the telemetry dropped out, and Bob Carlton was left to guess how much fuel they had left. He could do little more than say that the crew had roughly 12 minutes to reach the landing site. While Kranz and Duke each wondered whether they were doing the right thing in pushing forward despite the communication problems, Neil and Buzz were preoccupied with their own concerns.[30] Up to PDI, everything they had done had been tested on previous missions. Now, as their altitude dropped to 47,000 feet, they were descending into the unknown. In case of an emergency the crew chose to leave their rendezvous radar on, allowing it to send regular updates to the computer.

Buzz noticed an electrical meter was fluctuating, but Neil suddenly discovered they had a bigger problem. *Eagle*'s landing radar wouldn't begin operating until they descended to between 40,000 and 35,000 feet. Until then he needed to compare the time they arrived above familiar hills and craters with estimates that had been worked out previously. In doing this, Neil discovered that they were ahead of where they should be.

Armstrong: 'OK, we went by the 3-minute point early. A little off.'

Aldrin: 'Rate of descent looks real good. Altitude – right about on.'

Armstrong: 'Our position checks downrange show us to be a little long.'

Mission Control: 'Roger. Copy.'

The unexpected increase in speed Bales had noticed had now become apparent to Neil as he realised they were around three seconds further along the flight-path than they should have been. As each second equated to one mile, this meant they would be touching down at the far tip of the landing ground. They were heading towards the region Stafford had said was littered with rocks. Unknown to the crew or Houston, when the LM had undocked, oxygen escaping from the tunnel had given *Eagle* a slight shove. Neil had tried to cancel any residual rates of motion, but the tunnel vent and other manoeuvres had put him slightly ahead.

For the moment, however, he had other concerns. After passing over the crater Maskelyne-W he began to roll the spacecraft over by 180 degrees so that they would no longer face down but directly up. Initially this took much longer than expected, but once Neil adjusted the hand controller they began turning more quickly until they were looking straight up into space. They were now less than 40,000 feet above the Moon, low enough for the landing radar to begin sending information to the computer. In trying to estimate their height, the guidance system disagreed with the figures supplied by the radar, differing by 2,900 feet. Focusing on the instruments, Buzz reported the difference to Neil.

Aldrin: 'Delta-H is minus 2900. [D, or delta, stood for difference, and H for height.] We got the Earth right out our front window.'

Mission Control: 'Roger. We copy.'

Aldrin: 'Got the Earth right out our front window.'

Armstrong [to Aldrin]: 'Sure enough.'

While Buzz had set his microphone to 'vox', transmitting everything he said, Neil's was on 'push-to-talk', so that Houston only heard his words when he wanted them to. At one point during training, Neil's reluctance to share everything with the world had led him to mutter a comment to Buzz about 'that damned open mic of yours'.[31] Pushing the transmit button on his hand controller, Armstrong asked Houston to assess the difference in their altitude estimates. While managing a stream of data from the rendezvous radar, the computer was now also accepting updates from the landing radar. Neil and Buzz had the option of telling the computer to ignore the rendezvous updates, but they didn't choose to do this following advice received in training. However, the training had been devised for Apollo 10. With no intention of landing, Stafford knew he would rendezvous after a relatively short flight. He had no desire to switch the radar off and never got low enough for the landing radar to pose any problems. *Eagle*'s computer was now receiving data from both radar systems at once. When Buzz gave it the additional task of looking at the difference between the two altitude estimates, it began to perform a combination of tasks that had not been tried before. In checking the spacecraft's current position, firing thrusters and setting the forward trajectory, the computer was running out of spare capacity, and at five minutes into the burn it triggered a yellow warning light along with an intermittent alarm.

Armstrong [to Houston]: 'Program alarm.'

Mission Control: 'It's looking good to us. Over.'

Armstrong [to Houston]: 'It's a 1202.'

Aldrin: '1202.'

Armstrong [to Aldrin]: 'What is it?'

On the ground, Bales – who had been preoccupied with the navigation error – now needed to work out how much trouble the computer was in. He quickly talked over the internal radio loop to Jack Garman, his backroom specialist, who told him that 1202 was a reference to 'executive overflow'. The computer was struggling to complete some of its tasks, just as had happened prior to the 1201 alarm during training. To Neil and Buzz, however, the alarm code was unfamiliar, and Armstrong was forced to break his concentration and pay close attention to the spacecraft's systems. Without knowing what the problem was it was impossible to know how much danger they were in.

This time, unlike the training session, Bales looked at whether there were any actual problems with the guidance and navigation data. The telemetry suggested that everything seemed to be working well. Since the computer hadn't crashed altogether but had simply returned to the top of its list of tasks, Bales decided the alarm could be ignored. The computer could still function – as long as it wasn't pushed any further. If it began to trigger successive alarms he knew they would have to abort. Armstrong didn't know if they were at that point already, and Buzz later said that 'hearts shot up into throats while we waited to learn what would happen'.[32]

Bales told Kranz that the mission could continue, and Kranz instructed Duke to give the go-ahead to the crew.

Mission Control: 'Roger. We're go on that alarm.'

With *Eagle* now down to 27,000 feet, less than 30 seconds later the alarm rang out again. This time Buzz realised it sounded whenever he asked the computer how far they were from the landing site.

Aldrin: 'Same alarm, and it appears to come up when we have a 16-68 up.'

Mission Control: 'Roger. Copy.'

Armstrong [to Aldrin]: 'Were we – were – was it [their delta-H] coming down?'

Aldrin: 'Yes, it is coming down beautifully.'

Mission Control: '*Eagle*, Houston. We'll monitor your delta-H.'

The spacecraft was flying at 800mph, at an altitude of three and a half miles. Now that Houston was easing its workload, the computer was free to begin the next phase of the landing sequence. At six minutes and 25 seconds into the burn the digital autopilot slowed the engine. Still flying horizontally, feet first, Neil would soon have to slowly pitch up so that *Eagle* assumed more of an upright position.

At home in Houston, Janet Armstrong and 12-year-old Ricky sat on the floor listening to the television while studying lunar maps and diagrams. Thinking of Neil standing up like a trolley-bus driver as he flew towards the surface, Janet excitedly called out, 'Come on, come on, trolley!'[33]

In Mission Control, Jay Greene – his quickfire Brooklyn accent cutting across the radio loop – told Kranz that the trajectory looked good. At 5,000 feet above the ground Neil got ready to take over from the digital autopilot, and with less than four minutes remaining he briefly tested the hand controller. Satisfied with its response, he focused on the view ahead. The surface was filling more and more of his window as *Eagle* approached a vertical position, the Sun now directly behind them. At 4,000 feet Kranz polled the controllers ahead of the landing.

Mission Control: '*Eagle*, Houston. You're go for landing. Over.'

Aldrin: 'Roger. Understand. Go for landing; 3,000 feet.'

Mission Control: 'Copy.'

Aldrin: 'Program alarm – 1201.'

Alarms sounded a total of five times during the descent. They did not recur frequently enough to prompt an abort but they were a major distraction for Neil. The computer was bringing them down on a specific trajectory and would not swerve from its course despite the fact it couldn't tell whether it was taking them towards rocks or a crater. Neil needed to keep an eye on where they were heading. Yet as much as he wanted to monitor their descent, each time an alarm went off he was forced to look down at the instruments to see if everything was all right. As a result he missed many of the landmarks he had memorised. 'I just didn't get a chance to look out the window,' Armstrong later said.[34]

Armstrong [to Houston]: '1201.'

Mission Control: 'Roger, 1201 alarm. We're go. Same type. We're go.'

Aldrin: '2,000 feet; 2,000 feet.'

Armstrong [to Aldrin]: 'Give me an LPD.'

After interrogating the computer, Aldrin obtained a landing point designator angle of 47 degrees. By looking at this angle on the scale etched on his window Neil could see where the computer was leading them. As they came down to just a thousand feet above the surface, again there was a program alarm and again Neil was forced to shut it out of his mind as he focused on the landing. With the fuel decreasing all the time he couldn't afford to spend time on a problem that wasn't critical. The computer was bringing them down just short of a crater that was the size of a football field and surrounded by boulders, most of them as big as cars. The LM would survive a landing on sloping ground but rocks could damage its legs or tear open its fragile skin.

At around 600 feet Armstrong activated the hand controller and, following the pilot's maxim of 'when in doubt, land long', cut his rate of descent and tipped *Eagle* forward slightly. Flying the spacecraft like a helicopter, Neil allowed the main engine to carry them across the dangers below, at a speed of 40mph. Now entering the dead-man's box, if the engine failed there was little he could do about it. Come what may, in less than three minutes the limited amount of fuel would force him down. Yet looking at the ground ahead Neil still didn't like what he saw.

Armstrong [to Aldrin]: 'Pretty rocky area.'

Ignoring the difficulties below, Buzz continued to support Neil with a constant account of their progress, his life now in Armstrong's hands.

Aldrin: '600 feet, down at 19 [feet per second].'

Aldrin: '540 feet, down at 15.'

Aldrin: 'OK, 400 feet, down at 9; 58 [feet per second] forward.'

Armstrong [to Aldrin]: 'No problem.'

Aldrin: '350 feet, down at 4 ... 330, 3½ down. OK, you're pegged on horizontal velocity.'

Uncertain where he was and running low on fuel, Neil finally spotted a suitable area, sandwiched between more craters and another boulder field. By now 'quite concerned' about the fuel level, he still had some distance to cover to reach safety.[35] 'I was being absolutely adamant,' Armstrong later said, 'about my right to be wishy-washy about where I was going to land.'[36]

In Houston, Janet put her arm round Ricky's shoulder as she sat with a hand over her mouth. To most TV viewers there was barely any indication of just how much pressure the men were under.

As he cleared an 80-foot crater, Armstrong was still covering a greater distance horizontally than vertically. At less than 100 feet, with dust being blown aside and obscuring his visibility, he faced a multitude of competing demands. He needed to be edging forward at the moment of landing in order to stay clear of the dust kicked up by the rocket exhaust. The rate of velocity must not be fast enough to risk damaging the legs, and he would have to avoid a slope of more than 15 degrees. He could not land while drifting sideways, and he must avoid craters. At the same time he must remain aware of their abort options, his position relative to the Sun, and the fuel rate called out by Buzz. Above all he had to come down soon.

In Houston, the controllers could see the LM's odd trajectory and could not understand what was happening. Why wasn't he landing? Bob Carlton's figures showed there was just 5 per cent fuel remaining. In his relaxed southern drawl he called 60 seconds, Duke passing on the message. Later, Charlie Duke said the atmosphere was so tense you could have cut a chunk out of it. Anxious to do what he could to help the crew, at one point he was jabbed in the ribs by Deke who muttered, 'Shut up, Charlie, let 'em land!'[37]

Leaning against a doorframe in her living room, Joan Aldrin dabbed her eyes with a tissue.[38] In homes around the world millions of people listened to the sound of one of the spacemen calmly reading out some numbers, everything apparently going smoothly.

Aldrin: '40 feet, down 2½. Picking up some dust.'

There was no mistaking that comment by anybody: the Moon was real, and at last so was the chance of landing on it.

Aldrin: '30 feet, 2½ down. Faint shadow.'

Aldrin: '4 forward, 4 forward. Drifting to the right a little. OK. Down a half.'

Aldrin: '20 feet, down a half; drifting forward just a little bit. Good. OK.'

In Houston, Carlton counted down the seconds as the fuel supply reached a critical level. To Kranz he sounded completely unperturbed, as if 'out picking cotton'.[39] Other than Carlton, the MOCR was silent, the rest of the controllers almost not daring to breathe as they helplessly waited for *Eagle* to land. Carlton reported there were just 45 seconds remaining. No-one reacted. Kranz knew the crew must now either abandon it or come down immediately. He didn't know how high they were when they'd started picking up dust, but since they must be within reach of the surface he had to accept that the final decision was Armstrong's.

Fifteen seconds later, Carlton spoke again, and again Duke passed on the warning.

Mission Control: '30 seconds.'

Armstrong [to Aldrin]: 'Forward drift?'

Armstrong was struggling to see the ground through the clouds of dirt rising up from the surface. He was a little confused, he said later, about *Eagle*'s sideways motion and he tried to focus on anything that appeared to be static. 'I could see rocks and craters through this blowing dust,' he recalled.[40]

Aldrin: 'OK.'

Suddenly a blue light on Armstrong's instrument panel lit up as one of the six-foot probes beneath *Eagle*'s landing pads made contact.

Aldrin: 'Contact light.'

Armstrong [to Aldrin]: 'Shutdown.'

The right and forward landing pads reached the ground simultaneously as Neil brought *Eagle* smoothly down to the surface. He had intended to let the LM fall the last three feet but he didn't have time to switch the engine off early, as planned.[41] 'It just settled down like a helicopter on the ground and landed,' Armstrong later said.[42]

Aldrin: 'OK. Engine stop. ACA out of detent [the hand controller needed to be put in the correct position].'

Armstrong: 'Out of detent. Auto.'

Aldrin: 'Mode control, both auto. Descent engine command override, off. Engine arm, off; 413 is in [a reference to an AGS program].'

Armstrong [to Aldrin]: 'Engine arm is off.'

Neil, the soft-spoken auditor's son from small-town America, had landed on the Moon. It was later established that he had more fuel than he thought (which wasn't registered due to sloshing in the tanks). Nevertheless Armstrong had enough for only another 25 seconds of flight. Now, his immediate task was to confirm the landing for the benefit of everyone listening in. Reluctant to say 'Houston, *Eagle*, *Eagle* has landed', he had decided in advance what he was going to say and had warned Charlie Duke.

Duke: 'We copy you down, *Eagle*.'

Armstrong: 'Houston, Tranquility Base here. The *Eagle* has landed.'

Still wearing their helmets and gloves, Armstrong and Aldrin smiled at each other and warmly shook hands. Buzz later said, 'I had known what he was going to say, but he had never told me when he was going to say it.'[43]

While Buzz's emotional reaction to the landing was 'quickly suppressed', in Joan Aldrin's front room everyone burst into applause – everyone other than Joan, who left them to it and walked into Buzz's study in search of privacy.[44] In the Armstrong household, Janet and Ricky hugged each other in delight.[45]

In New York, an announcement was made at Yankee Stadium, where 16,000 people cheered and sang 'The Star-Spangled Banner'. In Moscow, cosmonauts – including Alexei Leonov, who had performed the world's first EVA – heard the landing on television and applauded their rivals' achievement. In Britain, TV viewers were glued to the country's first all-night broadcast, including coverage of jubilant scenes in Trafalgar Square. In Japan, Emperor Hirohito also followed the landing on television, and later cancelled his plans in order to watch the moonwalk. It was 3.17pm in Houston, where cheering and applause in Mission Control's viewing gallery took the controllers by surprise. 'There's nothing in training that prepares you for that second,' Kranz remembered.[46] John Houbolt, hoping the world would freeze at that moment, was congratulated by Wernher von Braun amid a frenzy of flag-waving and back-slapping. The euphoria threatened to catch on in the MOCR, but between them Slayton and Kranz brought the noise back to an acceptable level so that the team could establish whether *Eagle* was in any immediate danger.

Duke: 'Roger, Tranquility. We copy you on the ground. You got a bunch of guys about to turn blue. We're breathing again. Thanks a lot.'

Duke slumped back in his chair and grinned at Slayton.[47]

Armstrong: 'Thank you.'

Duke: 'You're looking good here.'

Armstrong [to Aldrin]: 'OK. Let's get on with it. [To Houston] OK. We're going to be busy for a minute.'

They needed to quickly check that the LM was safe. If an emergency rendezvous were needed *Eagle* would have to launch within the next 12 minutes, before *Columbia* flew out of reach. Prior to the mission, it had been agreed to make two successive decisions at this point as to whether it was safe to stay. Less than two minutes after the landing, the flight controllers quickly checked the LM's systems before announcing all was well. They confirmed their decision seven minutes later, after a more detailed study of the telemetry. Once Michael passed out of range he would not return for another two hours, so for a little while yet at least Neil and Buzz had the Moon to themselves.

Above: In Mission Control, Flight Director Cliff Charlesworth (centre) sits to the right of Gene Kranz.

Below: Soon after arriving in orbit, the crew's faces filled with blood until their bodies adjusted to weightlessness.

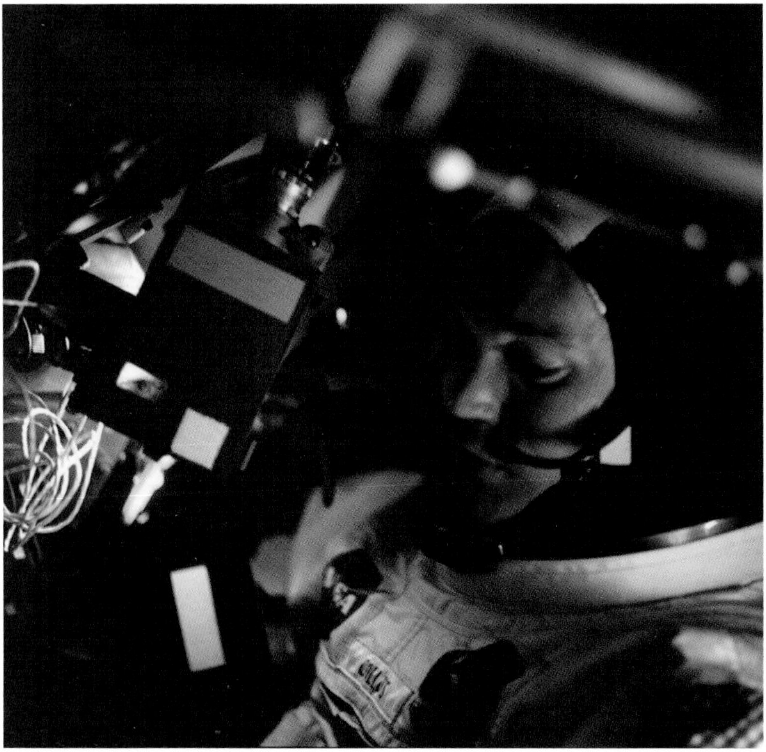

Above: Buzz Aldrin in the lunar module, photographed by Neil Armstrong during the long journey to the moon.

Above: The lunar module, *Eagle*, after undocking from the command module. The long rods under the landing pads are lunar surface sensing probes.

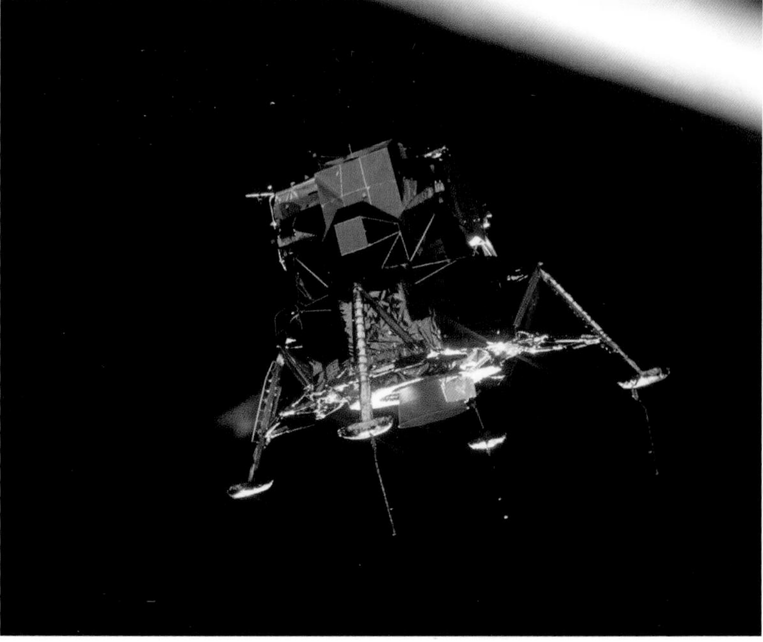

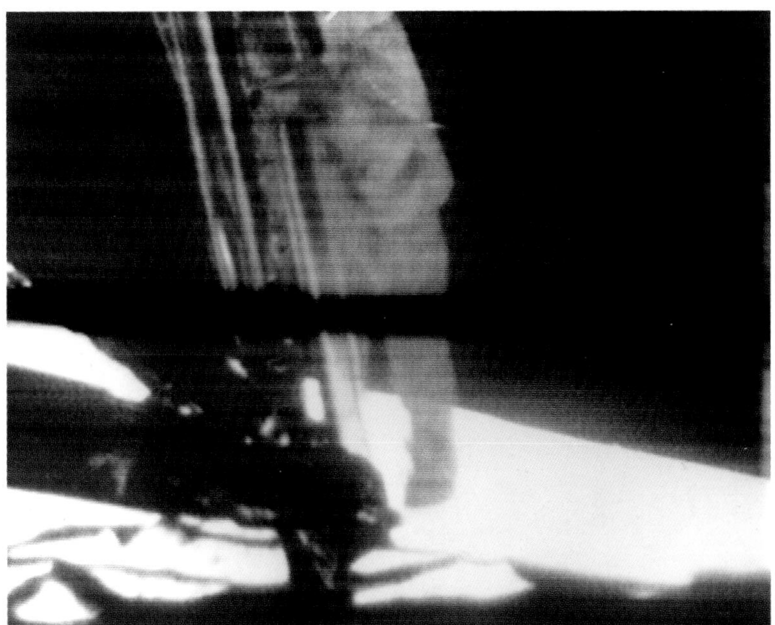

Above: The television image that millions around the world were waiting for on July 20th 1969. Armstrong steps off the ladder on to the lunar surface.

Right: Aldrin prepares to step on to the lunar surface.

Buzz Aldrin, in Armstrong's iconic picture of man on the Moon.

Above: Aldrin beside the US flag. The footprints of the astronauts are clearly visible in the soil of the Moon.

Right: One small step… Buzz Aldrin's bootprint.

Above: Buzz Aldrin and, to his right, the Solar Wind Composition experiment.

Above: A relieved Armstrong back in the LM after the moonwalk.

Right: Buzz's position on the right-hand side of the lunar module cabin. In the window is a 16mm film camera.

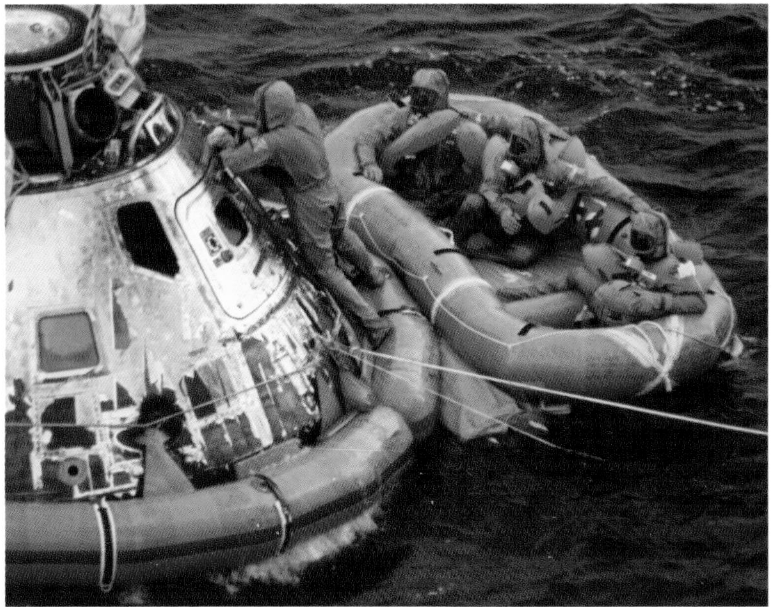

Above: Lt. Clancy Hatleberg closes the spacecraft hatch while the crew await rescue. Leaving *Columbia* Aldrin said he was struck by a 'peculiar sense of loss'.

Below: Officials join the flight controllers in celebrating the return of Apollo 11. Third from left (foreground) is Chris Kraft, fourth is George Low and fifth is Bob Gilruth.

Above: President Nixon welcomes the astronauts aboard the USS *Hornet*. The crew are already confined to the Mobile Quarantine Facility, MQF).

Above: Inside the quarantine facility.

Left: New York City welcomes the three astronauts, in a shower of ticker tape.

Chapter 13

SNEAKING UP ON THE PAST

For astronomers and geologists, Apollo 11 promised to offer a unique glimpse into the earliest years of the Moon, the Earth and the solar system. Relative to the Earth, the Moon is so big that some astronomers don't regard it as a moon at all but more the smaller partner in a binary planetary system. Many of the features on the near side are big enough to be seen with the naked eye, including mountainous regions rising to thousands of feet. But, since it orbits the Earth primarily (and does not orbit the Sun directly, in the way the Earth does), the Moon is not officially classified as a planet by the International Astronomical Union. It is better described as Earth's only natural satellite.

Information given to the press before the launch offered three competing theories for its origin.[1] While some experts believed the Moon evolved separately from (but at the same time as) the Earth, others thought its mass was once part of the Earth itself until driven into space by some cataclysmic impact. A third idea suggested it had wandered through space until captured by the Earth's gravitational field.[2] In the search for the truth, the Moon's most alluring feature was the promise it held of an unprecedented look into the long-lost history of the Earth. In the billions of years since our planet was formed, climate conditions and continental drift have erased important clues about the past. Seas have come and gone, coastlines have vanished and mountain ranges have been greatly eroded. The lunar surface, however, undisturbed by the processes alive on Earth, remains suspended in a deathly state of preservation. While the Earth's surface is rarely older than 500 million years, there was hope that an astronaut on a lunar mission might find rocks dating back to more than four billion years. In 1969, scientists imagined the Moon would reveal the dormant secrets of the solar system's formative years.

Quite how well preserved the Moon would prove to be depended partly on its history of seismic and volcanic activity. Geologists had been trying to land a seismometer on the surface since the Ranger 1 mission. It was hoped that the instrument carried by Apollo 11 would finally answer some of their questions about the Moon's internal structure. Whether they could find answers to other questions would depend on the astronauts' ability to find valuable examples of moon rocks and successfully bring them home. To stir things up a bit, Armstrong had considered sneaking a piece of limestone (the sedimentary product of sea creatures) into the LM and placing it into one of the two rock-boxes.[3] Samples of material were due to be sent to teams of scientists at 127 laboratories around the world, their research interests ranging from rare gases and metals to the analysis of lunar glass.[4] Looking for an exclusive insight into the earliest days of the Moon, they were hoping to be whisked away on a bountiful journey into the distant mists of time. It would all begin the moment someone stepped on to the surface.

For astronauts hoping to walk on the Moon, the most striking features were not the rocks found in a specific area but the life-threatening conditions prevalent across the entire lunar terrain. Unprotected by an atmosphere, during the height of the lunar day the ground soars to a temperature of 243°F. Radiation levels are significantly greater than on Earth, occasionally becoming dangerously high, and micrometeoroids regularly pelt the surface. Armstrong and Aldrin would have to overcome these dangers if they were to leave the relative safety of *Eagle*. And once outside, there was no certainty they would find what they were looking for. Their landing ground had been chosen largely because of its flat terrain rather than for any geological value. They had received little training specific to the site and they were not expected to retrieve much more than samples of whatever they found lying beside the spacecraft.[5] Yet slender as these pickings might be, once brought home to Earth they would be unique. Although the dangers were considerable, so were the potential rewards.

After being given permission to stay on the surface, Neil explained to Mission Control why he had taken his time to land: 'Hey, Houston, that may have seemed like a very long final phase. The auto-targeting was taking us right into a football-field-sized crater, with a large number of big boulders and rocks for about one or two crater diameters around it, and it required us going in [computer program] P66 and flying manually over the rock field to find a reasonably good area.' Meanwhile, in Houston, Joan Aldrin was passing round cigars when the TV coverage switched to a press conference being given by Janet. Deciding she ought to do the same, Joan left the revellers in her front room to join the reporters waiting outside.[6]

Much still needed to be done before Neil and Buzz could begin to relax. Soon after landing, they vented the descent engine's fuel tanks to prevent a dangerous build-up of vapour pressure. Since a leaking fuel tank on the ascent stage or a failure in their oxygen supply could force them to return to orbit sooner than planned, the next priority was to update their guidance systems with *Eagle*'s position relative to the stars. Releasing the cables holding him in position, and removing his helmet and gloves Buzz peered through *Eagle*'s alignment telescope. Determining relevant angles relative to specific stars, he updated the two computers. 'The first two hours on the lunar surface were, for me, the busiest part of the flight,' Buzz later said.[7] Neil tried to establish whereabouts they were on the ground. The navigation error they had encountered at the start of PDI had been stretched by his decision to fly virtually straight and level as they dodged the craters at the end of the flight. They had a rough idea of where they were, but neither the crew nor Mission Control could establish a precise position.

Armstrong: 'Houston, the guys that said that we wouldn't be able to tell precisely where we are, are the winners today. We were a little busy worrying about program alarms and things like that in the part of the descent where we would normally be picking out our landing spot. And aside from a good look at several of the craters we came over in the final descent, I haven't been able to pick out the things on the horizon as a reference as yet.'

Mission Control: 'Rog, Tranquility. No sweat. We'll figure out ... We'll figure it out. Over.'

Later, it was established that they had come down nearly four miles further west than expected. The landing site was roughly a third of a mile beyond the 'football-field-sized crater' that the radar had been bringing them towards. During their training this had been informally called West Crater. At some point in the Moon's history it had been gouged out of the landscape after a meteoroid smashed into the surface, creating an explosive force that had sent broken chunks of rock in all directions. Some could be seen through Buzz's window, away to the right of the spacecraft, while closer to the LM lay many smaller rocks, several up to three feet across.[8] Craters of all sizes lay everywhere, ranging from one to 100 feet wide. But the feature that dominated the landscape was the layer of dust blanketing the ground, which Neil compared to 'very fine silt'.[9] By making detailed assessments of what the surface looked like, the men were outstripping the capabilities of the Surveyor probes before they had even stepped out of the spacecraft. The LM was facing west, and while they could see ahead and much of the ground left and right, they couldn't look directly behind them, back towards the Sun.

Armstrong: 'The area out the left-hand window is a relatively level plain, cratered with a fairly large number of craters of the 5- to 50-foot variety; and some ridges which are small – 20, 30 feet high, I would guess; and literally thousands of little 1- and 2-foot craters around the area. We see some angular blocks out several hundred feet in front of us that are probably 2 feet in size and have angular edges. There is a hill in view, just about on the ground track ahead of us. Difficult to estimate, but might be a half a mile or a mile.'

Mission Control: 'Roger, Tranquility. We copy. Over.'

To Neil, the surface appeared warm and inviting. 'It looked as if it would be a nice place to take a sunbath,' he later remembered. 'It was the sort of situation in which you felt like going out there in nothing but a swimming suit to get a little sun.'[10]

Still passing across the near side, Michael Collins in *Columbia* had heard the exchange of transmissions during the landing. Twenty minutes after touchdown, he was encouraged by Neil's first impressions of the surrounding area.

Collins: 'Sounds like it looks a lot better than it did yesterday at that very low sun angle. It looked rough as a cob then.'

Armstrong: 'It really was rough, Mike. Over the targeted landing area, it was extremely rough, cratered, and large numbers of rocks that were probably some – many – larger than 5 or 10 feet in size.'

Collins: 'When in doubt, land long.'

Armstrong: 'That's what we did.'

Safely on the ground and reflecting on what had happened, Neil's heart-rate was now registering in the 90s; during the landing it was in the region of 150 beats per minute. While he continued to describe what he could see, Aldrin worked on the guidance systems. Now that they were on the surface they could see fewer stars than when coasting through space, and to enhance the accuracy of the updates Buzz used an estimate of vertical based on gravity.[11] Other tasks also demanded attention. *Eagle*'s mission timer was suggesting they had been in space for 902 hours, and after trying to reset it Houston asked the crew to vent the fuel tanks again.

At 3.59pm, 103 hours and 27 minutes into the mission, radio contact with *Columbia* was suddenly lost as the command module began its fifteenth orbit. For the first time on his own, Michael slipped behind the far side of the Moon. 'I am alone now,' he later wrote, 'truly alone, and absolutely isolated from any known life. I am it. If a count were taken, the score would be three billion plus two over on the other side of the Moon, and one plus God only knows what on this side.' Coasting through shadow, for 48 minutes Michael lay beyond the reach of any other human being. Gazing out of the window he could see nothing but stars; in the darkness even the Moon itself was concealed from him. Enveloped by a sense of freedom and peace, Collins regarded it as a magical experience that he described not as solitude but characterised more by a sense of confidence, 'almost exultation'.[12]

While waiting for the command module to return overhead, Neil and Buzz carried out a simulated countdown. All being well, this would serve as a rehearsal for the launch scheduled for the following day, although if they got into difficulty and needed to blast off as soon as possible they would be well prepared. The countdown was timed to reach zero upon *Columbia*'s return. This moment would be their third opportunity to leave the Moon earlier than planned, but again it wasn't needed. As Mike passed above it was clear that Armstrong and Aldrin would be staying where they were for a while longer yet, and they began to power down the LM.

Aboard *Columbia*, Collins approached the landing site from the direction of the Sun. Coasting at more than 3,600mph, 60 miles above the Sea of Tranquility, it took him just 13 minutes to pass above the general area of the landing ground. Before vanishing over *Eagle*'s western horizon, Michael used the sextant to look for the LM. By entering map co-ordinates into his computer, he hoped the sextant would be automatically aimed at the right spot on the surface. But the instrument was fitted at a steep angle and the presumed landing site crossed its field of view for just two minutes, giving him little time to find the LM. Houston later gave Michael new co-ordinates to check, and on each successive pass he searched up to two grid squares on his map, together totalling a square mile or so. Houston was giving him areas that were ten grid squares wide, and in the little time available he saw nothing but craters.[13] While coasting overhead, Collins could talk directly to Neil and Buzz, but once he sailed beyond their line of sight he relied on Houston to connect him. Of course, as soon as he passed round to the far side, Michael could talk to nobody.

During this period, Collins climbed out of his pressure-suit. By detaching the centre couch and placing it to one side, he made it easier to get in and out of the lower equipment bay where the sextant was installed. Turning up the lights and moving freely in the spacious cabin, Michael knew that TV commentators would be suggesting he was the loneliest man 'since Adam'. He didn't agree, and later wrote that 'Far from feeling lonely or abandoned, I feel very much a part of what is taking place on the lunar surface.'[14]

On the ground, the crew agreed to skip a four-hour rest period, following an idea they had discussed before launch. There had been concerns that it might take time to adjust to one-sixth gravity. But Neil felt they had done this remarkably quickly, and he advised Houston that the EVA would now begin in about three hours' time, at around 8pm.[15] The rest period had been included in the flight-plan partly to soak up any delays caused by technical difficulties. If the crew had lost time after the landing in dealing with a problem they might still have been able to begin the EVA on schedule. But since reaching the surface, Armstrong and Aldrin had not encountered any serious problems. They had the Moon at their feet and were keen to explore its surface.

Before preparing to leave the spacecraft they took their first meal break since breakfast, ten hours earlier. For Buzz this was an opportunity to pause and consider the almost unbelievable position they now found themselves in. After seeking the advice of Reverend Dean Woodruff, Aldrin had decided that at this point it would be appropriate to celebrate Holy Communion, and had agreed this in advance with Deke.[16] A leading atheist had taken NASA to court after the reading from Genesis by the Apollo 8 crew, consequently Slayton had advised Buzz not to broadcast the Communion text. Taking the wine and chalice from his personal preference kit, Aldrin read from a small card as he addressed Houston and the millions of people listening at home.

'This is the LM pilot. I'd like to take this opportunity to ask every person listening in, whoever and wherever they may be, to pause for a moment and contemplate the events of the past few hours and to give thanks in his or her own way. Over.' Buzz then took Communion in silence, the wine slowly swirling around the chalice in the Moon's low gravity.

Neil was left to his own thoughts, which soon he too would be sharing with the world. Only after they landed did he decide on what he would say once he stepped on to the surface.[17]

When they were ready, the men broke into the snacks they had brought with them and tucked into a brief cold meal. With empty food trays adding to the clutter in the cabin, they now found themselves up against an unexpected problem. In Houston, EVA training sessions had always begun with everything ready to hand. Now, their cramped cockpit was strewn with cameras and magazines, checklists and flight-plans and bulky equipment for extra-vehicular activity – and everything had to be either prepared for use on the surface or else stowed away.[18] In case the timer could not be restarted, Neil decided to leave his watch in the cabin rather than wear it during the EVA.[19] (Astronauts were given a standard-issue Omega Speedmaster Professional manual-wind watch, but Buzz considered it not up to the job.[20]) Tidying up the cabin, setting up cameras and retrieving kit from lockers, they took their time preparing everything carefully, wanting to get as much done as possible before they had to strap on their bulky backpacks.

Returning across the near side, Michael was trying to listen to their preparations. Later he said that the role of the command module at this point in the mission was to 'act like a good child and be seen and not heard'.[21] In single-handedly maintaining his position in orbit, and providing the closest thing Neil and Buzz had to a rescue agency, Collins himself was taking part in a test-flight. Armstrong later said, 'I think Mike's view, and I share it, was that his responsibility was to prove single-man operation of the command module – a very complex piece of machinery – for the first time, for an extended duration, and in conjunction with a spacecraft on the ground. He needed to demonstrate communications procedures and many other things.'[22] The dialogue between Houston and *Eagle* was initially transmitted to *Columbia*, but when Buzz complained that the relay signal was interfering with the LM's transmissions Houston switched it off. After losing contact with Tranquility Base, Michael felt 'somewhat cut out of the loop'.[23] Later he also inadvertently lost contact with the ground, and by the time the link was restored he was ready for something close to a chat.

Collins: 'Houston, *Columbia*. Over.'

Mission Control: 'Go ahead, *Columbia*.'

Collins: 'Roger. I finally got you back on [antenna] Omni D. I've been unsuccessfully trying to get you on the high gain, and I've gone command reset to process. How do you read me now?'

Mission Control: 'Roger. Reading you loud with background noise.'

Collins: 'Houston, *Columbia*. Could you enable the S-band relay at least one-way from *Eagle* to *Columbia* so I can hear what's going on?'

Mission Control: 'Roger. There's not much going on at the present time, *Columbia*. I'll see what I can do about the relay ... are you aware that *Eagle* plans the EVA about 4 hours early? Over.'

Collins: 'Affirmative ... I haven't heard a word from those guys, and I thought I'd be hearing them through your S-band relay.'

Mission Control: 'Roger. They're on about page Surface 27 in the checklist, proceeding in good time.'

Collins: 'Glad to hear it. You got a crowd there in MCC [Mission Control Center]?'

Mission Control: 'Roger your last [message], *Columbia*.'

Collins: 'Roger. I'd expect you probably have about nine CapComs and eleven flight directors with no place to plug in.'

Mission Control: 'Roger.'

Collins: 'That ratio might even be reversed ... glycol evaporator outlet temperature is 50 degrees and the comfort in here is just fine.'

Mission Control: 'Roger. We copy 50 degrees on the glycol – and comfort index fine.'

Collins: 'And, if you'll excuse me a minute, I'm going to have a cup of coffee.'

Neil and Buzz were struggling to keep abreast of their highly detailed EVA checklist. Since leaving Earth they had been relying on the life-support systems aboard *Columbia* and *Eagle* to supply them with oxygen, regulate the temperature and remove the threat of contaminants. Soon they would be dependent on their pressure-suits, and in making sure these were functioning properly they took all the time they needed.

The suits were made of layers of a range of materials, and after the Apollo 1 fire they were designed to be fireproof.[24] Closest to the body was a layer of Nomex material, designed for comfort, then came the rubber-coated nylon pressure bladder, followed by a nylon restraint layer. The pressure-suits used by all three crewmen were broadly similar, but those worn by Neil and Buzz had an integrated exterior cover protecting them from heat and micrometeoroids. This cover was made of two layers of rubber-coated nylon, followed by five layers of heat-resistant Mylar film, separated by four layers of Dacron spacer netting. These were covered by two layers of fireproof beta-cloth incorporating Kapton film, similar to the gold foil used on the LM's descent stage. The suit was then sealed in an outer shield of Teflon-coated beta-cloth. Worn outside the suit was a backpack which in NASA-speak was known as the portable life support system, or PLSS (pronounced 'pliss'). Secured to the suit by straps and clips, the PLSS pumped water through the thin tubes embedded in the astronaut's liquid-cooled underwear. It also supplied oxygen, which was released through a choice of vents at the neck and torso (Buzz preferred the former).[25] The PLSS removed carbon dioxide and other contaminants from inside the pressure helmet, and sent and received communications and telemetry to Earth (via the LM). Protected by a thermal insulation jacket, the Apollo 11 PLSS was able to support an astronaut for four hours. Coolant, oxygen and communications were supplied by tubes (their blue and red attachments becoming a characteristic of the suit), and all three could be adjusted using a remote control unit worn on the chest.

Above the PLSS was a second supply of oxygen that would last 30 minutes in an emergency, and on top of this was a communications antenna. Fitting over the bubble helmet (which Neil and Buzz treated with an anti-fog spray) was a protective polycarbonate shell, covered with layers of fabric. Held in place by straps, this was known as the lunar extra-vehicular visor assembly, or LEVA, and was equipped with two main visors. One protected the bubble helmet, while the other was gold-tinted and shielded the astronaut from sunlight (which could be further restricted using smaller side visors). The LEVA's gold visor was immediately distinctive, becoming the hallmark of pictures of men on the Moon.

Boots and gloves were already incorporated into the pressure-suits, but were supplemented by bulkier items designed to stand up to the harsh conditions of the surface. The over-gloves consisted of layers of thermal insulation, and included fingertips made of silicone rubber to provide a degree of sensitivity. Both Neil and Buzz had simple checklists sewn on to the gauntlet of their left glove. The exterior boots incorporated deep treads cut into a thick blue rubber sole, while the upper surfaces were made of Chromel-R woven steel. They rounded off the outfit, which in its entirety was known as the A7L extra-vehicular mobility unit (EMU). Weighing 183lb (on Earth), each EMU cost close to $1.5 million. Zips and hose connectors were locked in position, and these locks were then secured with additional 'snap locks', so that vital connections were doubly locked tight. 'I was pleasantly surprised by the quality of the environment inside the suit,' Armstrong later said.[26]

While preparing the two backpacks, Neil and Buzz discovered each had a control button that in all their simulations they had never encountered before. Worse, the remote control unit on the front of Neil's suit could not be secured to his PLSS. The 50-pin connecting cable had always proved tricky in training. Now that he was doing it for real, to Neil 'it began to look like we would never get those connectors made'.[27] On Earth the backpacks were worn with protective shoulder pads – but even without these, in reduced gravity they were still comfortable. *Eagle*'s small cabin had been tricky to operate in at the best of times. Now that Armstrong and Aldrin were wearing their PLSSs on top of their bulky suits, there was barely room to move. To Buzz, it felt like they were 'two fullbacks trying to change positions in a tent'.[28] They couldn't afford to damage anything in the fragile spacecraft so every move had to be made with great care.

Collins: 'Houston, *Columbia* on the high gain. How do you read?'

Mission Control: 'Roger, *Columbia*. Reading you loud and clear on the high gain. We have enabled the one-way MSFN relay that you requested. The crew of Tranquility Base is currently donning PLSSs. The LMP [lunar module pilot] has his PLSS on, comm checks out, and the CDR [commander] is checking his comm out now. Over.'

Collins: 'Sounds good. Thank you kindly.'

Eventually the men were ready to disconnect their suits from *Eagle*'s oxygen and water supplies. While preparing to switch over to their backpacks, they found that the PLSS cooling units were taking longer to start working than they had estimated. Depressurising the LM also took longer than expected. By the time they finished their preparations it was 9.36pm and they were more than an hour and a half over the time they had estimated for the beginning of their EVA. TV networks around the world were forced to wait for the sensational pictures they had promised their viewers. Without knowing what was holding things up it was hard to know when the moonwalk would actually start. Janet

Armstrong suggested the delay was caused by Neil thinking of something suitable to say. Joan passed the time listening to music. Pat Collins found the process frustrating and compared the uncertainty to labour pains. When someone pointed out that Michael would be behind the Moon when the door finally opened, Rusty Schweickart said he'd be back around again, then added, 'It's going to be a long night for these guys if he isn't.'[29]

Finally, Buzz was ready to open the hatch, down to the left of his knees. Given its narrow width it would have been impossible for the men to carry the TV camera, tools, flag and package of experiments with them, so these had been stored in compartments on the outside of the LM. Moving about in the awkward, stiff suit, Buzz was surrounded by scores of switches and circuit breakers, each set in a deliberate position. With a great deal of effort he bent down but found the hatch wouldn't open. Having not completely vented the oxygen from the cabin they found that pressure of just a tenth of a pound per square inch was still pushing the hatch shut against the vacuum outside.[30] Only by tugging on it could Buzz break its seal and allow the remaining oxygen to escape. Glittering ice crystals were instantly formed, vanishing through the broken seal as quickly as they were created.[31] Having successfully turned the handle, Buzz pulled the hatch in towards him – and there, outside, lay the surface of the Moon, now theirs to explore.

Chapter 14
A WALK ON THE MOON

By the time Apollo 11 was ready to launch, few people still believed that heavy objects settling on the Moon would sink into the dust. Yet in preparing to step on to the unfamiliar surface, Neil took the precaution of securing himself to the LM.[1] Before sliding through the hatch, he set up the lunar equipment conveyor (LEC), a strap and pulley system that would allow a camera, and other awkward items, to be hoisted to and from the cabin. With one end of the LEC secured to the cockpit and the other to his suit, Neil faced the rear of the cabin. Kneeling down, he pushed his feet out through the hatch until he found the porch at the top of the ladder. After testing his ability to pull himself back inside, Armstrong got down again and began to slide out backwards. Guided by comments from Aldrin, he moved slowly to avoid snagging his PLSS.

Aldrin: 'OK. You're not quite squared away. Roll right a little. Now you're even.'

Armstrong: 'OK, that's OK.'

Aldrin: 'That's good. You've got plenty of room to your left.'

Armstrong: 'How am I doing?'

Aldrin: 'You're doing fine.'

Aldrin: 'OK. You want this bag?'

Once outside on the porch, the first thing Neil did was throw out the bag, containing empty food trays and other equipment which couldn't be used again. After this he pulled a handle on the left of the porch which opened a compartment built into the hull of the LM beneath Buzz's window. Known as the MESA (modular equipment stowage assembly), it contained the crew's sampling tools and rock-boxes. As its door hinged down it exposed a TV camera fastened to its inside surface and aimed at the foot of the ladder. By closing a circuit breaker on the instrument panel Buzz sent power to the camera, allowing a snowy picture of Neil to be transmitted back to Earth.

( )

The decision to include television cameras on the mission had been controversial from the start. Transmitting and receiving live pictures from the Moon created complications on the ground and required equipment to be added to a spacecraft that was already severely restricted in the weight it could carry. In early 1969 George Low asked Chris Kraft to look into the subject. Kraft was anxious to see 'those first steps live' and tried to do what he could to build the necessary support.[2] Gene Kranz's unpredictable communications officer Ed Fendell was given the task of looking at the question in detail, with a view to producing a favourable report. 'I should have given them better direction,' Kraft later fumed.[3] At a meeting attended by almost everybody with an interest in the subject, Fendell finished his report with the thought that there was no reason to have television on the Moon. Kraft erupted. 'I can't believe what I'm hearing,' he shouted above a clamour of raised voices. 'We've been looking forward to this flight – not just us, but the American taxpayers and in fact the whole world – since Kennedy put the challenge to us.'[4] With the old hands leading the way, the pro-TV camp quickly gathered force and the room soon came round to their way of thinking. Once Armstrong and the crew gave them their support the matter was officially settled. But privately, reservations remained. Referring to it as 'a bloody nuisance of an afterthought', Michael Collins wrote that 'we simply didn't have time to fool around with it'.[5]

There wasn't time to develop a colour camera for use on the lunar surface; instead, the LM was equipped with a Westinghouse slow-scan model that shot ten frames a second in black and white. It was fitted with a bayonet mount, designed to allow the lens to be changed by an astronaut wearing a pressure-suit. Television pictures, transmitted via the LM, would be received by the Manned Space Flight Network tracking stations at Honeysuckle Creek in eastern Australia and Goldstone Lake, California. Due to the crew's four-hour rest, as scheduled in the flight-plan, the EVA would begin twenty minutes after the Moon had set at Goldstone. This meant NASA would be principally relying on the facilities in Australia. Honeysuckle was supported by the Parkes Radio Telescope in central New South Wales, which, like Goldstone, was equipped with a giant 210-foot antenna.

In eastern Australia the landing occurred at 6:17am local time on the morning of 21 July. Although it would be seven hours before the Moon was high enough to be seen from Parkes, this was anticipated in the flight-plan.[6] So when the crew decided to drop their rest period, the Parkes technicians feared the whole thing would be over before the Moon had risen above their part of the world. They would have to give way to Goldstone. But as the preparations aboard the LM dragged on, hope returned to Parkes. By the time Neil finally emerged from the hatch, six hours and 22 minutes after the landing, the Moon was just beginning to rise above New South Wales.[7] Yet now the Parkes technicians faced a new problem. Parkes scientist John Sarkissian recalled that the winds were so high the huge dish was forced to operate well outside safety limits.[8]

The signal from Parkes was sent to Sydney, and there it was converted into a format suitable for domestic television before being distributed to the Australian TV networks. At the same time, it was relayed to a communications satellite over the Pacific and then passed to Houston, where a six-second delay was added in case anything happened to the astronauts. The pictures were then ready to be released to the rest of the world. Parkes, Honeysuckle and Goldstone received television from the Moon simultaneously and Houston briefly distributed the picture from

Goldstone and Honeysuckle before deciding for technical reasons to stay with Parkes for the rest of the EVA.[9]

( )

Before a television audience of 600 million people, a fifth of the human population, Neil slowly climbed down the ladder on the leading leg of the LM.[10] The ladder stopped three feet above the ground to prevent it being bent by protruding rocks. In Mission Control the TV picture was projected on to a screen on the front wall, creating a ripple of excitement among Cliff Charlesworth's team of flight controllers.

Mission Control: 'OK. Neil, we can see you coming down the ladder now.'

Armstrong: 'OK. I just checked getting back up to that first step, Buzz. It's … the strut isn't collapsed too far, but it's adequate to get back up.'

Mission Control: 'Roger. We copy.'

Armstrong: 'Takes a pretty good little jump.'

Jumping down from the last rung, Neil found himself standing in the landing pad. Before he went any further he rehearsed the jump back on to the ladder to be sure it wouldn't be a problem later. He then jumped back down into the landing pad.

Armstrong: 'I'm at the foot of the ladder. The LM foot-pads are only depressed in the surface about one or two inches, although the surface appears to be very, very fine grained, as you get close to it. It's almost like a powder. Ground mass is very fine.'

Armstrong: 'I'm going to step off the LM now.'

Still tethered to the cabin by the LEC, Armstrong stepped off the landing pad, placing his left foot on the dust and tentatively shifting his weight. To Buzz it seemed like a 'small eternity' before he heard Neil say anything.[11]

Armstrong: 'That's one small step for man; one giant leap for mankind.'

In the years after the mission, Neil's apparently tautological historic words have become the subject of much debate.

Armstrong later said he intended to say 'one small step for a man' and believed he had done so. Yet, despite extended efforts by some to prove the contrary, the 'a' appears to be missing from the sound recording of Neil's transmission. Nevertheless, for most people his message was clear.[12]

Armstrong: 'The surface is fine and powdery. I can kick it up loosely with my toe. It does adhere in fine layers, like powdered charcoal, to the sole and sides of my boots. I only go in a small fraction of an inch, maybe an eighth of an inch, but I can see the footprints of my boots and the treads in the fine, sandy particles.'

Having put both feet on the surface, for the first time Neil let go of the ladder and disconnected himself from the LEC tether. In front of him stretched an arid desert, bathed in bright daylight beneath a dark night sky. The silent wastes appeared to be tan, but their colour dissolved to shades of grey the closer he looked towards areas of shadow. Armstrong thought the ground beside his feet was a charcoal grey, 'the colour of a lead pencil'.[13] Close to the spacecraft, light grey dust lay scattered across small rocks that had been thrown aside during the landing. Further away were two features that could be described as low hills, while several hundred feet to the right of the LM lay a boulder field. Without high ground or a hazy atmosphere to obscure his view Neil could see as far as the horizon, which curved away in all directions. For 360 degrees there was nothing but dust, rocks and craters. Only *Eagle* offered any relief from the stark landscape, its golden foil and silver-coloured components reflecting the dazzling light like a gleaming beacon of precious metal. Bathed in sunshine, the LM cast depths of shadow of breathtaking blackness.

Armstrong: 'There seems to be no difficulty in moving around – as we suspected. It's even perhaps easier than the simulations of one-sixth g that we performed in the various simulations on the ground. It's absolutely no trouble to walk around.'

Armstrong: 'OK. The descent engine did not leave a crater of any size. It has about one-foot clearance on the ground. We're essentially on a very level place here. I can see some evidence of rays emanating from the descent engine, but a very insignificant amount.'

The airy black and white TV pictures gave Neil a ghostlike appearance, and at first it was hard to make out what was happening. In the Armstrong household, six-year-old Mark heard his father describe the lunar dust, and asked, 'How come I can't see him?'[14] But to the technicians at Parkes, the controllers in Houston and fascinated TV viewers around the world, an astronaut was definitely moving about on the surface. The Moon was now within man's reach as much as next-door's back yard. Joan Aldrin clapped her hands and cried, 'I can't believe this.'[15]

While the TV pictures might have been a little murky, Neil and Buzz were equipped with a modified Hasselblad 500EL camera, capable of taking pinpoint photographs on 70mm film. Buzz used the LEC to lower the camera down to the surface, and once he had retrieved it Neil secured it to a mount on the remote control unit on his chest.

Armstrong: 'I'll step out and take some of my first pictures here.'

Mission Control: 'Roger. Neil, we're reading you loud and clear. We see you getting some pictures and the contingency sample.'

After taking a series of panoramic pictures while standing at the bottom of the ladder, Armstrong left the shadow of the LM and walked ten feet over to a sunlit area. Here, within the view of the 16mm film camera in Buzz's window, Neil took a tool from a pocket on his left leg and collected an initial sample of dust. He deposited the material into a bag, which he then returned to his pocket. If the EVA ended early, Armstrong still hoped to be able to bring home a small selection of material.

Armstrong: 'This is very interesting. It's a very soft surface, but here and there where I plug with the contingency sample collector, I run into a very hard surface. But it appears to be a very cohesive material of the same sort. I'll try to get a rock in here. Just a couple.'

Armstrong: 'It has a stark beauty all its own. It's like much of the high desert of the United States. It's different, but it's very pretty out here. Be advised that a lot of the rock samples out here – the hard rock samples – have what appear to be vesicles [small cavities] in the surface. Also, I am looking at one now that appears to have some sort of phenocrysts [crystals].'

Mission Control: 'Houston. Roger. Out.'

Aldrin: 'OK. Are you ready for me to come out?'

Armstrong: 'Yeah. Just stand by a second. I'll move this [the LEC strap] over the handrail. OK.'

Fifteen minutes after Neil arrived on the surface, Buzz emerged from the hatch, guided and photographed by Armstrong.

Aldrin: 'OK. Now I want to back up and partially close the hatch. Making sure not to lock it on my way out.'

Armstrong: 'A particularly good thought.'

As Buzz paused on the ladder, television viewers saw a man apparently taking time to reflect. In fact Buzz was relieving himself before jumping down to the landing pad. 'The whole world was watching, but I was the only one who knew what they were really witnessing,' he later remarked.[16] Still holding on to the ladder, Aldrin marvelled at the emptiness stretching before him.

Aldrin: 'Beautiful view!'

Armstrong: 'Isn't that something! Magnificent sight out here.'

Aldrin: 'Magnificent desolation.'

'I felt buoyant,' Buzz wrote, 'and was full of goose pimples.'[17] He was intrigued by the lunar dust; comparing it to sand on a beach he found it notably different. When kicking grains of sand, some quickly fall down while others scatter a little further, but Buzz discovered that in doing the same thing on the Moon *every* grain travelled the same distance. Both men found that as fine as the grains of dust were they had a tendency to stick together, forming clods of material that crumpled under their boots.[18]

Together with his suit and backpack, on Earth Buzz weighed a total of 360lb. On the Moon this was cut to 60lb. Taking his first few steps away from the LM, Aldrin found that it was easier to walk if he leant forward a little. With practice, he was able to move around as comfortably as if he were at home. When Buzz tried to run he felt himself to be much lighter, and realised that if he were to stop suddenly he would topple over. Instead he had to wind down slowly, being careful to avoid rocks near the LM which were slippery with dust. Neil tried jumping a few times but found that the PLSS had a tendency to make him tip over backwards, and after nearly falling he decided 'that was enough of that'.[19] In the piercing sunshine, Buzz thought that Neil's pressure-suit gleamed 'like no white I had seen before', making Armstrong stand out on the surface almost as brightly as the LM.[20]

Neil found that the suit was largely comfortable and allowed him to move around freely – with the exception of bending down to pick up things from the surface. This had already been established during practice sessions at home, influencing the design of the soil-sample tools. The suits also prevented the men kneeling, and this fact, together with the difficulty of retrieving things with their hands, led to concerns about dropping things. Objects could be scooped up using tools but this was a time-consuming process. 'The suit was cumbersome and bulky and not really easy to operate,' Neil recalled, 'but on the whole, it performed remarkably well. When you think that the surface temperature was something north of 100 centigrade, in terms of the [air] flow and the cooling, it was really doing an excellent job, and allowed us to really do most of the things we planned to do – although perhaps not as quickly as we would have liked to do them.'[21]

After familiarising himself with the surface and the suit, Aldrin watched Armstrong remove the cover of the commemorative plaque that was secured between the rungs of the ladder. Since the ladder was attached to the descent stage, the plaque would remain on the Moon.

Armstrong: 'For those who haven't read the plaque, we'll read the plaque that's on the front landing gear of this LM. First there's two hemispheres, one showing each of the two hemispheres of the Earth. Underneath it says "Here Men from the planet Earth first set foot upon the Moon, July 1969 A.D. We came in peace for all mankind." It has the crew members' signatures and the signature of the President of the United States.'

Aldrin later said, 'This was one place where I felt signing "Buzz" was too informal'.[22]

Neil then took the TV camera from the MESA and after changing its lens he carried it to a point some 60 feet away to the right of the LM, where it could cover a wider region of the surface. While looking for a suitable spot, something in a crater caught his eye. This was later thought to be a glassy material produced during the intense heat and shock of a high-velocity impact. 'We were supposedly in a nondescript area,' Aldrin recalled, 'but there was far more to investigate than we could ever hope to cover. We didn't even scratch the surface.'[23] The camera's white cable, leading back to the LM, retained a spiral kink that left it sticking up above the surface. Once it became dirty it was hard to see. Neil caught his foot in it and needed help from Buzz to untangle himself.

While Armstrong was working on the camera, Aldrin set up the solar wind collector about ten feet to the right of the LM. Looking like a narrow flag, one foot wide and four and a half feet tall, the SWC was made of thin aluminium foil. Deployed facing the Sun, it was designed to capture particles of helium, neon and argon that were found in the solar wind.

After setting up a table at the MESA, Buzz helped Neil remove the US flag from its case beneath the ladder. They carried it back towards the TV camera and chose a spot around 15 feet from the LM. The flag was designed to hang from a telescopic arm that extended perpendicularly from the pole. But despite pulling as hard as they dared, the arm wouldn't properly extend and Armstrong and Aldrin feared an imminent public relations disaster.[24] The flag was left distinctly ruffled – as were conspiracy theorists, who later wanted to know why it looked as if it were being blown by the wind. After coping with this problem, the flag still threatened to upstage the men when it refused to be pushed into the ground. The dust on the surface was relatively soft but deeper down it became hard to penetrate. Inside his gloves Neil's hands were sweating and he found it difficult to grip the staff and drive it into the soil.[25] At first the flag defied attempts to make it stand upright but eventually Armstrong forced it into the dust by about seven inches, far enough to prevent it toppling over live on television.

In the meantime Collins, now on his eighteenth orbit, returned from his enforced silence and began to pass across the near side once again.

Collins: 'Houston, *Columbia* on the high gain. Over.'

Mission Control: '*Columbia*, this is Houston. Reading you loud and clear. Over.'

Collins: 'Yeah. Reading you loud and clear. How's it going?'

Mission Control: 'Roger. The EVA is progressing beautifully. I believe they are setting up the flag now.'

Collins: 'Great!'

Mission Control: 'I guess you're about the only person around that doesn't have TV coverage of the scene.'

Collins: 'That's all right. I don't mind a bit. How is the quality of the TV?'

Mission Control: 'Oh, it's beautiful, Mike. It really is.'

Neil took a picture of Buzz saluting the flag and then he went back to the MESA to begin collecting more material from the surface.

Mission Control: 'Tranquility Base, this is Houston ... we'd like to get both of you in the field-of-view of the camera for a minute. Neil and Buzz, the President of the United States is in his office now and would like to say a few words to you. Over.'

Armstrong: 'That would be an honour.'

Mission Control: 'All right. Go ahead, Mr President. This is Houston. Out.'

Nixon: 'Hello, Neil and Buzz. I'm talking to you by telephone from the Oval Room at the White House, and this certainly has to be the most historic telephone call ever made. I just can't tell you how proud we all are of what you [unclear] For every American, this has to be the proudest day of our lives. And for people all over the world, I am sure they, too, join with Americans in recognising what an immense feat this is. Because of what you have done, the heavens have become a part of man's world. And as you talk to us from the Sea of Tranquility, it inspires us to redouble our efforts to bring peace and tranquility to Earth. For one priceless moment in the whole history of man, all the people on this Earth are truly one; one in their pride in what you have done, and one in our prayers that you will return safely to Earth.'

Armstrong: 'Thank you, Mr President. It's a great honour and privilege for us to be here representing not only the United States but men of peace of all nations, and with interests and the curiosity and with the vision for the future. It's an honour for us to be able to participate here today.'

Nixon: 'And thank you very much and I look forward, all of us look forward to seeing you on the Hornet on Thursday.'

Armstrong : 'I look forward to that very much, sir.'

Armstrong later told Aldrin that he had known the president might call. Buzz, who had had no such knowledge, wrote that the experience made him feel awkward. He felt he ought to have made some profound comment, but without wanting to intrude on the conversation he took what seemed to be the next best alternative and remained silent.[26]

After the call, the astronauts went back to the MESA where Buzz picked up the Hasselblad camera left there by Neil. While Armstrong collected samples of rocks, Buzz took pictures of the impression his boots made in the dust. As he set up collection bags and the sample return containers on the table, Neil found he was working in shadow. He wanted to avoid collecting material that had been contaminated by the exhaust from the descent engine, and in looking for an undisturbed sunlit area he walked back towards the solar wind collector. He tried to scoop up as many different types of rocks as he could before taking them back to the table and dropping them into a bag. Making around ten trips to this spot, Armstrong repeatedly crossed back and forth from harsh sunlight into the LM's stark shadow and he found his eyes were sometimes slow to adjust. During training it had been suggested that he could possibly twist the LM immediately before landing, to make sure the MESA was in sunlight. But Armstrong remembered that 'I was very reluctant to do any fancy manoeuvring on the first lunar touchdown'.[27]

Taking the camera from Buzz, Neil photographed the sample area before taking a full-frontal picture of Aldrin. Buzz, his gold visor pulled down, stands with his left arm raised as he prepares to read from the checklist on his glove, in what has since become one of the most iconic photographs of all time. Neil then gave the Hasselblad back to Buzz before taking from the MESA a stereoscopic camera, designed to snap close-up images of the lunar dust. It was a late addition to the flight, and Neil found it tricky to operate.[28] Now half an hour behind their timeline, Armstrong tried the stereoscopic camera while Buzz removed the seismometer and the laser reflector from the LM's scientific equipment bay.

Aldrin: 'OK; have you got us a good area picked out?'

Armstrong: 'Well, I think right out on that rise out there is probably as good as any.'

Buzz set up the seismometer about 50 feet to the left of the LM, placing it behind a large rock to shield it from the effects of lift-off. While he made sure it was level and that the solar panels were properly deployed, Neil set up the reflector. Made up of many finely machined quartz corners, the device would allow the measurement of small changes in the motion of the Moon or the Earth.

Mission Control: 'Neil, this is Houston. Over.'

Armstrong: 'Go ahead, Houston.'

Mission Control: 'Roger. We've been looking at your consumables, and you're in good shape. Subject to your concurrence, we'd like to extend the duration of the EVA 1-5 [i.e. 15] minutes from nominal. We will still give Buzz a hack at 10 minutes prior, for heading in. Your current elapsed time is 2 [hours] plus 12 [minutes]. Over.'

Armstrong: 'OK. That sounds fine.'

After setting up the experiments, their next task was to take a documented sample of the surface. This involved Buzz taking two core samples from an area that Neil would then closely photograph. While Aldrin prepared the tubes, Armstrong decided to break from the timeline and dash back to the 80-foot crater they had flown over just before landing. He knew this would be his best opportunity to take a look beneath the surface. The crater lay nearly 200 feet away to the east of the spacecraft, towards the Sun, and in the true spirit of exploration Neil freely ran across the ground, carrying the Hasselblad and the stereoscopic camera. He found that the crater was 20 feet deep, and after peering inside he spent a minute taking pictures.

Researchers Joe O'Dea and Thomas Schwagmeier have shown that if Neil had been standing on the penalty spot in front of the right-hand goal on a soccer pitch, the LM would be just in front and to the right of the other penalty spot.[29] The TV camera would be in the far right-hand corner, the flag would be between the camera and the LM, and the seismic and LRRR experiments would be over towards the left-hand boundary line.

Neil ran back to the LM just as Buzz was preparing to push in the first core sample, near the solar wind collector. Both Armstrong and Aldrin described attempts to run as more of a lope – somewhere between a run and a walk, where both feet would be off the ground at the same time. Finding that their actual 'foot motion' was quite slow, Neil said that while loping he would find himself 'waiting to come down' in between strides.[30] At home in Houston, Pat Collins exclaimed, 'Look at Neil move. He looks like he's dancing – that's the kangaroo hop.'

Joan Aldrin thought that Buzz too was doing a form of kangaroo bounce and she asked, 'How can you be serious about what you're doing when you're doing that?' For her, the moonwalk had an unreal quality about it, as if she were watching a Disney cartoon. In the Armstrong household, there was some debate as to who was saying what since Neil and Buzz sometimes sounded alike. Ricky suggested his father was easy to recognise since 'he always says uhhh'.[31]

Taking two core tube samples, Aldrin needed a hammer to drive them into the ground. Nearby, Neil used a pair of long-handled tongs to retrieve any unusual examples of rocks he could find. He dropped them into a collection bag which was then put into one of the sample return containers. Hammering as hard as he could, Buzz found it difficult to force the tubes into the ground. After retrieving them, he then took down the solar wind experiment, rolled it up and placed it back in its container. This was also put into a sample return container, then both were sealed.[32]

Mission Control: 'Buzz, this is Houston. It's about time for you to start your EVA close-out activities.'

Aldrin: 'Roger. That's in progress.'

Grabbing the magazine from the stereoscopic camera, Buzz put it in a pocket and started up the ladder, which he found was slippery now that his boots were covered in dust. Neil collected the magazine from the Hasselblad, attached it to the first rock-box, then secured both to the LEC strap so that he could haul them up to the cabin. Halfway up, the magazine fell off. Neil leant on the ladder, picked it up and attached it to the second rock-box while Buzz pulled the first into the cockpit. Neil then attached the magazine and the second box to the LEC. Coming at the end of the EVA, this was one of the most demanding moments during the walk on the surface. 'I worked real hard at a high workload,' Neil recalled.[33]

Armstrong: 'OK. I've got one side [of the LEC] hooked up to the second box and I've got the film pack on.'

Aldrin: 'OK. Good.'

Armstrong: 'Boy, that filth from on the LEC is kind of falling over me while I'm doing this.'

By the time they got the second box into the cabin everything was caked with dust, including the LEC. 'We all looked like chimney sweeps,' Armstrong later remarked.[34] Neil asked Buzz whether he had remembered to leave the Apollo 1 badge and the two Russian medals on the surface. They had imagined improvising some form of ceremony but Buzz described it more as an 'afterthought'.[35] Taking a pouch containing the items from his pocket, he threw it down on to the ground. Neil then jumped on to the ladder and climbed back into the spacecraft, once again guided by Buzz.

Locking the hatch shut at 12.09am, they completed their post-EVA checklist before re-pressurising the cabin. Both felt a little disappointed that they had barely succeeded in getting everything done. After removing their helmets, they discovered a strange smell which Neil described as 'wet ashes' and Buzz as slightly 'metallic'.[36] This smell was later noticed by other astronauts on subsequent lunar missions, one describing it as 'spent gunpowder'.[37]

Meanwhile, aboard *Columbia*, Michael, on his nineteenth orbit of the Moon, was just coming back into radio contact with Houston. He had taken photos of the surface but still hadn't located Tranquility Base.

Mission Control: '*Columbia*. *Columbia*. This is Houston. Over.'

Collins: 'Roger, *Columbia* on [omni antenna] Charlie. How do you read?'

Mission Control: 'Roger, *Columbia*. This is Houston. Reading you loud and clear on Omni Charlie. The crew of Tranquility Base is back inside their base, repressurised, and they're in the process of doffing the PLSSs. Everything went beautifully. Over.'

Collins: 'Hallelujah.'

Aboard *Eagle*, Neil and Buzz were collecting the items they wouldn't be needing again, and dumping them into a bag. This would be jettisoned, along with the backpacks, in an attempt to save as much weight as possible. The Hasselblad camera had already been abandoned on the surface. Using a second camera, Buzz took a picture of a very relieved-looking Neil, then looked back at the flag and at the boulder field beyond it.[38] The rocks appeared to be relatively close and the flag seemed to be right outside the window, but he knew that they hadn't got anywhere near the boulders and the flag was 15 feet away. With all available space now taken up by the bubble helmets, LEVAs, PLSSs, camera magazines and rock-boxes, the men tried to find space to eat. Armstrong later said that 'With all that stuff in the cockpit, there's really no place left for people to relax.'[39] They then read through a checklist of switch positions, and in doing so Buzz noticed what at first glance appeared to be a serious problem.

Aldrin: 'Houston, Tranquility. Do you have a way of showing the configuration of the engine arm circuit breaker? Over. The reason I'm asking is because the end of it appears to be broken off. I think we can push it back in again. I'm not sure we could pull it out if we pushed it in, though. Over.'

While wearing his PLSS, at some point Buzz had knocked off the switch that would send electrical power to the ascent engine – on which they were depending to get home. 'The little plastic pin simply wasn't there,' Buzz wrote.[40]

Nearly a minute after Aldrin reported the problem, Houston responded.

Mission Control: 'Tranquility Base, this is Houston. Our telemetry shows the engine arm circuit breaker in the open position at the present time. We want you to leave it open until it is nominally scheduled to be pushed in, which is later on. Over.'

The crew's next task was to depressurise the cabin in order to open the hatch and eject the backpacks and the bag of rubbish. Before they began, for the first time in the mission Deke Slayton came directly on the radio.

Slayton: 'Tranquility Base, Houston.'

Armstrong: 'Go ahead. Tranquility Base here.'

Slayton: 'Roger. Just want to let you guys know that, since you're an hour and a half over your timeline and we're all taking a day off tomorrow, we're going to leave you. See you later.'

Armstrong: 'I don't blame you a bit.'

Slayton: 'That's a real great day, guys. I really enjoyed it.'

Armstrong: 'Thank you. You couldn't have enjoyed it as much as we did.'

Slayton: 'Roger.'

Aldrin: 'It was great.'

Slayton: 'Sure wish you'd hurry up and get that trash out of there, though.'

Armstrong: 'Yes. We're just about to do it.'

Slayton: 'OK.'

In depressurising the cabin, this time they used a second valve to speed up the process, and with their suits connected to the LM's life-support system they opened the hatch. Neil threw the two backpacks down the ladder, along with their over-boots and the bag containing food trays and other litter.

Mission Control: 'Tranquility. We observed your equipment jettison on the TV, and the passive seismic experiment recorded shocks when each PLSS hit the surface. Over.'

Armstrong: 'You can't get away with anything any more, can you?'

Armstrong and Aldrin had now been awake for more than 21 hours, and with their last task of the day completed, at 3.23am Houston bid them goodnight. Although filthy with dust, the cockpit was tidier and there was now room to sleep. Settling down for the seven-hour rest period, Buzz lay on the floor while Neil sat on the ascent engine cover, his feet suspended by a cable lashed above the instruments. They kept their helmets and gloves on, hoping that this would shut out some of the whirring noise from the life-support system.[41] But as the temperature dropped, both men found it hard to doze.

On Earth, Pat Collins was also finding it hard to sleep, and in the small hours of the morning she strolled outside to gaze up at the Moon.[42] In a Vietnamese prison camp, air force pilot Sam Johnson – an old friend of Aldrin's – approached one of the guards and, pointing to the Moon, said, 'That's ours now.'[43]

Chapter 15

MISSION ACCOMPLISHED

Tired and still wearing their bulky pressure-suits, Armstrong and Aldrin shivered in the cold cabin of the LM. Warning lights and electroluminescent instrument panels could not be switched off and the surface reflected sunshine so brightly, light penetrated the thin window shades. Even the Earth kept Neil awake, since it lay directly in his line of sight through *Eagle*'s alignment telescope. 'It was just like a lightbulb,' he later recalled.[1] The cabin was shielded from the Sun by the bulk of the spacecraft, so without a heater it became uncomfortably chilly. Raising the temperature of their cooling systems had little effect and neither Neil nor Buzz could properly sleep.

Stretched out in the comparative luxury of the command module, Michael was woken by Mission Control at 9.31am on Monday, 21 July.[2] He was immediately given instructions on navigation tasks before vanishing behind the Moon at the start of his twenty-fourth orbit. Houston then called Tranquility Base, and after a breakfast of cold snacks Neil and Buzz powered up the computers and the rendezvous radar. Houston still hadn't established their position, and to provide further details Buzz was asked to track the command module using the rendezvous radar. Once he'd done this, Mission Control changed the checklist procedures and asked Buzz to switch off the radar until they reached orbit, to avoid overloading *Eagle*'s computer. During the descent the computer had been so busy it had triggered a series of alarms. During the ascent it would be busier still. 'We were concerned,' admitted Charlie Duke, 'very concerned.'[3]

In preparing the spacecraft for launch, Buzz had to find an alternative way to close the engine arm circuit breaker, which had been damaged the previous day by his PLSS. Looking for a suitable object that could be inserted into the hole, he found that a felt-tipped pen fitted perfectly, and he successfully pushed the circuit breaker into the correct position. Electrical power could now reach the engine when a switch was pushed by Neil. If they hadn't been able to close the circuit, they would have had to resort to more complicated ways to get round the problem. After preparing the 16mm camera in Buzz's window, they put their gloves and pressure helmets back on and waited for the countdown to end. Once again, timing was essential. They had to launch at precisely the right moment if they were to catch up with Collins before running out of electrical power.

When Michael approached the Sea of Tranquility on his twenty-fifth orbit, Houston asked him to look for *Eagle* one final time. The LM had been on the surface for a little over 21 hours, but Collins had not been able to spot it once. Mission Control had refined the search, and with less than 30 minutes to go before lift-off Collins was given a new location that later proved to be only 220 metres away from *Eagle*. By that point, feeling 'like a nervous bride',[4] Michael wanted to focus only on the launch. 'My secret terror for the last six months,' he wrote, 'has been leaving them on the Moon and returning to Earth alone.'[5] In Houston, Janet Armstrong believed that as long as *Eagle* lifted off from the surface, 'Mike will come and get them, wherever they are'.[6] Collins, however, knew that if Neil and Buzz failed to reach 50,000 feet, the lowest height he could descend to, there was little he could do to help them. 'One little hiccup and they are dead men,' he wrote.[7]

Mission Control: 'Tranquility Base, Houston.'

Aldrin: 'Roger. Go ahead.'

Mission Control: 'Roger. Our guidance recommendation is PGNS, and you're cleared for take-off.'

Aldrin: 'Roger. Understand. We're number one on the runway.'

While pressurising the two fuel tanks Buzz discovered that one failed to respond, which for him was 'the worst thing we could have seen'.[8] The problem began to resolve itself, however, and the flight controllers were not especially worried – but they were slow to reassure the crew.

At 12.54pm – 21 hours and 37 minutes after landing – the launch countdown reached zero. Neil pushed switches that ignited four explosive nuts and bolts and severed the electrical cable connecting the two stages of the spacecraft. After Armstrong pushed the engine arm switch, Aldrin then punched the computer's 'proceed' button, allowing the software to ignite the engine. A second went by and nothing happened. Then, in a sudden jerk of movement, the engine fired, and as the ascent stage smoothly rose vertically from the surface its exhaust plume knocked over the flag and shredded the foil on the descent stage. A swarm of sparkling ribbons of Kapton scattered sunlight in its wake.[9]

As they accelerated towards orbit, Neil and Buzz noticed that in the time they had been on the ground the terminator had crept back, revealing features they had not previously seen. Gravity gradually fell away as they raced towards the escape velocity of 3,400mph, and some of the lunar dust in the cabin began to float about. Although the ascent engine was relatively small, the ascent stage was by far the lightest spacecraft in the Apollo system, and compared to the pick-up truck characteristics of *Columbia* it handled like a sports car. 'It's a very light, dancing vehicle,' Armstrong later said.[10] Aldrin felt that 'each time you hit the thrust controller, the vehicle behaved as if somebody hit it with a sledge hammer, and you just moved'.[11]

After seven minutes the engine shut down, and at an altitude of ten miles above the Moon they entered orbit. Coasting at nearly 3,800mph towards their highest orbital point, 47 miles above the surface, the men removed their gloves and helmets as the spacecraft raced through shadow. Once they switched on the rendezvous radar, Armstrong and Aldrin began to play catch-up with the command module. *Eagle* would perform the rendezvous procedures while *Columbia*, coasting at an altitude of 60 miles, remained the passive partner. Mission Control took a back seat as Neil and Buzz pursued the command module around the Moon, progressively raising their orbital altitude over three hours, as perfected during the Gemini missions.[12]

With *Eagle* chasing him from below, Collins worked flat out to make sure he was holding a stable position. Operating on his own, during the course of the day he would have more than 850 key strokes to make on the computer. As the LM drew closer, Michael kept his eye glued to the sextant and was taken aback when he spotted *Eagle* coming up towards him. 'For the first time, I had the feeling that that son of a gun was really going to get there in one piece,' he wrote.[13] Relief was starting to replace his long-harboured anxiety. Having slowed to match *Columbia*'s speed, *Eagle* took up a position less than 100 feet from the command module. The two spacecraft were behind the Moon, and for the moment the crew were unable to tell Houston that everything was going to plan. As soon as they came back into radio contact Mission Control was anxious to know how things were developing.

Mission Control: '*Eagle* and *Columbia*, Houston. Standing by.'

Armstrong: 'Roger. We're station-keeping.'

It was the news the controllers had been waiting for, and relieved applause filled the Mission Operations Control Room.[14]

With the two spacecraft flying in formation, the three astronauts were ready to begin their docking manoeuvres. Neil was preparing to adjust *Eagle*'s position when he realised he was about to look directly into the Sun. In swiftly taking alternative action, he inadvertently jammed the LM's guidance system, triggering warning lights and freezing the autopilot. Just a few feet short of the command module, Armstrong and Aldrin were forced to switch to the backup computer. But they managed to hold their course, and at 4.35pm the combined command and service modules successfully docked with the lightweight ascent stage. Working on the probe and drogue assembly inside the tunnel, once again Michael smelt the odour of burnt material that he had noticed on the first day of the flight.[15]

As they prepared to enter the clean cabin of the command module, Neil and Buzz knew they risked carrying with them a quantity of lunar dust. To keep this to a minimum, they unstowed the LM's small vacuum cleaner and tried to collect as much dirt as possible. It wasn't only cleanliness they were concerned about. Before the mission, fears of so-called 'moon-bugs' had prompted NASA to adopt an extensive set of precautions. Virtually none of the 127 teams of scientists awaiting samples of moon rocks believed there was any point in testing the material for forms of life. Nevertheless, Congress was persuaded to hurriedly authorise the construction of a special quarantine facility in Houston, as part of the elaborate plan to isolate potential bugs. The plan also included protective rubber suits, the vacuum cleaner for *Eagle* and a period of quarantine for the crew – beginning the moment Neil and Buzz left the surface.[16]

Aboard *Columbia*, Michael raised the level of the cabin's oxygen supply. Once the hatches were open the increased pressure would flow into the LM, rather than the other way round.[17] As Armstrong and Aldrin returned through the tunnel he was ready to kiss his crew-mates, but settled for firm handshakes instead. Smiling and giggling like schoolboys, Neil, Buzz and Michael warmly congratulated each other and joked about the difficulties that had caused so much anxiety and which had now been successfully completed.[18] Later, Buzz returned to *Eagle*, and telling Mike to 'get ready for those million-dollar boxes' he passed the two sample containers through the tunnel. These were then zipped up in white cloth bags before being stored in the lower equipment bay. Since they had been sealed in the vacuum of space Michael was unable to open them, but Neil showed him the contingency sample so that he could see the dark powder for himself. 'Sort of like wet sand,' was his first impression.[19]

As part of their preparations to leave lunar orbit, the crew collected rubbish, urine bags and items they no longer needed and dumped everything inside the LM. *Eagle* was to be jettisoned and left to freely coast around the Moon. Its decaying orbit would eventually bring it crashing down to the surface. Once Neil and Buzz had taken a last look at the cabin of their spacecraft, the hatches were replaced and Collins fired pyrotechnics to separate the two vehicles. 'There she goes,' said Armstrong, 'it was a good one.'[20] At 6.41pm, Collins flew *Columbia* away from the LM, and as they began to leave it behind they saw its thrusters fire as *Eagle* loyally held its position.[21]

Two hours later, *Columbia* was passing the near side on the twenty-ninth orbit when Charlie Duke offered to read them some news.

> Starting off: Congratulatory messages on the Apollo 11 mission have been pouring into the White House from world leaders in a steady stream all day. Among the latest are telegrams from Prime Minister Harold Wilson of Great Britain and the King of Belgium. The world's press has been dominated by news of Apollo 11. Some newsmen estimate that more than 60 per cent of the news used in papers across the country today concerned your mission. The *New York Times* which, as we mentioned before, has had such a demand for its edition of the paper today – even though it ran 950,000 copies – said it will reprint the whole thing on Thursday as a souvenir edition. And Premier Alexei Kosygin has sent congratulations to you and President Nixon through former Vice President Humphrey who is visiting Russia. The cosmonauts have also issued a statement of congratulations. Humphrey quoted Kosygin as saying, 'I want you to tell the President and the American people that the Soviet Union desires to work with the United States in the cause of peace.

Duke then moved on to news from home.

> You're probably interested in the comments your wives have made. Neil, Jan said about yesterday's activities, 'The evening was unbelievably perfect. It is an honour and a

> privilege to share with my husband, the crew, the Manned Spacecraft Center, the American public, and all mankind, the magnificent experience of the beginning of lunar exploration.' She was then asked if she considered the Moon landing the greatest moment in her life. She said, 'No, that was the day we were married.' And Mike, Pat said simply, 'It was fantastically marvellous.' Buzz, Joan said – apparently couldn't quite believe the EVA on the Moon. She said, 'It was hard to think it was real until the men actually moved. After the Moon touchdown, I wept because I was so happy.' But she added, 'The best part of the mission will be the splashdown.'

After one more orbit, Michael was ready to make the final significant burn of the mission, the trans-Earth injection manoeuvre, which would launch them out of lunar orbit and send them on their journey home. At 11.55pm they ignited the engine, and for two minutes and 30 seconds a stream of flame accelerated them from less than 3,700mph to 5,900mph, enough to free them from the grip of the Moon. Coasting back to Earth, once again they maintained the passive thermal control roll – slowly turning the spacecraft in order to distribute evenly the impact of the Sun's heat. As on the outward journey, platform alignments, fuel cell purges and waste dumps needed to be regularly tended to, but other than their routine chores there was little to do beyond watching the Moon get smaller. 'What did we do with our free time?' Collins asked himself later. 'We mostly just waited. We had plenty of time to eat, had plenty of time to get rested up.'[22]

At last they had time to complete some minor tasks. It had been hoped that before *Eagle* parted from *Columbia*, prior to the descent to the surface, the crew would have time to frank a first-day cover commemorating a new 10-cent stamp showing an astronaut on the Moon. The idea was that the envelope would bear proof that it had been handled by the crew only hours before the landing. They had been given ink and a rubber stamp marked with the date 20 July, but they did not have a chance to use them until 22 July, the seventh day of the mission.[23]

That night, as they aimed their camera out the window during their TV broadcast, Charlie Duke identified what he could see.

Mission Control: 'We see the Earth in the centre of the screen ... and see some land-masses in the centre, at least I guess that's what it is. It's very hazy at this time on our Eidephor [screen]. Over.'

Collins: 'Believe that's where we just came from.'

Mission Control: 'It is, huh? Well, I'm really looking at a bad screen here. Stand by one. Hey, you're right.'

Collins: 'It's not bad enough not finding the right landing spot, but when you haven't even got the right planet!'

Mission Control: 'I'll never live that one down.'

Collins: 'We're making it get smaller and smaller here to make sure that it really is the one we're leaving.'

Mission Control: 'All right. That's enough you guys.'

On the following day, Wednesday 23 July, Houston informed the men that Nixon was planning to meet them on their return. The president was about to embark on a trip to seven nations and would begin his travels with a visit to the USS *Hornet*, the aircraft carrier that was waiting to recover the crew. As well as international updates there were also domestic headlines: 'A little closer to home here, back in Memphis, Tennessee, a young lady who is presently tipping the scales at eight pounds, two ounces, was named "Module" by her parents, Mr and Mrs Eddie Lee McGhee. "It wasn't my idea," said Mrs McGhee, "it was my husband's." She said she had baulked at the name Lunar Module McGhee, because it didn't sound too good, but apparently they have compromised on just Module. Over.' The crew were also told that the residents of Seattle, Portland, Vancouver and San Francisco were planning to make their cities visible by switching on all their available lights.

That evening Janet Armstrong and Pat Collins took their children to Mission Control to watch the crew's final TV broadcast.

With the mission drawing to a close, each of the men had prepared a personal statement. After Neil delivered a brief introduction, he handed over to Michael. Collins was conscious that while TV audiences around the world knew of the three astronauts, Apollo 11 represented the work of thousands of people who did not receive the same recognition. Paying tribute to those who had put together the hardware on which their lives depended, he thanked the 'American workmen' who had built the spacecraft, the technicians who had assembled and tested everything and everyone who had worked on the mission at the Manned Spacecraft Center. 'This operation,' said Collins, 'is somewhat like the periscope of a submarine. All you see is the three of us, but beneath the surface are thousands and thousands of others, and to all those, I would like to say, thank you very much.'

Buzz took a different tack, and suggested that the mission was representative of something more than the will of one nation. To him, Apollo 11 stood 'as a symbol of the insatiable curiosity of all mankind to explore the unknown'. He added, 'Neil's statement the other day upon first setting foot on the surface of the Moon, "This is a small step for a man, but a great leap for mankind," I believe sums up these feelings very nicely.' Buzz then finished with a verse from Psalms before handing back to Armstrong, who ended the broadcast with a farewell to everyone listening in: 'We would like to give a special thanks to all those Americans who built the spacecraft, who did the construction, design, the tests, and put their hearts and all their abilities into those crafts. To those people, tonight, we give a special thank you, and to all the other people that are listening and watching tonight, God bless you. Goodnight from Apollo 11.'

After the broadcast, looking down at the lights shining on the west coast of North America, the crew prepared for the final night of the mission.

By the morning of Thursday 24 July the crescent-shaped Earth was growing rapidly larger in the windows. Gravity was pulling the spacecraft towards the planet with ever-increasing speed. By the time the crew hit the atmosphere they would be travelling at nearly 25,000 miles per hour, 40 per cent faster than a Mercury capsule.[24] At this velocity, if they came in at too steep an angle they would burn up; if their approach were too shallow they risked bouncing off the atmosphere on a trajectory that would take them back into space. The acceptable gap between the two was just 40 miles wide. If the Earth were the size of a football, this re-entry corridor would be little thicker than the edge of a sheet of paper.

After securing loose items in the cabin, the men took seasickness pills while working their way through the re-entry checklist.[25] Sitting in the left-hand commander's seat, Michael kept an eye on their progress by monitoring the angle of the horizon, assisted by Neil in the middle couch who was reading from the DSKY. The computer would guide them down, but Collins had to be prepared to take over should anything unexpected develop. 'As our journey draws to a close,' he later wrote, 'the consequence of a screw-up looms as large as life, literally.'[26]

Columbia's shape was designed to produce a small amount of lift, like an aircraft wing. The angle at which the spacecraft fell could be altered by thrusters embedded in its hull, allowing some control over its path through the atmosphere. Collins had been expecting to fly just over a thousand miles during re-entry, but fearing turbulent weather in the landing zone Houston advised him to increase the ground-track to 1,500 miles. The *Hornet* had already moved to the new position, which was 800 miles southwest of Hawaii. By using the thrusters to change the angle of lift, the command module's flight-path could be extended. But the new landing point was at the far end of its range and Michael was concerned that should he need to take over from the computer he would be 'hard-pressed to come anywhere near the ship'.[27]

Twenty-seven minutes from re-entry, *Columbia* entered the Earth's shadow. Then, with just 14 minutes to go, the service module was jettisoned. After keeping the crew supplied with water, oxygen and electrical power throughout the mission, it was no longer needed, and the men watched it fly past their windows on its way to burning up in the atmosphere. At launch, Apollo 11 had been heavier than 3,300 tons; now all that remained was the command module, which weighed less than six. *Columbia*'s blunt side, previously hidden by the service module, was protected by a heat-shield. Made of resin, the shield was ablative, in that as the temperature rose pieces of it would gradually flake off, exposing cooler material underneath.

Once their altitude fell to 67 miles (400,000 feet) above the Earth, the crew began to be buffeted about as *Columbia* ripped a burning hole through the night sky above the Solomon Islands, north-east of Australia.[28] Wearing only their flight-suits, and sitting with their backs to the direction of travel, the men plummeted 33 miles towards the ocean while covering the first 500 miles of the ground-track. Falling too fast to push the air out of the way, *Columbia* hurtled through a blaze of colour as it collided with gaseous molecules beneath the heat-shield, smashing into them, generating friction and creating bursts of heat that accumulated into a fiery ball. 'We started to get all these colours past the windows,' Collins later remembered, 'subtle lavenders, light blue-greens, little touches of violet, and great variations mostly of blues and greens.'[29] As flames rolled back the blackness of space, Michael believed they were 'flooding the entire Pacific basin with light'.[30] The disintegration (or ionisation) of the molecules blocked radio signals, and for three minutes the crew were unable to talk to Houston. At 5,000°F, temperatures outside the spacecraft were hotter than the exhaust from the F-1 engines that had launched the men eight days earlier.[31] The command module's silver-coloured thermal shielding helped to prevent heat penetrating the cabin, and inside the crew were kept cool by the spacecraft's life-support system.

Eventually *Columbia* flattened out, at which point each man felt six and a half times heavier than his normal weight on Earth as the g-forces peaked at their maximum level. The spacecraft flew the next 500 miles more or less horizontally, but it was approaching the landing point too quickly and risked overshooting it. Following a predetermined plan, the computer shifted the command module's angle of attack, sending *Columbia* thousands of feet back up into the atmosphere. Then, as they dived down to cover the final 300 miles towards the landing point, the crew were given a second dose of high g-forces. By the time the spacecraft had descended to an altitude of 15 miles, it was plunging almost vertically.

At 24,000 feet, a cover protecting the apex of the command module was jettisoned and two small drogue parachutes were released, stabilising the descent.[32] At 10,000 feet, three much larger parachutes opened. Looking up out of the windows, Michael watched the orange and white streams of cloth blossom into three great canopies. Together they eased *Columbia* through banks of stratocumulus clouds. The men struggled to regain control of their arms and legs, now suddenly heavy with gravity.

Once radio contact resumed, Houston stayed off the air as much as possible while the navy prepared to retrieve the crew.

Rescue helicopter: 'Swim 1. Have a visual dead ahead about a mile.'

Hornet: '*Hornet*. Roger.'

Rescue helicopter: 'Roger. This is Swim 1, Apollo 11.'

Armstrong: '300 feet.'

Rescue helicopter: 'Roger. You're looking real good.'

Rescue helicopter: 'Splashdown!'

Less than ten minutes after beginning re-entry, *Columbia* plunged into the Pacific 812 miles south-west of Hawaii. While it was 11.50am in Houston, locally it was 7.50am, ten minutes before dawn. Splashing down into water was seen as a softer, and therefore safer, option than hitting the ground; even so, in coming down at 20mph they still landed with a solid jolt. Buzz needed to push in circuit breakers that would allow Michael to eject the parachutes, but he was thrown forward with the impact, and as they filled with water the parachutes dragged *Columbia* over before they could be cut. After eventually releasing the canopies,

Michael had to shut down the spacecraft's power. Before he could do this, however, he had to quickly close the vents that had allowed the cabin to match atmospheric pressure. This instruction on the checklist, circled and underlined, was intended to prevent the 'moon bugs' escaping, and in Michael's mind failure to carry it out would mean that 'the whole world gets contaminated, and everybody is mad at you'.[33]

The spacecraft was designed to float, either right way up in the 'stable 1' position or upside down in 'stable 2'. Suspended by their restraints in the uncomfortable stable 2 position, Buzz, Michael and Neil waited for three flotation balloons to roll *Columbia* over. In the intervening seven minutes a snorkel valve began to let in seawater, and while waiting for navy swimmers to be carried out to them by helicopter they took another seasickness pill. The spacecraft had landed within 12 miles of the *Hornet*, the prime component in an extensive recovery force that was directed from a room next to the MOCR in Mission Control. Consisting of two ships in the Pacific and three in the Atlantic, the force was supported by 13 aircraft at seven bases around the world.[34]

Briefly opening *Columbia*'s hatch, navy swimmer and decontamination specialist Lieutenant Clancy Hatleberg threw in three 'biological isolation garments', or BIGs. Rubber suits equipped with a hood, a visor and a biological filter, the outfits were the next stage in the plan to prevent the risk of contamination.

Standing in the lower equipment bay, the hatch closed once more, Neil put his on first, followed by Mike; Buzz slipped into his while sitting in a couch. After helping each other secure zips and fasteners, they scrambled out of *Columbia* and clambered into a raft bobbing in the purplish-blue water beside the spacecraft. While trying to ignore a growing sense of seasickness, the men sprayed each other with disinfectant, again as part of the decontamination regime. With their face-masks fogging up, they were then hoisted up into one of the Sea King helicopters hovering above, leaving the swimmers to shut the hatch and disinfect the command module.

The safe retrieval of the crew was filmed from another helicopter, and seeing the men on television, Janet, Joan and Pat allowed themselves to celebrate. In the Armstrong household, everyone jubilantly waved flags while drinking champagne.[35] The TV pictures were also shown in Mission Control, where huge cigars were handed out to the controllers, astronauts and VIPs cheering and applauding in the Mission Operations Control Room. Those who had watched the splashdown from the viewing gallery joined the party in the MOCR, and with the celebrations in full swing there was barely room to move.

Aboard the helicopter the men were greeted by NASA doctor Bill Carpentier, who would have jumped into the water and helped them to safety had one of them been injured. To Buzz, *Columbia* had represented safety and security; now, looking down on it from above, the spacecraft seemed small and helpless. He was struck by a 'peculiar feeling of loss'.[36]

After touching down on *Hornet*, the helicopter was lowered into one of the ship's vast hangars. Uncomfortably warm in their BIGs and struggling to keep their balance, Neil, Michael and Buzz stepped on to the deck to the accompaniment of a brass band. While waving to hundreds of sailors, and a sprinkling of VIPs, they briskly walked into a silver trailer set up 30 feet away. The Mobile Quarantine Facility (MQF) would be their home until they got to Houston, and only Carpentier and technician John Hirasaki were allowed to join them.

The crew had been living and working in virtual isolation since June, and now that they were home, for the moment nothing would change. Their period of quarantine had been set at three weeks, and after spending three days of this in space they would pass another three in the MQF. The airtight trailer contained a lounge area, a galley (complete with microwave oven), bunk-beds and washing facilities. After a series of hurried medical checks, the men showered and, for the first time in more than a week, put on clean clothes. When they were ready, a curtain was drawn back from a window and there, waiting outside to greet them, was Richard Nixon. The president was genuinely enthralled to meet them and during a short, light-hearted exchange he described himself as the 'luckiest man in the world'.[37]

Two hours after the men arrived aboard the ship, *Columbia* was hauled from the water and hooked up to the MQF via a plastic tunnel. With assistance from the crew, Hirasaki went into the spacecraft, and after making sure the thrusters and pyrotechnics were safe he retrieved the films and rock-boxes. These were passed to the outside world via an airlock in the MQF before being taken by separate helicopters to Johnston Island, from where they were flown to Houston.

As the ship sailed for Hawaii, the enormity of their mission struck Buzz once again, as it had during training.[38] Now, however, there was no longer a flight to focus on. Instead, there was a growing realisation that there would be months of public functions to attend. Later, Buzz came to realise that it was his time on the *Hornet* that marked the 'start of the trip to the unknown'.[39]

The following day Michael crawled back into *Columbia* to retrieve the flight-plans and checklists. Before leaving, above the sextant he wrote 'Spacecraft 107 – alias Apollo 11 – alias *Columbia*. The best ship to come down the line. God Bless Her. Michael Collins, CMP'.[40]

On arrival at Pearl Harbor the MQF was loaded aboard a flatbed lorry, and as it was gently driven to an airfield crowds of onlookers accompanied the crew's slow journey. It was then hoisted aboard a C-141 transport jet for the six-hour flight to Houston. Just after midnight on the morning of Sunday 27 July, Neil, Michael and Buzz landed at Ellington Air Force Base, near the Manned Spacecraft Center. The MQF was hauled out of the aircraft and taken to a brightly lit area where again another enormous crowd awaited them. This time, however, the well-wishers included friendly faces from home. Wearing Hawaiian carnation leis, Janet, Joan and Pat, accompanied by their children, could do little more than swap smiles through a window and hold stilted conversations over telephones. But the women could see for themselves that their men were safe, and that now they were in Houston they were home. 'Oh, thank God,' said Joan, through her tears.[41]

The rocks, the men and even *Columbia* were all to be accommodated in a purpose-built quarantine facility at the Manned Spacecraft Center known as the Lunar Receiving Laboratory (LRL). The three-storey LRL was based on plans drawn up in 1966 by an inter-agency committee composed of government departments, the National Academy of Sciences and NASA. As well as quarters for the crew – and the technicians, doctors, housekeepers and cooks looking after them – the LRL also contained elaborate facilities to store and analyse lunar material in vacuum conditions. Sealed from the outside world by biological barrier systems, the LRL's inhabitants would be held for the remaining two weeks of the quarantine period.

They could be held for longer if more time were needed to prove that anyone who had come into contact with the rocks posed no risk to Earth.[42] This would be established in the ultra-clean facilities of the sample operations area. Here, on 26 July, the rock-boxes were opened under vacuum, preserving them in their pristine state. After initial analysis, they were to be transferred, still under vacuum, to laboratories where their mineral and chemical content could be assessed. In examining the rocks for any evidence of life, samples would be exposed to plants, fish, birds, oysters, flies, cockroaches, prawns and germ-free mice, which would then be closely watched for evidence of a reaction. Fifty feet below the LRL, other samples would be assessed in a radiation laboratory using gamma ray spectrometry techniques. Meanwhile, *Columbia* would also be examined so that problems during the flight could be investigated. In designing and building the LRL, no expense had been spared. Nothing like it existed anywhere else in the world.

From Ellington, the MQF was driven by lorry along roads

packed with more excited onlookers before being parked beside the LRL. Once a germ-proof barrier had been set up, the men were released into their new home. In the following days they spent most of their time preparing written reports and delivering day-long debriefing sessions, attended by many different people. Sitting behind glass, they answered questions about every detail of the flight, for the benefit of Deke Slayton, the crew of Apollo 12, flight controllers, systems engineers, managers, mission planners and everyone else involved in returning to the Moon. The crew in turn were told the precise location of the landing site, determined by the film taken through Buzz's window. They were also given news that NASA had not wished to broadcast during the mission, including details of the fatal incident involving Senator Ted Kennedy at Chappaquiddick. By the time they came to be asked questions about the LRL itself, Collins simply replied, 'I want out.'[43]

Every now and again the LRL population was joined by people who had been accidentally exposed to lunar material. They too had to be confined to quarantine until the mice proved there was nothing to worry about. In the meantime a colony of red ants voluntarily broke in and the crew were happy to point out to the technicians in charge of the supposedly impregnable facility that the number of insects seemed to be steadily growing.[44] In between debriefings, and visits from family members (who were also held back by glass), the men tackled some of their burgeoning mail-bags, signing pictures and answering requests for autographs. They also discussed their future.

Collins had already told Deke that he would not be taking part in another flight, but he didn't yet know what he wanted to do. Nor did he know what Buzz and Neil were intending, 'but whatever it is, we should support each other', he wrote, adding, 'I'm not sure we have yet built the basis for that support'.[45] Buzz, however, was struggling to support himself emotionally. In a picture taken during the debriefings, he later came to believe that 'everyone else appears relaxed and there I am – eyes wide and looking frightened'.[46] At the centre of his worries lay concerns about what to do next. He was conscious that many public commitments were being planned for the crew and he saw it as his duty to accept them. Since these would keep him away from training for quite a while, he realised that the chances of flying again were shrinking. Decisions about his future were being made for him, and Buzz came to feel that things were slipping out of his control. It would be nearly three years before he felt able to make a new start.[47]

Earlier than anticipated, at 9pm on the evening of Sunday 10 August, the quarantine was declared over and the doors of the LRL were opened. Within two days Neil, Buzz and Michael would begin the first of many press conferences, speeches and guest appearances where they would be received as a team of dashing superheroes. For one last evening, however, they were still mere men. Taking what Collins described as 'their first smell of the earth in nearly a month', they went home to be reunited with their families.[48]

EPILOGUE

In all, Project Apollo lasted a total of 12 years, marshalling the industrial resources of a superpower in one of the biggest government enterprises mounted in peacetime. Apollo 11 represented only a fraction of the work that went into America's race to reach the Moon. *Eagle* was not the only lunar module NASA built, any more than Neil Armstrong was the only man able to fly it. While the crew were training for their mission, other astronauts were preparing for subsequent flights, and these preparations continued even after the race had been won by Neil and Buzz. In November 1969, Pete Conrad and the crew of Apollo 12 survived a lightning strike during lift-off, before landing with pinpoint accuracy beside Surveyor 3 in the Ocean of Storms. Conrad relished the chance to walk on the Moon and did so with an exuberance typical of his larger than life attitude.[1]

By the time Apollo 13 launched in April 1970, flying to the Moon was becoming old news and the TV networks struggled to provoke interest. Jim Lovell and Fred Haise (both of whom had been part of the Apollo 11 backup crew) planned to explore a highland region near the Fra Mauro crater but were lucky to make it home after an explosion crippled their service module. After Apollo 14 successfully landed in February 1971, NASA decided to press ahead with plans for more ambitious missions. The final three flights carried enough consumables for a three-day stay on the surface and were equipped with lunar rover 'moon buggies'. In April 1972, Charlie Duke got to see what the Moon was like for himself when he served as the lunar module pilot aboard Apollo 16.

NASA had planned to land on the surface a total of ten times.

But on 20 July 1969, the relentless drive to send a man to the Moon lost much of its energy in the enthusiastic cheering and flag-waving echoing through Mission Control. After all the political posturing, the hard work and the faith, the dream had finally been realised. With the space race effectively over, new priorities demanded attention and cash, and within six months missions began to be cancelled.

When Michael Collins was recovering from surgery in 1968 he had been offered a job at headquarters, in the Apollo applications programme.[2] This work focused on applying old Apollo hardware to new projects, and at the top of the list was a manned orbital space station. Unlike the lunar missions, the space station was dedicated to scientific research from its inception, a fact reflected in its name – Skylab. The Moon having been conquered, scientific research came to lead NASA's agenda, and since this was best done within easy reach of Earth, Skylab was confined to Earth orbit. Similarly, Skylab's successor, the International Space Station, operates at an altitude of 220 miles – little more than the distance between London and Paris. It is serviced by the space shuttle, which itself can fly no higher than 400 miles from the Earth. Since Apollo 17 returned from the Moon in 1972, no-one has travelled any further than a few hundred miles above the atmosphere.

In the years since Apollo came to an end, lunar samples have been studied in laboratories around the world. Neil and Buzz brought back 48lb of surface material, including 50 rocks of various sizes.[3] After initial analysis in the Lunar Receiving Laboratory, samples were distributed to international research teams, many of whom came to Houston in January 1970 for the first annual lunar science conference. Over four days, the conference heard that some of the rocks were basalts, formed from molten lava, but many were breccias – fragments of older rocks that had been fused together during the shock and heat of a meteoroid impact.[4] Some of the smaller samples were entirely different to the larger rocks and were thought to have come from the lunar highlands. More than 20 minerals known on Earth were identified, along with three new ones unique to the Moon. The basalts appeared to be between three and four billion years old, while the dust included particles believed to have been formed 4.6 billion years ago. The search for evidence of living organisms that had begun in the LRL failed to find any positive results.

For years after Apollo 11, scientists argued over the origin of the Moon. Based on evidence gathered by all the lunar missions, over time most came to believe that it was formed from the Earth. It appears that a huge asteroid, the size of Mars, collided with the Earth in its earliest years, sending an enormous amount of material into space which coalesced into the Moon.[5] The asteroid, meanwhile, slumped into the core of the Earth – where it remains. Today, the bulk of the material retrieved from the Moon is still stored in what was formerly the Manned Spacecraft Center and which in 1973 was renamed the Johnson Space Center. In total, Apollo astronauts gathered 842lb of rocks, more than a third of a ton of material. Collected from the pristine lunar surface, the rocks are protected in sterile conditions in order to preserve their purity.

Ironically, the Moon itself was not treated in the same way. In the quest for moon rocks, NASA left 118 tons of waste material on the lunar surface, including redundant Ranger, Surveyor and Lunar Orbiter probes, spent third stages of Saturn rockets (that were deliberately targeted at the Moon), abandoned LM descent stages, lunar rovers and other equipment, and the crashed remains of LM ascent stages. Untouched by wind or rain, Tranquility Base remains today as it was in 1969. Scattered pieces of Kapton litter a site marked by the presence of man. The overboots worn by Neil and Buzz, the food trays they ate from, their TV camera and its cable, the flag and their footprints, and of course the complete descent stage, all lie undisturbed.

While little may have changed at Tranquility Base, those involved in the mission have long since moved on. After leaving his post as MSC director in 1972, Bob Gilruth served at NASA headquarters before retiring in 1973. He died in 2000, still largely unrecognised outside NASA for the enormously influential role he played throughout the first decade of America's space programme. His former MSC role went to Chris Kraft, the 'father of Mission Control'. Kraft stayed with NASA until 1982, when he took on consultancy work. Gene Kranz worked on the remaining Apollo flights and in 1974 was promoted to the post of Deputy Director of Mission Operations, becoming director in 1983. Working on space shuttle flights, Kranz stayed with NASA until his retirement in 1994. Steve Bales also stayed with the agency, becoming Deputy Director of Operations at Johnson until he left NASA in 1996 to go into business.

Two days after they were released from the Lunar Receiving Laboratory, Neil, Michael and Buzz gave a detailed press conference in Houston. The next day, they took part in ticker-tape parades in New York and Chicago, accompanied by their wives and children. That night they attended a banquet in Los Angeles, hosted by Nixon, where each of them was presented with the Presidential Medal of Freedom, America's highest civilian honour. The same award was also collectively given to the flight controllers, the medal received on their behalf by Steve Bales.[6] In the following weeks there were further ceremonies and parades, in Houston and in the men's home towns. During a trip to Washington, on 15 September they returned the first-day cover commemorative envelope and stamp to the US Post Office, and the next day they delivered speeches to a joint session of Congress. There then followed the Giant Step Apollo 11 Tour. Visiting 26 countries in 38 days, Armstrong, Aldrin and Collins gave more speeches, received a variety of accolades and were greeted by heads of state including the Emperor of Japan, Queen Elizabeth, the Shah of Iran, General Franco, the Pope and Marshal Tito.

While Janet, Joan and Pat developed their genuine friendship, during this time the men themselves grew further apart. Removed from a uniting sense of purpose, Armstrong, Aldrin and Collins were confronted by an array of choices. As they began to consider their futures, they found they were looking in different directions and that gaps were beginning to open up between them. By the time they went their separate ways, their relationship was largely based on a shared past rather than ongoing mutual interests. Later, in looking back on his experiences with John Young during Gemini, and with Neil and Buzz during Apollo, Michael felt that the personality traits they had in common made it difficult to maintain an easy friendship. 'We are all four loners,' he wrote, 'and as a result I am not as close to any of them as the flight experiences we have shared might indicate.'[7] Collins, for one, was content to accept that it was time to move on from NASA and find a new challenge. He felt that 'Being an astronaut was the most interesting job I ever expect to have, but I wanted to leave before I became stale in it.'[8]

Taking up a post at the State Department as Assistant Secretary for Public Affairs, Collins retired from NASA in 1970. For a year he mixed in political circles but ultimately decided it wasn't for him and left to join the Smithsonian Institution. Collins became the director of the Air and Space Museum, overseeing the development of the monumental exhibition space that stands in Washington today. He stayed with the Smithsonian until 1980, and subsequently went into business. Today, retired and living in North Carolina and Florida, Michael fishes and paints, and continues to share life with Pat, to whom his 1974 book *Carrying the Fire* is dedicated.

For Buzz, moving on from Apollo proved to be more difficult. In striving to succeed at West Point, the air force, MIT and ultimately NASA, he dedicated himself to a lifetime of achievement. In making the most of a succession of opportunities to prove himself, he had little time to look at life from a broader perspective. When the workload eased off, Buzz lost a sense of direction. Following the triumphant Gemini 12 mission, he was confined to bed for five days.[9] During the aftermath of Apollo 11 he experienced a similar form of paralysis, this time lasting for years. 'Without a goal,' he later wrote, 'I was like an inert ping-pong ball being batted about by the whims and motivations of others.'[10] Having found himself removed from active participation in the remaining Apollo flights, in 1971 Buzz left NASA to become the commandant of the air force's test pilot school at Edwards (although he had never previously attended it).[11] He left the air force a year later. During this period Aldrin struggled with alcoholism and depression, and spent time in hospital in an attempt to regain a sense of control.[12] He began to accept he may have inherited something of the state of mind that had led to his mother and grandfather taking their lives.[13] Buzz eventually resolved many of the difficulties plaguing him, though not before he and Joan parted. Today he pursues an interest in developing techniques for further space exploration. He has remarried and lives in California.

Like Michael, Neil decided he too would not return to space. Throughout his time at NASA he considered himself first and foremost a test pilot involved in research and analysis. He was able to pursue these interests by taking up a post at headquarters, serving as Deputy Associate Administrator for Aeronautics in the Office of Advanced Research and Technology. Subsequently choosing to enter academia, Armstrong completed a masters degree in aerospace engineering at the University of Southern California (by submitting a thesis based on Apollo 11). Leaving NASA in 1971, he became a professor of aerospace engineering at the University of Cincinnati, and was involved in teaching and research until going into business in 1979. In 1970, Neil took a lead role in investigating the explosion that struck Apollo 13, and in 1986 he carried out similar work following the loss of the space shuttle *Challenger*. Like many Apollo astronauts, Neil's time at NASA didn't leave him unscathed. He and Janet subsequently parted, and on more than one occasion the man who for 15 minutes had the Moon to himself has had to be rescued from an excited mob. Neil later remarried, and today he spends much of his time travelling throughout the States and abroad.

Both Armstrong and Aldrin have been the subject of much misunderstanding regarding the mission, some of which began before they even left the LRL. Searching for a portrait shot of Neil on the Moon, *Life* magazine mistakenly believed there were no pictures of him on the surface at all.[14] While there was nothing to compare with the iconic full-frontal shot Armstrong took of Aldrin, there were at least five images showing Neil working in shadow beside the LM. Later he said, 'NASA kept putting out that there weren't any pictures of me. Because they believed that. But they didn't know [pictures did exist]. I don't think they probably ever asked Buzz or I.'[15]

In struggling to hold on to his privacy, Armstrong rarely publicly discusses the broader story of Apollo 11's journey. Inevitably, more than any other astronaut he has found himself the target of many rumours about what he apparently said, saw and did while on the Moon. Indeed, all three men have had to fend off questions about whether the mission in which they risked their lives even took place at all. Bold claims are made by people who have not always read everything, or anything, available to them, and their suggestions frequently fly in the face of reason. As Charlie Duke asked in the 2006 film *In the Shadow of the Moon*, if NASA hoaxed the landing, why did they fake it six times? In 1969, Russia tracked Apollo 11 to the Moon and back, as did astronomers at the UK's Jodrell Bank Observatory. Yet some suggest that thousands of US government politicians and officials, past and present, have together preserved the secret truth for 40 years, and that during the height of the Cold War they managed to persuade the Kremlin to join in. Those who believe NASA made it all up should perhaps visit the McDonald Observatory in Texas where laser beams are fired towards the lunar surface. Observers can watch the evidence of photons returning to Earth, which is only possible because Buzz left a reflector on the Moon. Even so, people continue to accuse him of 'faking the landing'. When filmmaker Bart Sibrel confronted Aldrin, in 2002, calling him 'a thief, liar and coward', Buzz (who was 72 at the time) punched him in the face.[16]

The truth is that during the Apollo programme NASA achieved far more than it expected to. In putting men on the Moon, the agency sent people 240,000 miles into space. This in itself enabled astronauts to take pictures of Earth from a distance that for the first time demonstrated just how fragile our planet really is. The famous Earthrise photograph, captured by Apollo 8, looks across the arid plains of the Moon towards Earth in the distance, and shows that the planet is a lonely drop of colour surrounded by endless depths of nothingness. Pictures such as this inspired the burgeoning green movement, which today has never been more active.

Another consequence of Apollo is perhaps even more significant. In 1969, the Cold War was inflamed by conflict in Vietnam and elsewhere, but in space it was a radically different story. When NASA asked Moscow for information on Luna 15, details of the probe's trajectory were sent promptly and without question. Luna 15 itself crashed in the Sea of Crisis a day after *Eagle* reached the surface, but it served a purpose in demonstrating that the two superpowers could work together in space. The relationship was greatly extended in 1975 when an Apollo command module successfully docked with a Russian Soyuz spacecraft. Paving the way towards later co-operation aboard the Mir Space Station, this political breakthrough was a triumphant moment for America and Russia – and also personally for Deke Slayton. Selected as an astronaut in 1959, then grounded three years later due to a heart condition, Deke was told he would never fly in space. But after medical treatment, in 1972 he was restored to full flight status. In looking for a crew for what was known as the Apollo-Soyuz Test Project, he selected himself as the docking pilot. Deke retired from NASA in 1982 and went into business. He passed away in 1993.

But perhaps the most significant achievement of Apollo is that in accomplishing its goal, it redefined humanity by proving we are capable of leaving our home planet. This will permanently be a defining characteristic of our capabilities – which is why, 40 years on, Neil Armstrong and Buzz Aldrin remain household names. In landing their gold and silver spacecraft on the surface of the Moon, Neil and Buzz proved something new about us. As they loped about in the dust years of work by thousands of people culminated in a mission flown by three men, who between them possessed the 'bright stuff' necessary to pull off what many said couldn't be done. The mission was to be repeated by others, but it was Neil, Michael and Buzz who led the way.

NOTES

Chapter 1: The Bright Stuff

1 Named Cape Kennedy in 1963, in 1973 the area reverted to its original name of Cape Canaveral.
2 Dr James Hansen, *First Man, The Life of Neil Armstrong* (Simon & Schuster, 2005), p.153.
3 Ibid.
4 Ibid., pp.29-32.
5 Ibid., p.48.
6 Ibid., p.31.
7 Ibid., pp.48-9.
8 Ibid., pp.49-50, 68.
9 Ibid., pp.80, 91-5.
10 Ibid., pp.124-7.
11 Ibid., pp.118-22.
12 Ibid., p.122.
13 Ibid., pp.127-8.
14 Ibid., pp.136-9.
15 Ibid., p.170.
16 Ibid., pp. 51, 96, 98, 108-9.
17 Ibid., pp.178-82.
18 Interview with Dr Robert Gilruth in Glen Swanson (ed.), *Before This Decade Is Out* (University Press of Florida, 2002), p.64.
19 Ibid., p.67.
20 Hansen, op. cit., p.169.
21 Stephanie Nolen, *Promised the Moon: The Untold Story of the First Women in the Space Race* (Penguin Canada, Toronto, 2002), p. 300.
22 Andrew Smith, *Moondust* (Bloomsbury, 2005), p.247.
23 Hansen, op. cit., p.189.
24 Deke Slayton, *Deke!* (Forge, 1994), p.82.

25 Hansen, op. cit., pp.139, 189.

26 Ibid., pp.194-6.

27 Ibid., p.8.

28 Phone-call between author and Dee O'Hara, 18/2/08.

29 Hansen, op. cit., p.8.

Chapter 2: Carrying the Fire

1 Armstrong, Aldrin, Collins, with Gene Farmer and Dora Jane Hamblin, *First on the Moon* (Little Brown and Company, 1970), p.106.

2 Of the various sources of statistics detailing the Apollo 11 spacecraft and booster, one of the most detailed is the contemporary press kit, published by NASA 6 July 1969. This is currently available online and also in print (published by Apogee Books, 1999, as *Apollo 11, The NASA Mission Reports, Volume 1*, edited by Robert Godwin. For references to propellants, Saturn V stages and construction of the stack, etc, see pp.51-68.)

3 Ibid., pp.88-92.

4 Guenter Wendt, *The Unbroken Chain* (Apogee Books, 2001), pp.112, 114, 127.

5 Michael Collins, *Carrying the Fire* (Cooper Square Press, 2001, originally published in 1974), p.126.

6 Ibid., pp.1-17.

7 Ibid.

8 Ibid., p.26.

9 Ibid., pp.27-8.

10 Dr James Hansen, *First Man*, p.195.

11 Collins, op. cit., pp.34-6.

12 Ibid., p.63.

13 Ibid., p.79.

14 Hansen, op. cit., p.224.

15 Collins, op. cit., p.121.

16 Ibid., p.122, and Hansen, op. cit., p.345.

17 Hansen, op. cit., p.2.

18 Ibid., p.6.
19 For gifts from Armstrong and Collins given to Wendt, see Guenter Wendt, op. cit., p.132.
20 Hansen, op. cit., p.407.
21 Armstrong, Aldrin, Collins, op. cit., p.96.
22 Collins, op. cit., p.xvi.

Chapter 3: Moving Targets

1 Michael Collins, *Carrying the Fire*, p.360.
2 Ibid., p.361.
3 Armstrong, Aldrin, Collins, with Gene Farmer and Dora Jane Hamblin, *First on the Moon*, p.96.
4 Robert Godwin (ed.), *Apollo 11, The NASA Mission Reports, Volume 1* (Apogee Books, 1999), p.18.
5 Armstrong, Aldrin, Collins, op. cit., p.100.
6 Buzz Aldrin and Wayne Warga, *Return to Earth* (Random House, 1973), p.219.
7 Collins, op. cit., p.364.
8 Dr James Hansen, *First Man*, p.408.
9 Ibid.
10 David Harland, *The First Men on the Moon* (Praxis Publishing, 2007), pp.129-30.
11 Aldrin and Warga, op. cit., p.220.
12 Harland, op. cit., p.137.
13 Collins, op. cit., p.387.
14 Aldrin and Warga, op. cit., p.159.
15 For details relating to Buzz Aldrin's background, see Aldrin and Warga, op. cit., pp.87-192, and Hansen, op. cit., pp.348-59.
16 Aldrin and Warga, op. cit., p.131.
17 Ibid., p.202.
18 Ibid., p.134.
19 Hansen, op. cit., p.203.
20 Aldrin and Warga, op. cit., p.42.
21 Hansen, op. cit., p.356.
22 Aldrin and Warga, op. cit., p.161.
23 Ibid., p.166.
24 Armstrong, Aldrin, Collins, op. cit., pp.98-9.

Chapter 4: Finding a Way Home

1 Michael Collins, *Carrying the Fire*, p.373.
2 David Harland, *The First Men on the Moon*, p.142.
3 Armstrong, Aldrin, Collins, with Gene Farmer and Dora Jane Hamblin, *First on the Moon*, pp.97-9, 104-5.
4 Collins, op. cit., p.374.
5 Interview with George Low in Glen Swanson (ed.), *Before This Decade Is Out*, p.317.
6 Dr James Hansen, *First Man*, p.319.
7 Interview with Wernher von Braun in Swanson (ed.), op. cit., p.41.
8 More than 3,000 V-2s were subsequently fired at Britain and other countries.
9 Interview with George Low in Swanson (ed.), op. cit., pp.320-3.
10 Ibid., p.322.
11 Robert Seamans, *Project Apollo, The Tough Decisions* (NASA, 2005), pp.13-15.
12 Interview with George Low in Swanson (ed.), op. cit., p.323.
13 Seamans, op. cit., p.45.
14 Special Message to the Congress on Urgent National Needs Page 4, John F. Kennedy Library.
15 Interview with George Low in Swanson (ed.), op. cit., p.318.
16 Seamans, op. cit., p.27.
17 http://history.nasa.gov/monograph4/against.htm, see note 55.
18 http://history.nasa.gov/monograph4/against.htm, see note 48.
19 http://history.nasa.gov/monograph4/against.htm, see note 72.
20 Seamans, op. cit., p.43.
21 Hansen, op. cit., p.318, and http://history.nasa.gov/monograph4/against.htm, see note 127.
22 Armstrong, Aldrin, Collins, op. cit., p.219.
23 Hansen, op. cit., p.258.
24 Armstrong, Aldrin, Collins, op. cit., p.220.
25 David Shayler, *Disasters and Accidents in Manned Spaceflight* (Praxis, 2000), p.156.
26 Hansen, op. cit., p.260.
27 Ibid., pp.263-5.
28 Buzz Aldrin and Wayne Warga, *Return to Earth*, pp.170-1.

29 Collins, op. cit., p.218.
30 Ibid., p.219.
31 Ibid., p.221.
32 Aldrin and Warga, op. cit., p.174.
33 Ibid., p.175.
34 Ibid., p.182.
35 Ibid., p.184.
36 Ibid., p.187.

Chapter 5: Nowhere to Hide

1 David Harland, *The First Men on the Moon*, p.366.
2 Ibid., p.26.
3 For descriptions of Mission Control, see Gene Kranz, *Failure Is Not an Option* (Berkley, 2000), pp.229, 248, 252, 278; and interview with Gene Kranz in Glen Swanson (ed.), *Before This Decade Is Out*, p.150.
4 Chris Kraft, *Flight, My Life in Mission Control* (Plume, 2002), pp.2, 114, 218.
5 Kranz, op. cit., p.274.
6 Kraft, op. cit., p.316.
7 Kranz, op. cit., p.256
8 Buzz Aldrin and Wayne Warga, *Return to Earth*, p.221.
9 Ibid., p.222.
10 Dr James Hansen, *First Man*, p.127.
11 Ibid., p.128; and Armstrong, Aldrin, Collins, with Gene Farmer and Dora Jane Hamblin, *First on the Moon*, p.150.
12 Hansen, op, cit., pp.160-8; and Armstrong, Aldrin, Collins, op. cit., pp.150-1.
13 Hansen, op. cit., p.165.
14 Ibid., p.166.
15 Ibid., p.167.
16 Ibid., pp.281-6; and Armstrong, Aldrin, Collins, op. cit., pp.218-19.
17 Hansen, op. cit., p.272.
18 Ibid., p.271.
19 http://history.msfc.nasa.gov/saturn_apollo/first_saturn_rocket.html
20 For North American and Grumman contracts, see http://history.

nasa.gov/SP-4205/ch2-5.html#source29 *and* http://history.nasa.gov/SP-4205/ch4-5.html

21 http://www.thespacereview.com/article/735/1

22 Interview with Robert Gilruth in Glen Swanson (ed.), op. cit., p.94.

23 Stan Redding and Walter Mansell, *Houston Chronicle*, 22 November 1963: http://www.chron.com/content/chronicle/special/jfk/houston/stories/dinner.html

24 http://www.britannica.com/eb/article-9057747/Outer-Space-Treaty#145193.hook

25 Hansen, op. cit., p.305.

26 http://www.lbjlib.utexas.edu/johnson/archives.hom/speeches.hom/670127.asp

27 David Shayler, *Disasters and Accidents in Manned Spaceflight*, pp.99-102; and Alan Shepard and Deke Slayton, *Moonshot* (Turner, 1994), pp.192-8.

28 Shayler, op. cit., p.102; and Shepard and Slayton, op. cit., p.198.

29 Hansen, op. cit., p.305.

30 Shayler, op. cit., pp.103-10; and Shepard and Slayton, op. cit., pp.200-4.

31 Hansen, op. cit., p.306.

32 Ibid., pp.305-7.

33 Ibid., pp.307.

Chapter 6: Grounded in Safety

1 Gene Kranz, *Failure Is Not an Option*, pp.202-3.

2 Michael Collins, *Carrying the Fire*, pp.254-68.

3 Deke Slayton, *Deke!*, pp.192-4; and Collins, op. cit., p.273.

4 Slayton, op. cit., pp.192-4.

5 Dr James Hansen, *First Man*, p.309.

6 Kranz, op. cit., p.206.

7 Slayton, op. cit., p.200.

8 Collins, op. cit., p.272.

9 Hansen, op. cit., p.310.

10 Ibid., p.311; and Andrew Chaikin, *A Man on the Moon* (Penguin,1994), p.27.

11 Chaikin, op. cit., p.55.

12 Hansen, op. cit., p.309.
13 Kranz, op. cit., p.207.
14 Hansen, op. cit., p.309.
15 Buzz Aldrin and Wayne Warga, *Return to Earth*, p.192; and Slayton, op. cit., p.205.
16 Kranz, op. cit., p.210.
17 Chris Kraft, *Flight*, p.278.
18 Collins, op. cit., pp.283-4.
19 Kraft, op. cit., p.284.
20 Collins, op. cit., p.335.
21 Ibid., p.384.
22 Aldrin and Warga, op. cit., p.223; also see Hansen, op. cit., p.418.
23 Hansen, op. cit., p.418.
24 Armstrong, Aldrin, Collins, with Gene Farmer and Dora Jane Hamblin, *First on the Moon*, p.159.
25 NASA's Lunar Surface Journal, at http://www.hq.nasa.gov/alsj/a11/a11.1201-fm.html; and http://en.wikipedia.org/wiki/Apollo_Guidance_Computer
26 Armstrong, Aldrin, Collins, op. cit., p.153; and Collins, op. cit., pp.285-7.
27 http://www.nasm.si.edu/exhibitions/attm/a11.jo.fc.1.html
28 Aldrin and Warga, op. cit., p.223.
29 Collins, op. cit., p.437.
30 Ibid., p.288.
31 Ibid.

Chapter 7: Risks and Risky Remedies

1 Deke Slayton, *Deke!*, p.196.
2 David Shayler, *Disasters and Accidents in Manned Spaceflight*, p.380.
3 Slayton, op. cit., p.217.
4 Ibid., pp.214-16.
5 Dr James Hansen, *First Man*, p.339.
6 Michael Collins, *Carrying the Fire*, pp.289, 294.
7 Ibid., p.294.
8 Ibid., p.300.

9 Frank Borman, roll 386, 06:30:10.
10 Collins, op. cit., pp.289-301.
11 Ibid., p.304.
12 Ibid., p.303.
13 Frank Borman, roll 386, 06:30:10.
14 Susan Borman, roll 388, 08:02:47:21.
15 Collins, op. cit., p.304.
16 Bill Anders, roll 1376, 16:14:22:28.
17 Andrew Chaikin, *A Man on the Moon*, p.96.
18 Ibid., p.97; and Bill Anders, roll 1376 16:39:02:27.
19 Hansen, op. cit., p.338.
20 Buzz Aldrin and Wayne Warga, *Return to Earth*, p.197; and Hansen, op. cit., p.358.
21 Hansen, op. cit., p.338; and personal conversation between the author and Neil Armstrong, Barcelona, 12/4/08.
22 Hansen, op. cit., p.339.
23 Ibid., p.338.
24 Ibid.
25 Ibid., p.358.
26 Ibid.
27 Armstrong, Aldrin, Collins, with Gene Farmer and Dora Jane Hamblin, *First on the Moon*, p.178.
28 Aldrin and Warga, op. cit., p.201.
29 Slayton, op. cit., p.224; and Hansen, op. cit., p.343.
30 Armstrong, Aldrin, Collins, op. cit., pp.131-2.
31 Slayton, op. cit., pp.191, 234.
32 Ibid., p.136.
33 Chris Kraft, *Flight*, p.304.
34 Aldrin and Warga, op. cit., p.201.
35 Ibid.
36 Hansen, op. cit., p.343.
37 Collins, op. cit., p.314.
38 Ibid., p.434.
39 Hansen, op. cit., p.228.
40 Collins, op. cit., p.434.
41 Hansen, op. cit., p.359.

42 Ibid, p.228.
43 Aldrin and Warga, op. cit., p.191.
44 Buzz Aldrin interview, roll 382, 22:29:40:29.
45 Hansen, op. cit., pp.343, 360.
46 Slayton, op. cit., p.233; Kraft, op. cit., p.323; Hansen, op. cit., p.361; and Andrew Smith, *Moondust*, p.99.
47 Aldrin and Warga, op. cit., p.205.
48 Kraft, op. cit., p.323; and Hansen, op. cit., p.361.
49 Buzz Aldrin, roll 383, 23:01:05:14.
50 Buzz Aldrin, roll 382, 22:13:01:17.
51 Aldrin and Warga, op. cit., pp.297-8.
52 Ibid., p.206.
53 Slayton, op. cit., p.234.
54 Aldrin and Warga, op. cit., pp.206-7.
55 Ibid., p.206.
56 Hansen, op. cit., p.363; and Collins, op. cit., p.347.

Chapter 8: A Tissue-paper Spacecraft

1 The space shuttle does not make a powered landing, but instead relies on its aircraft-style design to glide through the lower parts of the atmosphere.
2 Dr James Hansen, *First Man*, p.425.
3 Ibid., p.430.
4 For references to the unidentified object, see Hansen, op. cit., p.430; and Godwin (ed.), *Apollo 11, The NASA Mission Reports, Volume 2*, p.38.
5 Buzz Aldrin and Wayne Warga, *Return to Earth*, p.207.
6 Deke Slayton, *Deke!*, p.34.
7 Chris Kraft, *Flight*, p.249.
8 Ibid., p.248.
9 Godwin (ed.), *Apollo 11, The NASA Mission Reports, Volume 1*, pp.50, 63.
10 http://history.nasa.gov/SP-4205/ch6-2.html
11 Kraft, op. cit., pp.248-51.
12 Hansen, op. cit., p.321.
13 Ibid., p.447.

14 For references to technical details regarding the LM, see Godwin (ed.), *Apollo 11, The NASA Mission Reports, Volume 1*, pp.56-62.
15 David West Reynolds, *Apollo, The Epic Journey to the Moon* (Tehabi, 2002), p.119.
16 Michael Collins, *Carrying the Fire*, pp.59-60.
17 Gene Kranz, *Failure Is Not an Option*, p.254.
18 http://history.nasa.gov/SP-4205/ch12-5.html
19 Kraft, op. cit., p.306.
20 Re. Apollo 10, see Slayton, op. cit., p.229; and Andrew Chaikin, *A Man on the Moon*, pp.151,152.
21 Reynolds, op. cit., p.119.
22 Buzz Aldrin, roll 382, 22:31:12:09.
23 Hansen, op. cit., pp.370-2.
24 Kraft, op. cit., p.323.
25 Deke being outvoted: conversation between the author and Chris Kraft, Houston, October 2007.
26 Hansen, op. cit., p.365.
27 Slayton, op. cit., p.234.
28 Hansen, op. cit., p.366.
29 Ibid., p.314.
30 Ibid., p.316; and http://history.nasa.gov/SP-4205/ch4-5.html
31 Hansen, op. cit., pp.314, 326.
32 Ibid., p.317.
33 NASA's Lunar Surface Journal, at http://www.hq.nasa.gov/alsj/frame.html
34 Hansen, op. cit., pp.321, 323.
35 Ibid., p.314.
36 Ibid., p.324.
37 Ibid., p.326.
38 Ibid., pp.325, 328.
39 Ibid., p.328.
40 Ibid., pp.328-30, 333.
41 Godwin (ed.), *Apollo 11, The NASA Mission Reports, Volume 2*, p.39.
42 Ibid.
43 Ibid.

44 Bill Anders, roll 1376, 16:12:38:11.
45 David Harland, *The First Men on the Moon*, p.175.

Chapter 9: Into the Darkness

1 Michael Collins, *Carrying the Fire*, p.387.
2 Ibid.
3 Ibid.
4 Dr James Hansen, *First Man*, p.382.
5 Ibid.
6 Ibid.
7 Andrew Chaikin, *A Man on the Moon*, p.156.
8 Hansen, op. cit., p.383.
9 Chaikin, op. cit., p.156.
10 Gene Cernan, roll 322, 00:06:42:20.
11 Chris Kraft, *Flight*, p.309.
12 Deke Slayton, *Deke!*, p.232; Chaikin, op. cit., p.159; Kraft, op. cit., p.310; and David West Reynolds, *Apollo, The Epic Journey to the Moon*, p.128.
13 Hansen, op. cit., p.378.
14 Gene Cernan, roll 322, 00:06:42:20
15 Reynolds, op. cit., p.128.
16 David Harland, *The First Men on the Moon*, pp.28, 233.
17 Hansen, op. cit., pp.329, 330.
18 Ibid., p.332; and email to the author from Alan Bean, 11/7/08.
19 http://history.nasa.gov/alsj/LLTV-952.html
20 Collins, op. cit., p.339.
21 Harland, op. cit., p.297.
22 Armstrong, Aldrin, Collins, with Gene Farmer and Dora Jane Hamblin, *First on the Moon*, p.284.
23 Ibid., p.245.
24 W. Safire, *NY Times*, 12 July 1999, via NYTimes.com.
25 Hansen, op. cit., pp.377, 378.
26 Collins, op. cit., p.329.
27 Gene Kranz, roll 367, 07:36:00:09.
28 Collins, op. cit., pp.318, 337.
29 Ibid., p.330.

30 Ibid., p.336.
31 Ibid., p.350.
32 Ibid., p.330.
33 Ibid., p.344; and Harland, op. cit., p.73.
34 Gene Kranz, *Failure Is Not an Option*, p.17.
35 Ibid., p.44.
36 Hansen, op. cit., p.384.
37 Ibid.
38 Kranz, op. cit., pp.220-1.
39 Gene Kranz, roll 367, 07:30:34:16.
40 Ibid.
41 Kraft, op. cit., p.309.
42 Ibid., p.89.
43 Kranz, op. cit., pp.33, 83.

Chapter 10: Pushed to the Limit

1 Dr James Hansen, *First Man*, p.374.
2 Gene Kranz, *Failure Is Not an Option*, pp.259, 262.
3 Interview with Gene Kranz in Glen Swanson (ed.), *Before This Decade Is Out*, p.150.
4 Hansen, op. cit., p.387.
5 Kranz, op. cit., p.267.
6 Ibid., p.262.
7 Ibid.
8 Hansen, op. cit., p.387.
9 Ibid.
10 Interview with Gene Kranz in Swanson (ed.), op. cit., p.141.
11 Kranz, op. cit., p.263.
12 Ibid.
13 Frank Borman, roll 386, 06:34:57.
14 Hansen, op. cit., p.381.
15 Kranz, op. cit., p.262.
16 Ibid., p.265; and Hansen, op. cit., p.317.
17 Chris Kraft, *Flight*, pp.2, 314.
18 Ibid., p.313.
19 Ibid., p.314.

20 Hansen, op. cit., p.378.
21 Ibid., p.333; Kraft, op. cit., p.312; and David Harland, *The First Men on the Moon*, pp.69, 73.
22 Hansen, op. cit., p.334.
23 Kraft, op. cit., p.313.
24 Hansen, op. cit., p.334.
25 Michael Collins, *Carrying the Fire*, p.344.
26 Ibid., p.345.
27 Buzz Aldrin and Wayne Warga, *Return to Earth*, p.208.
28 Hansen, op. cit., p.149.
29 Ibid., p.378.
30 Ibid., pp.379, 380.
31 Collins, op. cit., p.347.
32 Hansen, op. cit., p.465.
33 Collins, op. cit., p.347.
34 Hansen, op. cit., p.378.
35 Kranz, op. cit., p.270.
36 Ibid., pp.268-71.
37 Hansen, op. cit., pp.463-5.
38 Kraft, op. cit., p.314.
39 Ibid.
40 Harland, op. cit., p.183.
41 Collins, op. cit., p.392.
42 Hansen, op. cit., p.437.
43 Collins, op. cit., p.391.
44 Harland, op. cit., pp.19-20.
45 Ibid., pp.21-8.
46 Ibid., pp.25-8.
47 Armstrong, Aldrin, Collins, with Gene Farmer and Dora Jane Hamblin, *First on the Moon*, p.205; and Harland, op. cit., p.188.
48 Collins, op. cit., p.350.
49 Aldrin and Warga, op. cit., p.227.
50 Collins, op. cit., p.391.
51 Aldrin and Warga, op. cit., p.234; and Hansen, op. cit., p.493.
52 Kraft, op. cit., p.314; and Hansen, op. cit., p.394.

Chapter 11: A Place in History

1 David Harland, *The First Men on the Moon*, pp.101,104; Armstrong, Aldrin, Collins, with Gene Farmer and Dora Jane Hamblin, *First on the Moon*, pp.147, 148; and Dr James Hansen, *First Man*, pp.420-2.
2 Michael Collins, *Carrying the Fire*, pp.278-80.
3 David Shayler, *Disasters and Accidents in Manned Spaceflight*, p.76; and http://www.jamesoberg.com/usd10.html
4 Shayler, op. cit., p.376; and Deke Slayton, *Deke!*, p.197.
5 Slayton, op. cit., p.217; and http://www.thespacereview.com/article/188/3
6 http://www.thespacereview.com/article/735/1; and interview with Robert Gilruth in Glen Swanson (ed.), *Before This Decade Is Out*, p.98.
7 Hansen, op. cit., p.421; and Slayton, op. cit., p.240.
8 Collins, op. cit., p.97.
9 Hansen, op. cit., p.120; and Godwin (ed.), *Apollo 11, The NASA Mission Reports, Volume 1*, p.77.
10 Collins, op. cit., p.54.
11 htp://www.pbs.org/wgbh/amex/moon/peopleevents/p_wives.html
12 http://news.bbc.co.uk/1/hi/magazine/7085003.stm
13 Hansen, op. cit., p.291.
14 Buzz Aldrin and Wayne Warga, *Return to Earth*, p.185.
15 Hansen, op. cit., p.278.
16 Aldrin and Warga, op. cit., p.165.
17 Ibid.
18 Ibid, p.202.
19 Collins, op. cit., p.352.
20 Hansen, op. cit., p.289.
21 Ibid., p.277.
22 Ibid.
23 Ibid., p.278.
24 http://www.hq.nasa.gov/pao/History/SP-4204/ch20-4.html
25 Collins, op. cit., p.348.
26 Hansen, op. cit., p.394.
27 Harland, op. cit., p.14.

28 Hansen, op. cit., p.514.
29 For details of EVA training, see Godwin (ed.), *Apollo 11, The NASA Mission Reports, Volume 1*, pp.29, 30, 32, 79-84.
30 Hansen, op. cit., p.375.
31 Armstrong, Aldrin, Collins, op. cit., p.213; and Hansen, op. cit., p.320.
32 Hansen, op. cit., p.376.
33 Armstrong, Aldrin, Collins, op. cit., p.211.
34 Hansen, op. cit., p.375.
35 Collins, op. cit., p.50.
36 Ibid., pp.333-5; and Hansen, op. cit., p.393.
37 PPK details from Hansen, op. cit., pp.522-8.
38 Collins, op. cit., p.426; and Hansen, op. cit., pp.522-8.
39 Hansen, op. cit., pp.522-8; Collins, op. cit., p.331; and Armstrong, Aldrin, Collins, op. cit., pp.127-8.
40 Hansen, op. cit., pp.522-8.
41 Armstrong, Aldrin, Collins, op. cit., p.47.
42 Collins, op. cit., p.434.
43 Hansen, op. cit., p.358.
44 Collins, op. cit., p.434.
45 Aldrin and Warga, op. cit., p.215; and Hansen, op. cit., p.390.
46 Hansen, op. cit., pp.390-402; and Gene Kranz, *Failure Is Not an Option*, pp.268-71.
47 Collins, op. cit., p.343.
48 NASA's Lunar Surface Journal, at http://history.nasa.gov/alsj/a11/a11.landing.html
49 Hansen, op. cit., p.367.
50 Collins, op. cit., p.349; and Hansen, op. cit., p.388.
51 Harland, op. cit., p.104.
52 Armstrong, Aldrin, Collins, op. cit., p.51.

Chapter 12: The Eagle has Wings

1 Robert Godwin (ed.), *Apollo 11, The NASA Mission Reports, Volume 2*, p.47.
2 Gene Kranz, roll 368, 08:18:22:13.
3 Buzz Aldrin and Wayne Warga, *Return to Earth*, p.228.

4 Michael Collins, *Carrying the Fire*, p.396.

5 Armstrong, Aldrin, Collins, with Gene Farmer and Dora Jane Hamblin, *First on the Moon*, p.226.

6 Godwin (ed.), *Apollo 11, The NASA Mission Reports, Volume 2*, p.49.

7 Collins, op. cit., p.398.

8 David Harland, *The First Men on the Moon*, p.214; David West Reynolds, *Apollo, The Epic Journey to the Moon*, p.138; and Gene Kranz, *Failure Is Not an Option*, p.286.

9 http://www.pbs.org/wgbh/amex/moon/peopleevents/p_wives.html

10 Armstrong, Aldrin, Collins, op. cit., pp.23, 271.

11 Ibid., p.276.

12 Ibid., pp.278, 279.

13 Ibid., pp.97-9.

14 Ibid., p.138.

15 Ibid., pp.157-8.

16 Ibid., p.168.

17 Ibid., p.181.

18 Ibid., p.261.

19 Ibid., pp.273-7.

20 Kranz, op. cit., p.283.

21 Descriptions of white team from: interview with Gene Kranz in Glen Swanson (ed.), *Before This Decade Is Out*, pp.149-150; and Kranz, op. cit., pp.258-60.

22 Gene Kranz, roll 368-01, 08:18:22:13.

23 Kranz, op. cit., p.279; interview with Gene Kranz in Swanson (ed.), op. cit., p.153; and Gene Kranz, roll 368, 08:18:22:13.

24 Harland, op. cit., p.193.

25 Collins, op. cit., p.399.

26 Gene Kranz, roll 368, 08:18:22:13; and interview with Gene Kranz in Swanson (ed.), op. cit., p.155.

27 Dr James Hansen, *First Man*, p.452.

28 Ibid., p.454; and Harland, op. cit., p.226.

29 For Armstrong's and Aldrin's accounts of the descent, see Godwin (ed.), *Apollo 11, The NASA Mission Reports, Volume 2*, pp.62-7.

30 Interview with Gene Kranz in Swanson (ed.), op. cit., p.157; and Armstrong, Aldrin, Collins, op. cit., p.282.

31 Aldrin and Warga, op. cit., p.230.
32 Ibid., p.230.
33 Armstrong, Aldrin, Collins, op. cit., p.22.
34 Ibid., p.288.
35 Ibid., p.289.
36 Ibid.
37 Deke Slayton, *Deke!*, p.244.
38 Armstrong, Aldrin, Collins, op. cit., p.23.
39 Interview with Gene Kranz in Swanson (ed.), op. cit., p.149.
40 NASA's Lunar Surface Journal, at http://www.hq.nasa.gov/alsj/a11/a11.html
41 Ibid.
42 Godwin (ed.), *Apollo 11, The NASA Mission Reports, Volume 2*, p.65.
43 Aldrin and Warga, op. cit., p.231.
44 Ibid., p.232.
45 Armstrong, Aldrin, Collins, op. cit., pp.24, 291.
46 Interview with Gene Kranz in Swanson (ed.), op. cit., p.162.
47 Harland, op. cit., p.242.

Chapter 13: Sneaking Up on the Past

1 Robert Godwin (ed.), *Apollo 11, The NASA Mission Reports, Volume 1*, p.49.
2 Ibid.
3 Dr James Hansen, *First Man*, p.376; and David Harland, *The First Men on the Moon*, p.41.
4 Armstrong, Aldrin, Collins, with Gene Farmer and Dora Jane Hamblin, *First on the Moon*, p.214; and Harland, op. cit., p.354.
5 Hansen, op. cit., p.376.
6 Armstrong, Aldrin, Collins, op. cit., p.298.
7 Buzz Aldrin and Wayne Warga, *Return to Earth*, p.232.
8 Apollo 11 Preliminary Science Report, at NASA's Lunar Surface Journal http://www.hq.nasa.gov/alsj/a11/a11.html
9 Godwin (ed.), *Apollo 11, The NASA Mission Reports, Volume 2*, p.69.
10 Armstrong, Aldrin, Collins, op. cit., p.306.

11 NASA's Lunar Surface Journal, at http://www.hq.nasa.gov/alsj/a11/a11.html

12 Michael Collins, *Carrying the Fire*, p.402.

13 Godwin (ed.), *Apollo 11, The NASA Mission Reports, Volume 2*, p.96; Collins, op. cit., p.404; and NASA's Lunar Surface Journal, at http://www.hq.nasa.gov/alsj/a11/a11.html

14 Collins, op. cit., p.402.

15 Godwin (ed.), *Apollo 11, The NASA Mission Reports, Volume 2*, pp.69, 74; and Aldrin and Warga, op. cit., p.233.

16 Buzz Aldrin, roll 383, 23:04:43:07.

17 Armstrong, Aldrin, Collins, op. cit., p.320; and Godwin (ed.), *Apollo 11, The NASA Mission Reports, Volume 1*, p.239.

18 Aldrin and Warga, op. cit., p.233.

19 Godwin (ed.), *Apollo 11, The NASA Mission Reports, Volume 2*, pp.68, 70.

20 NASA's Lunar Surface Journal, at http://www.hq.nasa.gov/alsj/a11/a11.html; and see also http://history.nasa.gov/alsj/omega.html

21 Godwin (ed.), *Apollo 11, The NASA Mission Reports, Volume 2*, p.97.

22 NASA's Lunar Surface Journal, at http://www.hq.nasa.gov/alsj/a11/a11.html

23 Godwin (ed.), *Apollo 11, The NASA Mission Reports, Volume 2*, p.97.

24 For further details on the pressure-suit, see Godwin (ed.), *Apollo 11, The NASA Mission Reports, Volume 1*, pp.68-70.

25 NASA's Lunar Surface Journal, at http://www.hq.nasa.gov/alsj/a11/a11.html

26 Ibid.

27 Godwin (ed.), *Apollo 11, The NASA Mission Reports, Volume 2*, p.71.

28 Aldrin and Warga, op. cit., p.233.

29 Armstrong, Aldrin, Collins, op. cit., pp.309-10.

30 NASA's Lunar Surface Journal, at http://www.hq.nasa.gov/alsj/a11/a11.html

31 Godwin (ed.), *Apollo 11, The NASA Mission Reports, Volume 2*, p.73.

Chapter 14: A Walk on the Moon

1 NASA's Lunar Surface Journal, at http://history.nasa.gov/alsj/a11/a11tether.html

2 Chris Kraft, *Flight*, p.307.

3 Ibid., p.308.

4 Ibid.; and Report by John Sarkissian, Parkes Observatory, October 2000, available at http://www.parkes.atnf.csiro.au/news_events/apollo11/

5 Michael Collins, *Carrying the Fire*, p.350.

6 Report by John Sarkissian, Parkes Observatory, October 2000, available at http://www.parkes.atnf.csiro.au/news_events/apollo11/

7 David Harland, *The First Men on the Moon*, p.368.

8 Report by John Sarkissian, Parkes Observatory, October 2000, available at http://www.parkes.atnf.csiro.au/news_events/apollo11/

9 NASA's Lunar Surface Journal, at http://www.hq.nasa.gov/alsj/a11/a11.html

10 For further details of the EVA, including verbatim accounts from Armstrong and Aldrin, see Godwin (ed.), *Apollo 11, The NASA Mission Reports, Volume 2*, pp.70-91; and NASA's Lunar Surface Journal, at http://www.hq.nasa.gov/alsj/a11/a11.html

11 Buzz Aldrin and Wayne Warga, *Return to Earth*, p.234.

12 Andrew Chaikin, *A Man on the Moon*, p.209; and NASA's Lunar Surface Journal, at http://www.hq.nasa.gov/alsj/a11/a11.html

13 Godwin (ed.), *Apollo 11, The NASA Mission Reports, Volume 2*, pp.69-70.

14 Armstrong, Aldrin, Collins, with Gene Farmer and Dora Jane Hamblin, *First on the Moon*, p.320.

15 Ibid.

16 Aldrin and Warga, op. cit., p.235.

17 Ibid.

18 Apollo 11 Preliminary Science Report, via NASA's Lunar Surface Journal, at http://www.hq.nasa.gov/alsj/a11/a11.html

19 Godwin (ed.), *Apollo 11, The NASA Mission Reports, Volume 2*, p.76.

20 Aldrin and Warga, op. cit., p.236.
21 NASA's Lunar Surface Journal, at http://www.hq.nasa.gov/alsj/a11/a11.html
22 Aldrin and Warga, op. cit., p.237.
23 Godwin (ed.), *Apollo 11, The NASA Mission Reports, Volume 2*, p.78.
24 Aldrin and Warga, op. cit., p.237; and Godwin (ed.), *Apollo 11, The NASA Mission Reports, Volume 2*, p.82.
25 Harland, op. cit., p.273; and Godwin (ed.), *Apollo 11, The NASA Mission Reports, Volume 2*, p.75.
26 Aldrin and Warga, op. cit., p.238.
27 Godwin (ed.), *Apollo 11, The NASA Mission Reports, Volume 2*, p.81.
28 Ibid., p.78.
29 NASA's Lunar Surface Journal, at http://www.hq.nasa.gov/alsj/a11/a11.html
30 Godwin (ed.), *Apollo 11, The NASA Mission Reports, Volume 2*, p.77.
31 Armstrong, Aldrin, Collins, op. cit., pp.323, 329, 340.
32 Apollo 11 Preliminary Science Report, via NASA's Lunar Surface Journal, at http://www.hq.nasa.gov/alsj/a11/a11.html; and Godwin (ed.), *Apollo 11, The NASA Mission Reports, Volume 2*, p.88.
33 Godwin (ed.), *Apollo 11, The NASA Mission Reports, Volume 2*, p.93.
34 Ibid.
35 Aldrin and Warga, op. cit., p.238.
36 Apollo 11 Preliminary Science Report, via NASA's Lunar Surface Journal, at http://www.hq.nasa.gov/alsj/a11/a11.html
37 Gene Cernan, roll 322, 00:32:09:02.
38 Harland, op. cit., p.290; and Godwin (ed.), *Apollo 11, The NASA Mission Reports, Volume 2*, p.69.
39 Godwin (ed.), *Apollo 11, The NASA Mission Reports, Volume 2*, p.91.
40 Buzz Aldrin and Malcolm McConnell, *Men from Earth* (Bantam, 1989), as quoted by NASA's Lunar Surface Journal, at http://www.hq.nasa.gov/alsj/a11/a11.html

41 Godwin (ed.), *Apollo 11, The NASA Mission Reports, Volume 2*, pp.52, 93, 94.
42 Armstrong, Aldrin, Collins, op. cit., p.359.
43 Aldrin and Warga, op. cit., p.120.

Chapter 15: Mission Accomplished

1 Robert Godwin (ed.), *Apollo 11, The NASA Mission Reports, Volume 2*, p.94.
2 Michael Collins, *Carrying the Fire*, p.411.
3 Armstrong, Aldrin, Collins, with Gene Farmer and Dora Jane Hamblin, *First on the Moon*, p.287.
4 Collins, op. cit., p.411.
5 Ibid., p.412.
6 Armstrong, Aldrin, Collins, op. cit., p.361.
7 Collins, op. cit., p.412; and David Harland, *The First Men on the Moon*, p.296.
8 Godwin (ed.), *Apollo 11, The NASA Mission Reports, Volume 2*, p.93.
9 For the LM's launch from the Moon, see NASA's Lunar Surface Journal, at http://www.hq.nasa.gov/alsj/a11/a11.html; Godwin (ed.), *Apollo 11, The NASA Mission Reports, Volume 2*, pp.99-101; Buzz Aldrin and Wayne Warga, *Return to Earth*, p.240; and Harland, op. cit., p.298.
10 Godwin (ed.), *Apollo 11, The NASA Mission Reports, Volume 2*, p.102.
11 Ibid.
12 For further information on rendezvous, see NASA's Lunar Surface Journal, at http://www.hq.nasa.gov/alsj/a11/a11.html; Harland, op. cit., p.299; Collins, op. cit., pp.411-13, 448; Godwin (ed.), *Apollo 11, The NASA Mission Reports, Volume* 2, pp.100-5; and Aldrin and Warga, op. cit., p.240.
13 Godwin (ed.), *Apollo 11, The NASA Mission Reports, Volume 2*, p.107.
14 Harland, op. cit., p.306.
15 Godwin (ed.), *Apollo 11, The NASA Mission Reports, Volume 2*, p.109.

16 For further information on the docking procedure, see Aldrin and Warga, op. cit., p.240; Harland, op. cit., p.307; and Godwin (ed.), *Apollo 11, The NASA Mission Reports, Volume 2*, pp.104-9.
17 Harland, op. cit., p.307.
18 Collins, op. cit., p.417.
19 Mission transcript at 131:07:07.
20 Mission transcript at 130:11:05.
21 Godwin (ed.), *Apollo 11, The NASA Mission Reports, Volume 2*, p.111.
22 Ibid., p.117.
23 Collins, op. cit., p.426.
24 Interview with Max Faget in Glen Swanson (ed.), *Before This Decade Is Out*, p.355.
25 For further details on re-entry, see Godwin (ed.), *Apollo 11, The NASA Mission Reports, Volume 2*, pp.119-22.
26 Collins, op. cit., p.438.
27 Godwin (ed.), *Apollo 11, The NASA Mission Reports, Volume 2*, p.119.
28 Armstrong, Aldrin, Collins, op. cit., pp.415, 416.
29 Collins, op. cit., p.440; and Godwin (ed.), *Apollo 11, The NASA Mission Reports, Volume 2*, p.120.
30 Collins, op. cit., p. 440.
31 Armstrong, Aldrin, Collins, op. cit., p.414; and David West Reynolds, *Apollo, The Epic Journey to the Moon*, p.218.
32 NASA's Lunar Surface Journal, at http://www.hq.nasa.gov/alsj/tnD7141ApPyrotchnc.pdf
33 Godwin (ed.), *Apollo 11, The NASA Mission Reports, Volume 2*, p.122.
34 For further details on the recovery, see Armstrong, Aldrin, Collins, op. cit., p.407; Godwin (ed.), *Apollo 11, The NASA Mission Reports, Volume 1*, p.39; Harland, op. cit., p.325; and http://www.uss-hornet.org/history/apollo/
35 Armstrong, Aldrin, Collins, op. cit., p.419.
36 Aldrin and Warga, op. cit., p.4.
37 Armstrong, Aldrin, Collins, op. cit., p.424.
38 Aldrin and Warga, op. cit., pp.9-10.

39 Ibid., p.10.
40 Collins, op. cit., p.446.
41 Aldrin and Warga, op. cit., p.13.
42 For further information on the Lunar Receiving Laboratory, see Godwin (ed.), *Apollo 11, The NASA Mission Reports, Volume 1*, pp.40, 100-5; Collins, op. cit., p.445; Harland, op. cit., p.326; and http://history.nasa.gov/SP-4205/ch8-5.html
43 Godwin (ed.), *Apollo 11, The NASA Mission Reports, Volume 2*, p.166.
44 Aldrin and Warga, op. cit., p.14.
45 Collins, op. cit., p. 435.
46 Aldrin and Warga, op. cit., p.16.
47 Ibid., pp.23-4.
48 Collins, op. cit., p.452.

Epilogue

1 Once on the surface Conrad discovered that pictures of semi-naked girls had been squeezed into the pages of his checklist by the backup crew. See NASA's Lunar Surface Journal, at http://history.nasa.gov/alsj/a12/a12_lmpcuff.pdf
2 Michael Collins, *Carrying the Fire*, p.298.
3 David Harland, *The First Men on the Moon*, p.349; and http://www.lpi.usra.edu/lunar/missions/apollo/apollo_11/samples/
4 http://www.lpi.usra.edu/lunar/missions/apollo/apollo_11/samples/
5 David West Reynolds, *Apollo, The Epic Journey to the Moon*, p.231; and http://en.wikipedia.org/wiki/Moon
6 Harland, op. cit., pp.339-40.
7 Collins, op. cit., p.460.
8 Ibid.
9 Buzz Aldrin and Wayne Warga, *Return to Earth*, p.187.
10 Ibid., p.300.
11 Ibid., pp.275, 278.
12 Ibid., pp.281-338; http://technology.timesonline.co.uk/tol/news/tech_and_web/specials/space/article2582966.ece; and http://en.wikipedia.org/wiki/Buzz_Aldrin
13 Buzz Aldrin, roll 382, 22:13:01:17.

14 Harland, op. cit., p.335.

15 Neil Armstrong in conversation with Eric Jones, at NASA's Lunar Surface Journal http://www.hq.nasa.gov/alsj/a11/a11.html

16 BBC News, at http://news.bbc.co.uk/1/hi/world/americas/2272321.stm; and http://news.bbc.co.uk/1/hi/sci/tech/2410431.stm

GLOSSARY

AGS	Abort Guidance System
AOS	Acquisition of Signal
BIG	Biological Isolation Garment
CapCom	Spacecraft Communicator
CMP	Command Module Pilot
CSM	Command and Service Module
DAP	Digital Autopilot
DOI	Descent Orbit Insertion
DPS	Descent Propulsion System
DSKY	[Computer] Display and Keyboard
EASEP	Early Apollo Surface Experiment Package
EMU	Extra-vehicular Mobility Unit
EVA	Extra-vehicular Activity
FIDO	Flight Dynamics Officer
GET	Ground Elapsed Time
IMU	Inertial Measurement Unit
LEB	Lower Equipment Bay
LES	Launch Escape System
LEVA	Lunar Extra-vehicular Visor Assembly
LLTV	Lunar Landing Training Vehicle
LM	Lunar Module
LMP	Lunar Module Pilot
LOI	Lunar Orbit Insertion
LOS	Loss Of Signal
LRL	Lunar Receiving Laboratory
RRR	Laser Ranging Retro-Reflector
MCC	Mid-Course Correction
MESA	Modular Equipment Stowage Assembly

MOCR	Mission Operations Control Room
MQF	Mobile Quarantine Facility
MSFN	Manned Space Flight Network
NASCOM	NASA Communications Network
PDI	Powered Descent Initiation
PGNS	Primary Guidance and Navigation System
PLSS	Portable Life Support System
PPK	Personal Preference Kit
PSE	Passive Seismic Experiment
PTC	Passive Thermal Control
S-IC	First Stage of the Saturn V
S-II	Second Stage of the Saturn V
S-IVB	Third Stage of the Saturn V
SWC	Solar Wind Composition (Collector)
TEI	Trans-Earth Injection
TLI	Trans-lunar Injection

BIBLIOGRAPHY

Books, focusing on contemporary works and first-hand accounts

Buzz Aldrin and Wayne Warga, *Return to Earth*, Random House, 1973

David A. Anderton, *Man in Space*, 1968

Armstrong, Aldrin, Collins, with Gene Farmer and Dora Jane Hamblin, *First on the Moon*, Little Brown and Company, 1970

Piers Bizony, *The Man Who Ran the Moon*, Icon Books, 2006

Andrew Chaikin, *A Man on the Moon*, Penguin,1994

Michael Collins, *Carrying the Fire*, Cooper Square Press, 2001 (originally published in 1974 by Farrar, Straus, and Giroux)

Michael Collins, *Liftoff: The Story of America's Adventure in Space*, Grove Press, 1988

Peter Fairley, *Man on the Moon*, Arthur Barker Limited, 1969

Robert Godwin, *Apollo 11, First Men on the Moon*, Apogee Books, 2005

Robert Godwin (ed.), *Apollo 11, The NASA Mission Reports, Volumes 1, 2 and 3*, Apogee Books, 1999

Richard P. Hallion and Tom D. Crouch (eds), *Apollo: Ten Years Since Tranquility Base*, Smithsonian Institution Press, 1979

Dr James Hansen, *First Man, The Life of Neil Armstrong*, Simon & Schuster, 2005

David Harland, *The First Men on the Moon*, Praxis Publishing, 2007

Edwin P. Hoyt, *The Space Dealers: A Hard Look at the Role of Business in the U.S. Space Effort*, The John Day Co., 1971

Chris Kraft, *Flight, My Life in Mission Control*, Plume, 2002
Gene Kranz, *Failure Is Not an Option*, Berkley, 2000
Norman Mailer, *Of a Fire on the Moon*, Little, Brown, 1970
Stephanie Nolen, *Promised the Moon: The Untold Story of the First Women in the Space Race*, Penguin Canada, Toronto, 2002
Rod Pyle, *Destination Moon*, Carlton Publishing Group, 2005
David West Reynolds, *Apollo, The Epic Journey to the Moon*, Tehabi, 2002
Robert Seamans, *Project Apollo, The Tough Decisions*, NASA, 2005
David Shayler, *Disasters and Accidents in Manned Spaceflight*, Praxis, 2000
Deke Slayton, *Deke!*, Forge, 1994
Andrew Smith, *Moondust*, Bloomsbury, 2005
James C. Sparks, *Moon Landing, Project Apollo*, Dodd, Mead, 1970
Glen Swanson (ed.), *Before This Decade Is Out*, University Press of Florida, 2002
Loyd Swenson, James Grimwood and Charles Alexander, *This New Ocean*, NASA, 1998
Guenter Wendt, *The Unbroken Chain*, Apogee Books, 2001

Websites

history.nasa.gov/monograph4
history.msfc.nasa.gov/saturn_apollo/first_saturn_rocket.html
history.nasa.gov/SP-4205
www.thespacereview.com/article/735/1
www.chron.com/content/chronicle/special/jfk/houston/stories/dinner.html
www.britannica.com/eb/article-9057747/Outer-Space-Treaty#145193.hook
www.lbjlib.utexas.edu/johnson/archives.hom/speeches.hom/670127.asp
www.hq.nasa.gov/alsj/a11/a11.1201-fm.html
en.wikipedia.org/wiki/Apollo_Guidance_Computer
www.nasm.si.edu/exhibitions/attm/a11.jo.fc.1.html
www.thespacereview.com/article/188/3
www.thespacereview.com/article/735/1
www.pbs.org/wgbh/amex/moon/peopleevents/p_wives.html
news.bbc.co.uk/1/hi/magazine/7085003.stm
www.hq.nasa.gov/pao/History/SP-4204
www.parkes.atnf.csiro.au/news_events/apollo11
www.uss-hornet.org/history/apollo
www.lpi.usra.edu/lunar/missions/apollo/apollo_11/samples
news.bbc.co.uk/1/hi/world/americas/2272321.stm
news.bbc.co.uk/1/hi/sci/tech/2410431.stm

Use the following NASA link to find out when the International Space Station can be seen with the naked eye above your home town: spaceflight.nasa.gov/realdata/sightings/index.html

INDEX

Aaron, John 201
Abernathy, Reverend Ralph 19–20, 40
Agena target vehicle 64, 65, 66, 67
Air and Space Museum *see* Smithsonian Institution
Aldrin, Buzz (Edwin Eugene Aldrin Jr) 35–6, 42–3, 44, 45, 93, 99, 175, 225, 247
  Apollo 8 106, 122
  career post-Apollo 11 269–73, 274
  character 26, 46, 47, 49, 50–1, 66, 69, 110, 111, 116, 133, 151, 191, 270–1, 272–3
  childhood 46–7
  Gemini flights 50–1
  landing on the moon 1, 2–3, 171–6, 193–4, 198, 200–1, 203–16
  launch, Apollo 11 38, 40
  launch preparation, Apollo 11 24, 25, 35–6, 37
  MIT 48
  moon, on appearance of 140–1, 168, 176
  moon walk, 218, 225, 226, 227–8, 229, 230–47
  NASA, joins 48–50
  Neil Armstrong and 50, 110–11, 118–19
  pictures, TV and camera, Apollo 11 55, 101–2, 112–13, 120–1
  position in Apollo program 88, 106
  PR duties, Apollo 11 180
  quarantine, Apollo 11 190, 252, 261–5
  re-entry and landing, Apollo 11 257–61
  rendezvous expert 46, 49–50, 51, 64, 66, 151, 249–50, 251, 252
  return to *Eagle*, Apollo 11 244–5
  return to earth, Apollo 11 261–5
  selected for Apollo 11 51, 110–11, 114, 115
  selection for moon walk117–19, 122, 133
  on surface of moon, Apollo 11 219, 220, 221, 222–4
  training 6, 151, 157, 159–71, 185–7, 190
  undocking, Apollo 11 command and lunar modules 195, 196, 197, 198
  US Navy 47–8
Aldrin, Gene 46, 47–8, 49, 118
Aldrin, Joan 33, 48, 49, 52, 53, 69, 89, 115, 116, 181, 182, 199, 200, 213, 215, 229, 235, 243, 254, 261, 262–3, 269, 271
Algranti, Joe 162
Anders, Bill 24, 86, 91, 106, 107, 108, 109, 115, 136, 137, 199, 202
Apollo, Project 266
  Apollo 1 tragedy, effect upon 83–5, 86, 87–9, 105, 114, 179, 188, 226
  birth of 79–80
  costs of 80, 81, 179–80, 191–2
  Kennedy and *see* Kennedy, John F.
  Soviet Union and *see* Soviet Union
Apollo 1 83–5, 86, 87, 88, 89, 105, 114, 179, 188, 226

Apollo 2 88
Apollo 3 88
Apollo 4 88, 89–90
Apollo 5 88, 90, 129, 130
Apollo 6 88, 90
Apollo 7 36, 88, 90–1, 105–6
Apollo 8 106, 107, 108, 109, 110, 111, 114, 122, 137, 141, 144, 155, 159–60, 167, 172, 223, 273
Apollo 9 88, 106, 110, 114, 130, 133, 141, 147, 189, 199
Apollo 10 34, 110, 114, 132, 133, 141, 142, 143, 144, 147, 153–4, 157, 167, 172, 200
Apollo 11 1, 2
- abort procedures 41, 128, 149–50, 158, 160, 196, 197
- adapter 23, 54, 111
- alarms 164–5, 190, 209
- command module *Columbia* 23, 54–6, 70, 91, 92, 123, 157, 164, 187, 194, 195, 198, 203, 204, 216, 221, 222, 225, 226, 228, 244, 250, 251, 252, 253, 254, 257, 258–65
- Command Module Pilot (CMP) 110, 111 *see also* Collins, Michael
- communications 53–4, 72–6, 151–4, 167–9, 171–2, 202, 203, 224–5, 232–3
- computers and computer programs 75, 95–8, 100, 127, 128, 153, 166–7, 175, 179, 186, 196, 208, 209, 210–11, 219, 248, 251, 257, 259
- conspiracy theorists and 239, 272–3
- contractors, role in building of 79–80, 87, 88–9, 107, 122, 191–2
- descent from lunar orbit to moon surface (DOI) (PDI) 134, 135, 136, 144–5, 157–65, 170–1, 172–6, 198, 200–1, 202, 203
- disaster, preparation for 146
- experiments, scientific 184–5, 186, 217–18, 240–1, 242, 243, 246, 267–8
- flight-plan 151
- launch vehicle/fuel tanks 20, 22–4, 33, 36, 42, 44–5, 53, 54, 56, 59, 70, 79, 89–90, 94, 121, 123–4, 129, 130, 178, 179, 266
- joystick 6–7
- landing sites 170–1, 172–3, 218, 211–16, 218, 220
- launch 38–44
- launch preparation 18–21, 24, 25–6, 33–4, 35–7
- life support system, portable (PLSS) 43, 128, 226–7, 228, 230, 237, 244, 245, 246, 249
- lunar extra-vehicular visor assembly (LEVA) 227, 245
- lunar orbit insertion (LOI) 154–6, 166–7, 172
- LOI-2 174–5
- lunar orbit rendezvous (LOR) 61–2, 63, 64, 80
- lunar orbit, getting into 154–5
- lunar orbit, leaving 252–3
- meals 93–4, 100, 102, 223
- mission patch 187, 189, 244
- Mobile Quarantine Facility (MQF) 261–5
- modular equipment stowage assembly (MESA) 230–1, 238, 240, 241
- Official Flight Kit 188–9
- 'parking orbit' 44
- passive thermal control (PTC) 93, 95, 96, 99, 121, 153–4, 156
- personal preference kits (PPKs) 187–9

PR and press 115, 177, 179–83, 269
primary guidance and navigation system (PGNS) 128, 249
readiness review 149–50, 192
re-entry and landing 1–5, 256–61
rendezvous 46, 49–50, 51, 57–69, 160, 249–52
rest periods 136–7, 223, 246, 248
rockets 20, 22, 23, 24, 36, 42, 44 *see also* Saturn V
rules, mission 150–1, 160–1, 165
selection process for mission 114–15, 116, 117–19, 122, 133
service module 23, 54–6, 70, 72, 79, 98, 257–8
solar wind collector (SWC) 238, 239, 242
stack ('space vehicle') 23–4
suits, pressure 25, 25–6, 74–5, 194, 223, 228, 237–8, 246, 248
toilet facilities 34, 74–5, 100
training for mission 134, 135, 136, 144–5, 157–71, 185–6
trans-lunar injection (TLI) 44–6, 53, 70, 74, 98, 123, 145, 254
pictures, TV and camera 4, 43, 52, 75–6, 101, 120–1, 142, 169, 173–4, 185, 189, 201, 212, 219, 223, 228, 229, 230–3, 235, 238, 240, 241, 242, 243, 244, 249, 255, 256, 272, 273
UFO sighting, possible 121–2, 136–7
washing facilities 93
water supply 99
Apollo 12 164, 264, 266
Apollo 13 111, 266, 271
Apollo 14 266
Apollo 15 266
Apollo 16 266
Apollo 17 267
Apollo Spacecraft Program Office 82, 88, 116, 123
Apollo-Soyuz Test Project 273
Armstrong, Eric ('Ricky') 11, 76, 77, 210, 215, 243
Armstrong, Janet 10, 11, 18, 21, 33, 40, 51, 53, 76, 77, 84, 181, 182, 189, 192, 199–200, 210, 212, 215, 219, 228–9, 249, 253–4, 255–6, 261, 262–3, 269, 271
Armstrong, Karen 11, 76–7, 78, 85, 189
Armstrong, Mark 11, 78
Armstrong, Neil 41, 45, 54, 93, 100, 112, 141, 176
Aldrin and 50, 110–11, 118–19
ambition to be an astronaut 17–18, 28, 29, 76, 78
Apollo 8 106, 109–10
career post-Apollo 270, 271, 272
character 7, 26, 47, 270
college 9, 10
Collins and 54, 55, 224
early life 7–9, 27
Ed White and 78–9, 84–5
Gemini flights 64–5, 68–9, 79
heart rate on landing, Apollo 11 221
landing on/descent to the moon (DOI) (PDI), Apollo 11 1–5, 171, 172–6, 193, 198, 200–1, 203–16, 219
launch, Apollo 11 41
launch preparation, Apollo 11 18, 24, 25, 35, 37
lunar landing research vehicle and 134, 135, 136, 144–5
lunar orbit insertion, Apollo 11 166, 167
moon walk, Apollo 11 218, 225, 226–9, 230–47
navy service 9–10

on chances of survival, Apollo 11 184
'one small step' line 224, 229, 233–4
pictures, TV and camera, Apollo 11 74, 101–2, 113, 120
position in Apollo program 88, 106, 109–10
PR duties, Apollo 11 180
quarantine, Apollo 11 190, 252, 261–5
re-entry and landing, Apollo 11 257–61
rendezvous techniques 64–5, 67, 68–9, 79, 249, 250, 251, 252
return to *Eagle*, Apollo 11 244–5
return to earth, Apollo 11 261–5
selected for Apollo 11 109–10
selected to be first man to walk on the moon 117–19, 133
test pilot 10, 11–14
training 31, 134, 135, 136, 144–5, 151, 157–71, 185–7, 190
undocking, Apollo 11 194, 196, 197, 198
view from Apollo 11 44, 70–1, 75, 139, 154, 168
X-15 7
Armstrong, Stephen 7, 18
Armstrong, Viola 7, 18

Bales, Steve 164, 165, 202, 205, 209, 269
Bassett, Charlie 50–1, 182, 187
Bassett, Jeannie 51–2, 182, 199
Bean, Alan 144
Bell Aerosystems 11, 134, 136
Belyaev, Pavel 177, 178
Beregovoi, Georgi 105
Bondarenko, Valentin 178
Borman, Frank 88, 90–1, 102, 106, 107, 108, 114, 146, 159, 177, 188
Braun, Dr Wernher von 57–8, 61, 62, 79, 89, 202, 215
Brown, Dick 201

Calle, Paul 24–5
CapCom 71–2, 73, 94, 99, 108, 133, 120, 153, 157, 201, 205, 225 *see also* Mission Control Center, Houston
Cape Kennedy *see* Kennedy Space Center
Carlton, Bob 201, 206, 212–13
Carpentier, Bill 261
Cernan, Gene 32, 34, 51, 65–6, 142, 143, 133, 202
Chaffee, Roger 82, 84, 88
Charlesworth, Cliff 71, 72, 73–4, 155, 233
CIA 179
Cobb, Jerrie 15
Cold War 74, 177, 272, 273 *see also* Soviet Union
Collins, Major General James 26, 27
Collins, Michael 32, 45, 99, 112, 140, 189
Air Force 27
Apollo Project, position within 88, 91
Buzz Aldrin and 116, 119
career post-NASA 267, 270
character 26–8, 47, 151, 270
childhood 26–7
command module pilot (CMP) 70, 66–7, 69, 86–7, 98, 110, 111, 145–8, 164, 172–6, 205, 224–5
Gemini flights 33, 66–7, 68, 69
health 103, 106, 107, 109, 110
joins NASA 28–9
launch preparation, Apollo 11 24, 25, 35, 37–8
lunar orbit insertion (LOI), Apollo 11 145, 154–6, 166–7, 200

LOI-2, Apollo 11 175–6
meals on Apollo 11 93, 94, 194, 224, 248
moon, on appearance of 140
moon orbit, Apollo 11 221–3, 224–5, 226, 228, 229, 239, 248
Neil Armstrong and 115–16, 224
pictures, TV and camera, Apollo 11 101, 102, 113, 120
PR duties, Apollo 11 177, 180
pressure suits, hatred of 26
quarantine, Apollo 11 190, 252, 261–5
re-entry and landing, Apollo 11 257–61
retirement from NASA 190
return to earth, Apollo 11 255. 256, 259–60, 261–5
selected for mission, Apollo 11 110, 111, 114
task list, Apollo 11 145–6, 147
trans-lunar injection (TLI), Apollo 11 44–5, 53, 254
training, Apollo 11 30–1, 49, 147–9, 151, 157–71, 190
undocking, Apollo 11 195–6, 197, 198
views from Apollo 11 44, 71, 75, 154, 167, 168
weightlessness, Apollo 11 43
Collins, Patricia 27–8, 29, 33, 53, 54, 78, 89, 181, 182, 183, 199, 200, 229, 242, 247, 254, 255–6, 261, 262–3, 269, 270
command modules 23, 54–6, 72, 79
Block I 86, 87, 88–9
Block II 86, 88, 88–9, 91, 105–6
see also Apollo 11
Conrad, Pete 88, 125, 202, 266
Cooper, Gordon 84
Cronkite, Walter 34, 90
Cunningham, Walter 36
Day, Dick 29
Deiterich, Chuck 202
descent orbit insertion (DOI) 198, 200–1, 202, 203
direct ascent 57, 59, 61
Duke, Charlie 133, 120, 157–8, 201, 203, 204, 206, 213, 214, 248, 253–4, 255, 266, 272

Early Apollo Scientific Experiments Package (EASEP) 185
earth orbit rendezvous (EOR) 57, 58–9, 61, 62
Edwards Air Force Base 10, 11–12, 28, 30, 77, 134, 135, 163, 271
Ellington Air Force Base 135, 144, 262, 263
extra-vehicular activities (EVAs)
early NASA 31, 32–3
Apollo 11 46, 113, 117, 122, 124, 127, 128, 131, 178, 185, 186, 215, 223, 224, 225, 226, 228, 232, 233, 235, 239, 242, 244, 254
Gemini 63, 66–9, 104
Soviet 31, 32, 104
Explorer 1 58

F-1 engine 59, 89–90
Faget, Max 58–9
Fendell, Ed 201, 231
Feoktistiv, Konstantin 177, 178
Freeman, Ted 187
free return 45–6, 154–5
Frick, Charles 123, 126

Gagarin, Yuri 15–16, 58, 59, 188
Garman, Jack 165, 209
Gemini, Project 31, 33, 49, 50–1, 59, 69, 73, 81, 92, 105, 106, 109, 110, 117, 119, 120, 123, 130, 133, 180, 270
Gemini 4 63, 72

Gemini 5 63, 64, 79
Gemini 6 64, 68, 131
Gemini 7 64, 68, 100, 131
Gemini 8 64, 76, 79, 136
Gemini 9 142, 182
Gemini 10 51, 66, 67–8
Gemini 11 79
Gemini 12 51, 66, 270
Gemini 13 51
Gilruth, Dr Robert 56–7, 60, 61, 62, 66, 69, 73, 80, 114, 115, 133, 145, 162, 183, 269
Glenn, John 77–8, 202
Goodard Space Flight Center, Maryland 153
Goldstone communications station, California 74, 76, 152, 232, 233
Gordon, Dick 67–8, 69, 84
Greene, Jay 202, 205, 210
Grissinger, John 36
Grissom, Gus 82, 83, 86, 88, 90, 114
Grumman Corporation 79, 90, 122, 123, 124, 126, 130, 132, 157, 186, 192, 194, 198

Haise, Fred 35, 106, 110, 111, 115, 202, 266
Hamblin, Dora Jane 33, 182–3, 186
Hatleburg, Lieutenant Clancy 260
Hinch, Derryn 40
Hirasaki, John 261, 262
Honeysuckle communications station 232, 233
Hornet, USS 255, 257, 260, 261, 262
Houbolt, John 61, 62, 111, 202, 215
Humphrey, Hubert 81

In the Shadow of the Moon 272
International Space Station 267
Irwin, Jim 164

Jodrell Bank Observatory 272
Johnson, Lyndon 15, 34, 60, 81, 82, 83
Johnson, Sam 247
Johnson Space Center, Houston 268, 269 *see also* Manned Spaceflight Center, Houston
Jupiter booster 79

Kelly, Tom 122, 123, 125, 126, 127, 129, 132, 169, 194
Kennedy Space Center, Florida 6, 18, 23, 24, 80–1, 82, 124, 182–3, 190
Kennedy, John F. 59–61, 62, 80–1, 89, 104, 116–17, 131, 134, 142, 169, 178, 184, 231
Khrushchev, Nikita 80, 178
Khrushchev, Sergei 80
King, Dr Martin Luther 192
King, Jack 38
Kissinger, Henry 177
Komarov, Vladimir 104, 105, 178, 188
Koos, Dick 159, 161, 164, 165
Korolev, Sergei 104, 105
Kosygin, Alexei 253
Kraft, Chris 72–3, 74, 79, 90, 91, 107, 115, 117, 123, 126, 127, 132, 133, 143, 145, 149, 150, 151, 152, 161, 162, 165, 177, 183, 192, 231, 269
Kranz, Gene 8, 73–4, 79, 87, 150, 152, 157, 158–9, 161, 164, 165, 190, 194, 201, 202, 203, 204, 205, 206, 209, 210, 213, 215, 231, 269
Langley Research Center 56, 61, 149, 162
Lederer, Jerry 108
Leonov, Alexei 31, 32, 215

Lewis, Charles 'Skinny' 152, 201
Life 180–1, 182–3, 272
Lovell, Jim 18, 38, 68, 84, 88, 98, 99, 100, 106, 107, 108, 109, 110, 115, 187, 199, 202, 266
Low, George 58, 59, 61, 63, 88–9, 90, 91, 107, 119, 122, 133, 176, 183, 231
Luna probes 171, 177, 192, 273
lunar extra-vehicular visor assembly (LEVA) 227, 245
lunar landing research vehicle (LLRV) 134–5
lunar landing training vehicle (LLTV) 135–6, 144, 145, 162
lunar module (LM) *Eagle* 1, 4, 112–3, 120, 266, 272, 273
  communications with MOCR 72, 73, 74
  decision to include in mission 56–7
  development of 79–80, 122–32 *see also* lunar modules, development of
  ejection/jettisoning of 54, 55, 56, 70, 111, 253, 254
  fuel 206–7, 214
  inspection of 111–13
  descent towards and landing on the moon 198, 199, 202, 203 205, 207, 211, 214, 216
  launch from moon 222, 249–50
  lunar gravity and 141–4
  powered descent capability 120, 204, 205, 206–7
  rendezvous with *Columbia* 145, 250–2
  simulators 157, 158, 159–60, 161–2, 163–5, 174, 175, 185, 189
  surface of moon, time spent on 218, 220, 222, 224, 225, 226, 228, 230, 231, 232, 233, 234, 237, 238, 241, 242, 246
  training to land *see* LLTV *and* simulators
  undocking with *Columbia* 153, 193, 194, 195–8
lunar modules, development of:
  LEM 124–8
  LM-1 128–30
  LM-2 130
  LM-3 131
  LM-4 132
  LM-5 122, 132
lunar orbit insertion (LOI) 155, 156, 166, 172
lunar orbit rendezvous (LOR) 61–2, 63, 64, 80
Lunar Orbiter 170, 171, 184, 266
Lunar Receiving Laboratory (LRL) 263, 264, 265, 266, 272
Lunex Project 58

Manned Space Flight Network (MSFN) 152, 206, 228, 232
Manned Spacecraft Center (MSC), Houston 18, 33, 49, 62, 79, 80, 84, 89, 114, 127, 132, 133, 144, 149, 162, 185, 254, 256, 263, 268, 269 *see also* Johnson Space Center
  Lunar Receiving Laboratory (LRL) 263, 264, 265, 266, 272
  Mission Control Center *see* Mission Control Center, Houston
Marks, Jay 20
Marshall Space Flight Center, Alabama 58, 62, 79
Massachusetts Institute of Technology (MIT) 46, 48, 96, 97, 167, 186, 270
McCandless, Bruce 41, 42, 71, 94, 95, 174, 175

McDivitt, Jim 63, 88, 106, 114, 126, 130–1, 132, 141–2, 149, 202
McDonald Observatory, Texas 272
Mercury, Project 15, 16, 20, 24, 29, 30, 31, 48, 56, 57, 58, 59, 60, 72, 73, 79, 82, 88, 109, 114, 120, 150, 151, 257
Mir Space Station 273
Mission Control Center, Houston 3, 4, 5, 30, 31, 32, 41, 45, 50, 74, 76, 92, 108, 111, 113, 132, 143, 151, 153, 155, 159, 161, 165, 168, 173, 175, 182, 194, 203, 210, 215, 219, 220, 225, 233, 248, 250–1
  Mission Operations Control Room (MOCR) 109, 153, 154, 194, 201, 202, 204, 260, 261
modular equipment stowage assembly (MESA) 230–1, 238, 240, 241
moon:
  Apollo Project and *see* Apollo Project
  dangers of landing on 29–30
  far side of 168, 169
  finding 45
  gravitational influence 137, 138, 141–4
  Kennedy's project for landing on *see* Kennedy, John F.
  landing sites 170, 171
  'mascons' 141
  origin of 217, 268
  surface 139, 141, 142–3, 168, 169, 170, 174, 217–19
  temperature 218
  waste on 268
Mueller, George 89, 107, 115, 117, 132, 182

N-1 booster, Soviet 178–9
NASA 7, 8, 14, 15, 16, 17, 20, 26, 27, 28, 29, 31, 32, 33–4, 36, 42, 45, 48–9, 50, 51, 56–9, 61–3, 67–9, 72, 74, 76, 79–80, 81, 87, 88, 89, , 90, 91, 95, 97, 102, 104, 105, 106, 107, 109, 111, 114, 118, 119, 120–1, 123, 126, 130, 132, 133, 134, 137, 142, 144, 149, 150, 152, 153, 157, 169, 170, 171, 177–8, 179, 180, 181, 182, 183, 184, 185, 186, 187, 191, 192, 201, 202, 223, 226, 232, 252, 261, 263, 264, 266–7, 268, 269, 270, 271, 272, 273 *see also under individual NASA craft, project and site*
National Academy of Sciences, US 263
National Advisory Committee for Aeronautics (NACA) 10, 12, 14
Neutral Buoyancy Facility, Houston 185–6
Nixon, Richard 34, 146, 240, 253, 255, 262, 269
North American Aviation/Rockwell 13, 79, 87, 88, 91, 123, 147, 186, 191–2, 194
Nova rocket 57, 59, 61, 62

O'Dea, John 242
O'Hara, Dee 18, 40
Outer Space Treaty 81

Paine, Thomas 20, 34, 192, 202
Parkes communications station 232, 235
passive thermal control (PTC) 93, 95, 96, 99, 121, 153–4, 156
Paules, Gran 202
Phillips, Sam 149, 202
'plugs out test' 82–4

portable life support system (PLSS) 128, 226–7, 228, 230, 237, 244, 245, 246, 249
powered descent initiation (PDI) 204, 206, 219
Project Horizon 58
Puddy, Don 201–2

Ranger probes 45, 169, 218, 266
Redstone rocket 16, 38–9, 58
Rusk, Dean 81

Safire, William 146
Sarkissian, John 232
Saturn I rocket 79
Saturn IB rocket 82, 90
Saturn V rocket 20, 22, 23, 24, 33, 36, 56, 59, 89–90, 94, 123–4, 129, 130, 178, 179, 266
Scheer, Julian 91
Schirra, Wally 64, 88, 90, 105–6
Schmitt, Joe 35
Schwagmeier, Thomas 242
Schweickart, Rusty 130, 131–2, 199, 229
Scott, Dave 33, 65, 130, 131, 132, 164, 177, 178
Seamans, Robert 62
See, Elliot 51, 187
Sevareid, Eric 34
Shaffer, Philip 137
Shea, Joe 82, 88, 126
Shepard, Alan 16, 38, 56
Sherrod, Robert 183
Sibrel, Bart 272–3
Skylab 267
Slayton, Deke 24, 49, 50, 51, 66, 69, 82, 84, 87–8, 89, 107, 109–10, 111, 114–15, 116, 118, 133, 135, 148, 149, 183, 187, 190, 201, 215, 223, 245, 246, 264, 273
smell of space 55–6, 244
Smith, Andrew 15
Smithsonian Institution 270
Soviet Academy of Sciences 177
Soviet Union 14, 15–16, 59, 60, 80, 81, 104, 105, 107, 169, 171, 177–9, 192, 272, 273
Soyuz 1 105, 178
Soyuz 2 105
Soyuz 3 105
Space Task Group, NASA 56–7, 62
Sputnik 14
Sputnik 2 14
Stafford, Tom 32, 34, 51, 65–6, 142, 143, 144, 149, 200, 202
sub-orbital flights 59
Surveyor probes 169, 171, 220, 266

UFO sighting, possible Apollo 11 and 121, 122, 137

Van Allen belts 108
Vietnam War 34, 81, 114, 191
'vomit comet' *see* 'zero-g airplane'
Voskhod 2 31
V-2 58

Walker, Joe 77
Webb, James 60
Wendt, Guenter 33, 35, 37, 68, 189
White, Ed 32, 63, 67, 72, 78, 82, 83–4, 88, 116, 117
Willoughby, Buck 201
Woodruff, Reverend Dean 223

X-15 7, 12–14, 79, 134

Yeager, Chuck 11, 15, 16
Young, John 66, 67, 142, 144, 147, 154, 270

'zero-g airplane' 30–1
Zieglschmid, John 201
Zond 5 105